Four Roman Comedies

Plautus **The Haunted House,**
Casina, or A Funny Thing Happened
on the Way to the Wedding
Terence **The Eunuch, Brothers**

Titus Maccius Plautus was born in Umbria in about 254 BC and
worked as an actor and stage carpenter before turning to writing. Of
well over a hundred plays attributed to him, an authentic twenty-one
were collected after his death, almost all of which are preserved on a
single manuscript. His comedies, like those of Terence, were all based
on Greek New Comedy from the previous century, translated or
transformed into a Roman setting. They show considerable evidence of
his experience in the popular theatre of his time, relying heavily on
their performance potential. They provide the earliest surviving
literature in Latin. Plautus died in 184 BC.

Publius Terentius Afer (Terence) was born between 195 and 185
BC in Africa and brought to Rome as a slave. The story has it that he
read one of his plays to a Roman official who was so impressed that
Terence was immediately invited to sit down and join him at dinner.
Though linked with Plautus as a comic playwright, Terence wrote
more subtly, concentrating on nuances of character rather than on the
farcical situations which drove the work of Plautus. All his six plays
survive complete. He died young, apparently drowned in the sea near
Greece while trying to recover more manuscripts of the dramatist
Menander, on whom he based most of his work.

Four Roman Comedies

PLAUTUS

The Haunted House
translated by Kenneth McLeish and Michael Sargent

Casina, or a Funny Thing Happened on the Way to the Wedding
translated by Richard Beacham

TERENCE

The Eunuch
translated by Kenneth McLeish
(edited by Michael Sargent)

Brothers
translated by J. Michael Walton

introduced by
J. Michael Walton

METHUEN DRAMA

Methuen Drama

1 3 5 7 9 10 8 6 4 2

This collection first published in the United Kingdom in 2003 by
Methuen Publishing Ltd

A CIP catalogue record for this book is available from the British Library

ISBN 0 413 77296 9

Typeset by Wilmaset Ltd, Birkenhead, Wirral
Printed and bound in Great Britain by
Cox & Wyman Ltd, Reading, Berkshire

CONTENTS

INTRODUCTION

The Greek background

Benjamin Disraeli's wife, Mary Anne, would have had difficulties with Roman comedy. Her husband patronisingly described her as an excellent creature but unable to remember which came first, the Greeks or the Romans. The plays of Plautus and Terence could only have added an extra dimension to her confusion. Written in Latin for performance in Rome during the second century BC they are set in Greek cities with Greek characters and a thoroughly Greek morality. In fact they were all based on Greek Middle and New Comedies written anything up to two hundred years earlier. So close do they seem to have been to the originals that they might almost count as translations had any of those Greek originals survived for a direct comparison to be possible. And yet they were in Latin – in Plautus we have the earliest surviving Latin literature; they offer Greek cities which are run as though they were under Roman control; and they are clearly aimed at a Roman holiday audience. There is a mix of culture here, Italian and Greek, which takes some unravelling. A historical perspective may help. For that we need to go back to the Athens of the fifth century BC.

The comedy of classical Athens divides itself neatly into periods. Achieving respectability and status at the Athenian festivals of the Lenaia and the Great Dionysia rather later than did tragedy, the form known as Old Comedy is represented for posterity by nine plays of the comedian Aristophanes, produced between 425 BC (*Acharnians*) and 405 BC (*Frogs*). Two further plays of his survive from the last years of his life, *Women in Power* and *Wealth*. Aristophanes wasn't born until after the death of Aeschylus. When he started to write for the stage, probably in 427 BC, it was for a theatre which was dominated, as far as tragedies were concerned, by Sophocles and Euripides; and politically, by the Peloponnesian War which lasted, albeit intermittently, from 431 to 404 BC. Many of Aristophanes' comedies used the war and the reactions of the Athenians. *Acharnians*, *Knights*, *Peace*, *Lysistrata*, *Frogs* offer a kind of running commentary on Athens' decline to military defeat at the hands of the Spartans. There was a sizeable opposition to the war from the ordinary citizens, an opposition which was effective only in the fantasies of the comic stage.

Other plays of Aristophanes satirised a variety of local issues, anything from education and the legal system to corruption in politics and women-only festivals. The point about all this is that Old Comedy, at least according to the work of the only exponent whose plays we have, was immediate, political and often parochial. After the defeat of Athens in 404 BC and the consequent turmoil, drama in Greece was never to pack the same punch. Not a single new tragedy in Greek survives from the fourth century onwards. The last two plays of Aristophanes, *Women in Power* (c.392 BC) and *Wealth* (c.388 BC), contain something of his whimsical vision but without the immediate spark. They are sometimes identified as Middle Comedy, sometimes as New Comedy, either label marking them out as the first moves towards a kind of social comedy, rooted in everyday concerns. The rest of this transitional stage towards domestic, what may even be called 'situation', comedy, during the fourth century BC survives only in the names of its authors. Alexis, Antiphanes and Eubulus are reputed to have written between them a staggering six hundred plays, all lost.

Philemon, Diphilus, Apollodorus and Menander, from the end of the fourth century BC and the beginning of the third, are slightly less shadowy figures, if only because it was to them that Plautus and Terence principally turned when creating Roman comedies based on Greek originals. The actual plays of Philemon, Diphilus and Apollodorus are gone, almost certainly beyond recall: the slight note of optimism contained in 'almost' is because for many hundreds of years the plays of Menander too were thought lost. A hundred years ago Menander, the comic writer with the finest reputation in the ancient world, was represented by bits and pieces, quips and quotations: plus four of the six plays of Terence, all known to be based on original Menanders. These include both *The Eunuch* and *Brothers* in the present volume.

The history of the recovery of two complete, or virtually complete, plays of Menander and major sections of four others, reads like something devised by a cross between Umberto Eco and Simon Raven. Alongside chance discoveries of segments of miscellaneous text wrapped as protective coverings round legal documents and even an Egyptian mummy, the two plays turned up in the possession of a Swiss bibliophile in circumstances which have never been fully revealed. So who knows what else may be waiting in some vault; misplaced in a dry and dusty volume; or part of a private collection to which most of the world has never had access?

Of the two Plautus plays in the present collection, *Casina* was based on a Diphilus original. *The Haunted House* is usually believed to be from Philemon's *Phasma* (*The Ghost*) but Menander wrote a *Phasma* too. An illustration from that is included among the Mytilene mosaics of scenes from Menander preserved in the House of Menander on the island of Lesbos, so it is possible that Menander too had some unwitting input into *The Haunted House*

What we have, then, in the plays of Plautus and Terence are works which not only derived from Greek material but where their Greek pedigree was paraded almost as a guarantee of quality. At the same time accusations of plagiarism and shifty practice were clearly flying about, a paradox that will be addressed below, but only after the circumstances of the writing of the plays has been more fully considered.

Plautus and Terence

All the plays of Plautus and Terence are examples of what was known as the *fabula* or *comoedia palliata*, a comedy wearing the *pallium*, the *pallium* being a Greek cloak, as opposed to the *fabula togata*, a story 'wearing the toga'. The two Roman comedians both wrote 'comedies in Greek dress': but they were not even contemporaries. Linking them does little service to either. Plautus sometimes gets blamed for not being Terence, Terence for not being Plautus. They tend to be linked because they are the only two comic playwrights writing in Latin any of whose complete plays survive. The only other extant Latin playwright of any sort is Seneca who was writing more than two centuries later, when the Roman republic had given way to the time of the emperors, whose erratic and maniacal rule was reflected in Seneca's dramatic output. Plautus and Terence, despite some similarities in their use of source material, are very dissimilar in comic style. Plautus, the elder, is the darling of the market-place, the crowd-pleaser, so popular that his name was pirated in later times and appended to any old play as a way of pulling in an audience. Terence had a much more uneasy relationship with both his audience and his fellow-playwrights, being more at home with a thoughtful maxim than with the slapstick.

Details of the lives of both are sketchy though there was a biography of Terence, a lot of it missing, attributed, a little doubtfully, to Suetonius, the same author who has provided posterity with the scandalous set of lives of the twelve Caesars. The *Life* of Terence is anecdotal, though not necessarily the worse for that, but what we know of both playwrights is at best second-hand. At least the circumstances of Plautus' life that have been handed down suggest good reasons for the differences of approach between the two comedians.

Titus Maccius Plautus was born in Umbria at Sarsina, a small town near Rimini, sometime around 250–240 BC. To give this a time-frame, Menander in Greece had been dead for about thirty years. More significantly, the first tragedies and comedies in Latin were written about 240 BC by one Livius Andronicus. Though brought to Rome as a slave, Andronicus was freed and translated Homer's *Odyssey* into Latin. This was the time of the First Punic War against Carthage and Andronicus' first plays, mainly on mythological themes relating to the Trojan War, may have been presented to celebrate the Roman victory. None has been preserved but his long career and high reputation gave Roman drama some status and led in 207 BC to the Collegium of Playwrights being given the right to meet at the Temple of Minerva on the Aventine Hill.

Plautus by this time had become an actor, perhaps in the localised comedy from southern Italy known as the Atellan farce (*fabula atellana*). Apart from the mythological plays that Livius Andronicus was writing, a number of indigenous Italian dramatic forms had emerged, the comedies in local dress known as *togatae* and Roman history plays called the *praetextae* or *praetextatae*. This latter form is credited to a contemporary of Livius Andronicus called Gnaeus Naevius who may also have been the first to write the *comoedia palliata* using Greek material translated into a Roman context. Naevius got himself into trouble for attempting to incorporate personal satire into his plays, the long-term fallout from which probably accounts for the lack of contemporary reference in either Plautus or Terence.

The Atellan was true theatre of the streets, a masked form as, of course, was the *palliata*, but the kind of popular entertainment that was not based on any formal script, thus difficult to trace. It seems from what evidence there is that a small number of fixed characters might appear in a series of different situations: Pappus, the foolish old man; Bucco, the glutton or braggart; Manducus or Dossenus, a clever swindler, often a hunchback; and Maccus, the fool. The obvious similarities between this form and what would emerge in sixteenth-century Italy *commedia dell' arte* are too strong to ignore, though theatre historians are divided over the closeness of such an association. If Plautus' middle name, Maccius, was taken as a result of his specialising in the role of the fool, Maccus, that would help to explain the way in which he was to write his plays. Plautus survives on the page but his texts are notable for concealing a range of potential physical action. There is plenty of leeway in and around any Plautus text for the *lazzi* of *commedia dell' arte*, gags and set routines which arise out of the moment. The *commedia* of the sixteenth century may be traced to northern rather than southern Italy but the actors, just as the actors of the Atellan, were renowned for the bank of tricks, jokes and devices which they developed as part of the comedy of improvisation.

The story has it that Plautus only became a writer of plays after he had put all his savings as an actor into a business venture which failed. It is certainly easy enough to see the influence of a player of improvised farce in the construction of his comedies. And those plays became the staple of the repertoire. Plautus was said to have written 130 plays but some hundred or so years after his death the grammarian Marcus Terentius Varro took it upon himself to establish what of the mass of material that people claimed as genuine Plautus really was genuine Plautus. Varro rejected a great number, reserved judgement on others and compiled a list of twenty-one plays which he classified as the real thing. A manuscript of those twenty-one survives, with one play partially damaged and another no more than fragmentary.

When Plautus died around 184 BC, his mantle as most popular playwright was taken over by a freed slave from Gaul, Caecilius Statius. Terence (Publius Terentius Afer) was born sometime between 195 and 185 BC and also came to Rome as a slave, in his case from Carthage – hence the cognomen Afer, the African. Bought into the household of the senator Terentius (hence the middle name) Lucanus who educated him, he was eventually freed to become the author of six plays, all written between 166 and 160. On a trip to Greece in 159 BC to recover new Menander manuscripts, he was drowned in a boating accident. That is one version, at any rate, though some historians are dubious, disposing of his reputation as anything between a mere contributor to the plays of some of the great men of the time and a front for those who were anxious to avoid the stigma attached to the profession of playwriting. The more charitable version has the young man reading his first piece to Caecilius at a dinner party and the famous playwright being so impressed he invited Terence to sit down with him. Even more romantic is an account of his death according to which he dropped all the manuscripts he had collected overboard by mistake and was so upset he jumped in after them.

Whatever the detail, the main differences between him and Plautus are exemplified by the company they kept. Plautus was at home with farce actors, Terence an adjunct to posh soirées. Plautus is the professional, Terence the amateur. Terence's six plays are more cultivated than those of Plautus in every way. His debt to Menander is shown not only by the use of Menander as source material but also in the manner in which he takes his characters seriously. In Plautus it is difficult not to feel that the characters often react according to the requirements of the scene and the situation. Their continuity is based on neither consistency nor plausibility, only on the exploitation of the comic scene. The characters of Terence develop as the play develops, learning from their experience and offering portraits from life as it might have been lived, at least in this strange, hybrid Graeco-Roman world that was Roman comedy. But if Terence's world was Graeco-Roman that of Plautus was more Romano-Greek, banging against the funnybone of the street audience out enjoying themselves but well aware that the sort of behaviour they were witnessing would never be condoned in the Rome of 200 BC. For Terence the public theatre was not the ideal medium.

The difference between the essentially farce texts of Plautus and the more sophisticated plays of Terence should not hide the fact that much of Plautus' wordplay is brilliant. So, it would appear, was his use of music. None of it survives but to ignore the likely contribution of music to the performance would be as foolish as to ignore the physical energy that is inherent in the text but which can only be released through performance. Plautus makes use of *cantica*, elaborate set pieces designed to have a musical accompaniment. Michael Grant went so far as to speak of Roman New Comedy as Roman opera and it was perhaps here in the Italy of the third century BC that *opéra bouffe* was born.

Terence relied less on music but his truthfulness and moral sense made him appeal to later centuries. In the six plays there is a humanity which struck a chord, especially with Cicero and Horace, and ensured his survival in schoolroom and in performance. Numbers of superb illustrations survive in the medieval manuscripts of Terence, providing as many as half a dozen different versions of specific moments throughout the plays. Though these can hardly offer evidence as to how the plays were first performed in second-century BC Rome, they provide between them a wonderful library of the whole iconography of masked and gestural acting.

Both playwrights wrote in verse with considerable metrical variation but Terence is more carefully contrived. Despite Plautus' more elaborate use of music his characters seem to speak colloquially, particularly when addressing the audience direct, almost as though they genuinely expect the audience to respond.

The Roman stage

When thinking about where and how classical plays were first staged it is only natural for those massive outdoor theatre buildings to come to mind, the ruins of which are scattered all over what was the Greek and Roman world from Turkey to Jordan to Tunisia: there is an ancient theatre at St Albans in England and there was reputed to be one in Babylon. Athens has two such theatres. It was for the Theatre of Dionysus on the slope below and to the south-east of the Acropolis that the Greek playwrights, tragic and comic, wrote most of their plays. This theatre, however, went through a number of structural alterations from being the initial venue for the surviving plays of Aeschylus; through the Periclean building programme of the latter part of the fifth century to the first stone theatre constructed under Lycurgus at the time when Menander was starting to write; and on to various modifications under Roman rule. The remains that can be seen in Athens today were overtaken as a performance space by the construction of a new theatre about 160 AD by Claudius Atticus Herodes, half a mile to the west of the Theatre of Dionysus. It is at Herodes Atticus that performances are still given of all manner of entertainment from the revival of ancient tragedies and comedies to performances by ballet companies and major orchestras, while the theatre precinct that saw the birth of western drama lies in ruins, as unkempt and undercared for as a neglected graveyard: which, effectively, is what it is.

It was, apparently, for the Theatre of Dionysus, in its first stone incarnation, that Menander originally wrote his plays. That poses a problem. The plays were for masked performance but they are also of a subtlety that a massive stone theatre would seem to militate against. If that is not the immediate issue here, it inevitably ties in to the question of how and where the plays of Plautus and Terence were staged, if only because they were all based on Greek comedies. One thing is certain. The plays of Plautus and Terence were not first played in one of these huge theatres. At the time when they were written no permanent theatre was permitted in Rome. Five years after Terence's death in 159 BC, two of Rome's elected magistrates, known as censors, attempted to build a stone theatre and were prevented by the doughty Publius Scipio Nasica on moral grounds. The Senate then passed a decree forbidding the provision of seats at public entertainments. It was another hundred and ten years before Pompey built a permanent stone theatre in Rome; and he only got away with it by putting up a shrine at the top and pretending that this was a shrine with a theatre attached rather than a theatre with a shrine.

The plays of Plautus and Terence were never intended for performance in what we now think of as a Roman theatre in the mould of Herodes Atticus in Athens, or Orange in southern France. They were made for, and played in, temporary theatres, made of wood, easily constructed and just as easily demolished. In fact, to describe them as theatres at all, in the sense of a theatre building constructed to house and control an audience, is probably something of a misrepresentation. Roman comedy was presented on temporary stages in an open space where dramatic performance was only one part of an entertainment. Plays were put on to mark special occasions, public festivals in honour of gods – Jupiter, Apollo or the Great Mother. These were under direct control of the *aediles*. They might also be funded by a wealthy individual to mark a family occasion, a wedding or a funeral, but always they had to compete for attention. The Games (*Ludi*), whether public or private, included dramatic performance as part of the available entertainment, alongside sporting contests and other exhibitions of skill. Plautus and Terence wrote not for the opera house but for the fairground booth. Some idea of the pressures and the competition can be found in the two prologues to Terence's *The Mother-in-Law* (*Hecyra*). In the first, whoever is delivering it complains that 'when this play was first put on it ran into unprecedented bad luck and never got a hearing. The stupid audience got distracted by some rope-dancer'. A second prologue has the theatre-manager, Lucius Ambivius Turpio, railing against 'the racket made by prize-fighters and their supporters: and the shouting of the women'. Scrutiny of the plays and the occasions may have been under strict magisterial control in a Rome that was at this time noted for its severity and respectability, but for the players this was the roughest of rough theatres.

The likelihood of any traces remaining of such theatres is nil even though some of the temporary theatres that were built in Rome could be huge. Pliny talks of one that was three storeys high and built on three hundred and sixty pillars. But this too was dismantled the following day and was anyway a product of less austere times. Though there can be no archaeological remains, in recent years a careful investigation has been made into the precise nature of the temporary stage. Richard Beacham, translator of *Casina* in the present volume, has related the requirements of the plays of Plautus to wall-paintings found in Rome and Pompeii. Using the visual evidence of similar paintings in the Room of the Masks, excavated in Rome in 1960, and more recent discoveries in the Villa of Oplontis and at the House of the Gladiators in Pompeii, amongst others, he has come up with a highly plausible reconstruction of a Plautine stage. The virtue of this reconstruction is the way in which it marries simplicity to versatility. A basic façade offers the kind of street front that almost all the scenes in Plautus and Terence require, with two adjoining houses and a central area that could be curtained off or used for a pathway between the houses. His evidence is strengthened by the large number of illustrations on vases from southern Italy. These celebrate a variety of fairly crude theatrical performances played on a raised stage with a playing space often flanked by two doorways and with some decoration involving painted panels and porticos. It would appear that a tradition of such temporary stages was already well established in Italy. Plautus may well have learnt his craft on such. Much of the apparent repetition in the scripts seems to relate to the

way in which an actor may have to engage and hold an
audience for whom the distractions of the fit-up stage were
exaggerated by a far from favourable acoustic. (See Beacham,
The Roman Theatre and its Audience, London, 1991.)

Beacham's reconstruction of this stage for actual production, originally tried out indoors, was given its major
theatrical test in a double bill performed in the Inner
Peristyle of the J. Paul Getty Villa at Malibu in 1994. The
variety of levels and alcoves offered by a series of steps and
inset doorways gave ample room for any and all the required
stage action, including eavesdropping, interruptions, running and false exits, plus all the physical business, pushing
and shoving that make up the plays' dynamic action. If each
and every play of Plautus and Terence were performed on
what was basically the same stage and with the same setting
then this reconstruction offers a perfect template.

Inside the plays

If the circumstances of performance received little attention
from writers of the time, and this is almost as true of the
Roman theatre as it was of the Greek, then the texts
themselves become even more important. What will not be
found in Plautus or Terence is much indication of the
political background of the first quarter of the second
century. There are distant references to foreign war – one
Plautus play is called *The Carthaginian* (*Poenulus*) and
contains a curious speech of some twenty lines in a foreign
tongue which is certainly not Latin. A few subtle references
may reflect recent legislation, usually to control extravagance, but there is little of any substance. Nor, because of the
blend of social and cultural worlds inherent in a play that is
part Greek and part Roman, will much impression be on
offer about what it would have been like to live either in the
Greece of the source or the Rome of the target culture. These
are stage worlds with one foot in the real world, the other
somewhere in the clouds.

The contemporary world does occasionally surface,
usually in the prologues where the playwright is most

likely to reveal himself and the circumstances of the performance. Even there a degree of caution needs exercising. The authenticity of the prologues as being by the playwrights remains unconfirmed. Nonetheless, the sideswipe at the behaviour of the audience of *The Mother-in-Law*, referred to above, does have the ring of truth and would be pretty pointless if it were not true. Much of the other prologues of Terence seems taken up with a series of personal feuds over the originality of his material. The key word in any such squabble is *contaminatio*. This, as its anglicisation would imply, can have the derogatory sense of 'debasing' or 'corrupting'. But when it is used to describe the process of relocating a Greek original in a Roman context then the meaning is more subtle. After all, this is what Plautus and Terence habitually did and in complex ways. Both frequently took more than one Greek original and mixed them together, sometimes introducing characters from one play into another. They can even make claims for the quality of their work because it involves *contaminatio*. This has a direct bearing on exactly what it is that Plautus and Terence were doing when they took a Greek original and 'converted' it into a Latin play. Would we identify it as a 'translation' or a 'version' or an 'adaptation'? There seems to be no doubt that Terence and those around him made strong distinctions, the detail of which has been most carefully sifted through by Sander Goldberg. (See Goldberg, *Understanding Terence*, Princeton, 1986; also Niall Slater, *Plautus in Performance*, Amsterdam, 2000, and Kenneth McLeish, *Roman Comedy*, Bristol, 1986.)

The plays of Terence caused controversy in their own times, at least in part as a result of differing responses to these very issues. A defence of his approach is lodged firmly in the prologues to four, arguably five, of his six plays. All deal with the accusation of plagiarism. In the prologue to his first play, *The Girl from Andros*, he records that Menander wrote two plays which were very similar and that he has made a single play from them. He has been roundly criticised for this but maintains that Naevius, Plautus and Ennius did the same.

In *Self-Tormentor*, the same Ambivius as delivers the

Mother-in-Law prologue defends the playwright for changing a Greek original into a play with a double plot. He also responds to the accusation that Terence has 'contaminated' (*contaminasse*) many Greek plays to make a small number of Latin ones. *The Eunuch* prologue is largely an attack on another playwright who is accused, despite being a decent translator (*vortendo*), of turning good Menander plays into bad Latin ones by poor construction. Terence had reason to dislike this other playwright, Luscius Lanuvinus, who was so incensed by what Terence was up to as to have interrupted a rehearsal of *The Eunuch* by shouting out that the author was not a playwright but a thief. Terence offers, within his play, or at least as a prelude to it, a complicated defence based on where he claimed he got certain characters from.

The prologue of *Phormio* is another attack on Lanuvinus, though a comparatively muted one, but in the last play, *Brothers*, Terence is back, all guns blazing, defending himself against having 'stolen' a scene from a Diphilus play which Plautus had left out in his Latin version of the Diphilus original. He prefers to consider what he had done, not as 'plagiarism' but as 'recovery' (*reprensum*).

So what does this add up to, apart from showing that the Roman theatre scene was even more of a snake pit than most? What it does seem to imply is that the process of using Greek originals was virtually a requirement, a guarantee of quality, but that such material was in short supply. Terence and Plautus may well have headed for the Greek repertoire but their originality as dramatists allows for the criticism by Terence of his rival in *The Eunuch* as a decent translator but a poor playwright: to put it literally, '... in translating well, he has written badly and from good Greek plays has made Latin ones that are not any good'.

Plautus seems to have been less troubled about any accusations of malpractice. His prologues do offer some information about contemporary stage conditions but primarily through inviting the audience's goodwill. Three of his plays have a prologue delivered by a non-human, including Mercury for *Amphitryon*, the only Roman comedy to survive based on a story from mythology; seven move straight into the first scene; the rest have a goodwill encounter between an actor and the audience, sometimes in character, sometimes not. After reading some of the extended introductory scenes in both playwrights it is difficult to resist the one play, Plautus' *Pseudolus*, with a two-line prologue: 'You'd best get up and give your balls a jiggle. It's a Plautus. And it's long.'

Plautus, *The Haunted House* (*Mostellaria*)

Mostellaria or *The Haunted House*, as it is better known, is a play with strong narrative and a number of stock characters. Beyond that, it exemplifies the Plautine plot about family relationships, where the driving factor in life is less love than money: who has it – a wealthy father; who is spending it – a wastrel son; who wants it – who doesn't? The setting is Athens but a heavily stage-Athens. A cast of a dozen includes four slaves, two courtesans and the maid of one of them, two young men, two old men and a moneylender. That is a lot of characters for an audience to distinguish, made more difficult in this case by the way in which the play is introduced. There is no prologue, normally a useful device, amongst other things, for trying out the mood of the audience and letting them know where the play is coming from.

The Haunted House opens instead with a routine. The first words are from a character whose name we don't know knocking on the door of the house of someone equally unknown. Grumio, as he turns out to be, would be identified as a slave by his costume, so the person against whom he is railing within the house is likely to be a slave too. The exposition that follows gradually, and quite cleverly, reveals where the play is set and what is happening. The two slaves both belong to the same household, that of Theopropides and his son Philolaches. The father has been away on business for three years in Egypt. His son, meanwhile, has been living a life of total debauchery, aided and abetted by several disreputable friends and, especially, by Tranio, the slave indoors. All this is much to the disapproval of Grumio who has just arrived from the country estate. After this opening exchange, Philolaches emerges from indoors and engages the audience in a kind of delayed prologue, a drunken and rambling assessment of his own life all revolving around the confused conviction that 'Man is like a house'. Despite his dissipation and, in the absence of his parents, turning their house into 'a ruin', he claims that he has now been redeemed by love.

The object of his attentions, Philematium, now emerges from inside with her maid Scapha, and Philolaches eavesdrops on their conversation. The enamoured Philolaches has bought Philematium and freed her. Scapha sees no reason for her to remain exclusively with him but Philematium feels she owes Philolaches a certain loyalty. Here, in these early scenes, the playwright offers a crosstalk act; a stand-up drunk scene; a mistress and maid scene overheard by the mistress's lover who eventually makes his presence known. All of these would have been familiar routines, full of comic potential and establishing the central characters. The odd thing here, however, is that though the five characters do offer a frame for the play, only one of them, and that the apparently less important indoor slave, returns to the stage. Grumio, Philematium and Scapha have a single entrance and that is it. More bizarrely, the young man, Philolaches, hears that his father has returned to Athens and departs indoors, letting his slave Tranio get on with sorting everything out. The rest of the play revolves around Tranio's attempts to cover up what has been going on at home during the three-year absence of the father, Theopropides.

The nub of the play has nothing to do with the relationship between father and son, as it has in, for example, Menander's *The Woman from Samos* which is based on a similar return from abroad. Father and son in *The Haunted House* never even meet. Instead, everything turns on the machinations of the slave, Tranio, to avoid the father finding out what in the end he is inevitably going to find out.

Several scenes follow hard on one another's heels, involving a moneylender, a friend of Philolaches called Callidamates and his servants, and the next-door neighbour, Simo. Tranio comes up with the story that the family home is haunted, which accounts for why the father cannot go indoors and, incidentally, for the drunken noises offstage.

His story gets more and more complicated and improbable when he tries to explain away a debt by saying the son has put down a deposit on the house next door. The scenes revolving around the bemused neighbour, Simo, are among the best in the piece when Theopropides starts to look round his prospective purchase, but without talking about it in case he upsets the ladies. The truth about Philolaches' lifestyle during his father's absence comes to light, a little lamely from a pair of Callidamates' slaves and it is Callidamates who persuades Theopropides to forgive not only the devious Tranio but also the absent son.

Character is definitely subordinate to incident here but there is no doubt that the play has a strong comic drive. The lack of concern with anything but plot allows the audience to concentrate exclusively on Tranio's latest twist. That he escapes with his hide intact is a tribute more to the play wright's sense of goodwill than the slave's gift for intrigue. This sense of living in the moment is almost a hallmark of the Plautine comedy. No matter that a situation is established which might interest the audience in discovering how a dissipated son is redeemed through the woman he loves; or perhaps, how he is reconciled with a stern father, dismayed to discover what the young man has been up to; or even how a clever slave reconciles the two. Here incident follows incident, nobody changes, nobody learns anything about themselves. This, though, is not what Plautus is aiming at. His dramatic achievement might even be typified by his ability to set up possible plots of the kind that are all too familiar, and drop them in favour of a driving sense of narrative in which the laugh is hearty but heartless. There is an audience for this sort of farce, particularly played in the sort of circumstances with which Plautus was familiar. There always has been, and no one should underestimate the skill required in writing material on which the natural comic actor can impose his comic personality. *The Haunted House* is a vehicle for the actor playing Tranio. In the hands of Frankie Howerd or a Zero Mostel, no one would be looking for sentiment and certainly not subtext, except as *double entendre*.

Plautus, *Casina,* or *A Funny Thing Happened on the Way to the Wedding*

If it is true of *The Haunted House* that it is a prime example of writing directed at the skills of the actor, how much more should *Casina* be judged on its performance potential and *joie de vivre* rather than on its morality. A rather charming book on Plautus and Terence written in the nineteenth century by the Reverend W. Lucas Collins has problems with several individual plays of both writers. As there are only six Terence plays he can hardly ignore any of them, but admits that he can only bring himself to write about *The Eunuch* when he has changed the plot and retitled it *The Ethiopian Slave*. Fortunately for the good cleric, Plautus offers him more to choose from and he is able to dismiss *Casina* and five others in the following words: 'Six more plays make up the list of Plautus' surviving comedies, and if these had not survived, we should certainly have had no loss.' He then goes on, reluctantly, to admit that *Casina* 'seems to have furnished Beaumarchais with the plot of his *Mariage de Figaro*'. He could with rather more conviction have suggested that *The Eunuch* supplied Wycherley with his plot for *The Country Wife*.

Napoleon is reputed to have described Beaumarchais' *Mariage de Figaro* as 'already the revolution in action'. *Casina* would have posed little similar threat to the powers-that-be in Rome. It revolves around a Roman father and son who both lust after the same slave girl and who both hope to get access to her by marrying her off to a complaisant slave: except that in a Plautus play the Roman is not a Roman at all but a Greek living in Athens, a Roman by proxy for the sake of a comic occasion. *Casina* was in fact based on an original play by Diphilus written around the time of the death of Alexander the Great in 323 BC and performed in Rome some hundred and fifty years later. This goes some way to disarming a fairly seedy tale. Father and son as rivals for the same girl has enough dramatic parallels: each championing her being married off to a different servant so that they can get sexual access to her offers another dimension, especially when the cause of the son is being promoted by his mother who has discovered her husband's infatuation.

But, once the scene is set, the play does turn into a romp where, as in *The Haunted House*, it is the plot that drives with the characters reacting as the moment requires. The play as we have it opens with a prologue, a long one – the present translator suggests using a dumbshow to give the exposition a theatrical thrust. One of the things revealed in the prologue, which was clearly added later, is that the play has been changed by Plautus and the son delayed so that he will not be one of the characters: 'Plautus changed his mind and dropped him from our play – by washing out a bridge that lay upon his way.' This immediately removes one possible dimension from the plot. Son and father will not come into direct competition, at least not in front of the audience. The focus instead turns on the wife, Cleostrata, and her support for the younger slave, as a means of foiling her husband, Lysidamus.

After revealing the entire situation and its ramifications, the prologue, who has no character apart from that of a knowing observer, reveals that the girl is not a slave at all but a free woman, thus paving the way for a somewhat ambivalent ending whereby she will end up married to the absent son. Cue for a sequel, you might think.

The plot is rather less cavalier than in *The Haunted House* about introducing characters and then forgetting about them, but it has a similarity in the manner by which it throws so much emphasis on the central character. *The Haunted House* is a vehicle for the slave, Tranio. *Casina* revolves around Lysidamus, a foolish old man whose determination to marry the girl off and thereby to bed her himself has the air of total fixation. The comedy derives in huge measure from his frustration at every turn. Fairly early in the play he has a song aimed at the audience, all about love and about his love in particular. It ends with him catching sight of his wife, 'that rugged old cross that I bear'. The effect is dramatically interesting, isolating him rather than allowing the audience to sympathise with him. There is a disarming quality to the unsavoury nature of most of what is going on, in the knowledge that he is never going to get the girl. Without that the play would descend into something simply sleazy.

Plautus ensures too that the rival slaves have none of the

humanity that might be found in Beaumarchais. In them self-interest overtakes all else. Lysidamus' triumph, when he succeeds in manipulating the lottery in favour of his candidate for the girl's husband, is short-lived. Everyone in the play knows what he is up to and his gullibility makes him the easiest of targets. A particularly Greek feature here is the way in which the slave and slave-owning class interact, part of the process of playing with an audience by the make-believe of contrasting stage and real life, Greeks and Romans. The wedding-scene with the young slave Chalinus disguised as a bride and being fondled by both the putative husband Olympio, and by his even more putative lover, Lysidamus, is a masterpiece of camp – there is no other way to describe it. And as Olympio discovers that his bride has a bristly beard and hands her over to Lysidamus, Plautus' own background finally and fully surfaces. This is the province of Pappus, Maccus, Dossenus and Bucco referred to above (p. xi). Diphilus may have supplied the original plot but *Casina* ends up much closer to the *comoedia atellana*.

Terence, *The Eunuch*

The Eunuch is often thought of as the most Plautine of Terence's six plays. It was first presented at the Megalensian Games (in honour of the Great Mother) in the spring of 161 BC. This was less than a quarter of a century after the death of Plautus and the circumstances of festival production had not greatly changed. The performance details of most of Plautus' plays are hazy. Terence is better documented, often by the author himself, or his producer, complaining about the way he is being treated by fellow professionals or by his audience. We know not only when *The Eunuch* was performed but under whose management, who were consuls and aediles at the time and even who the musician was.

The attitude in Rome towards Greece and Greek culture had become more positive and the prologue concentrates less on the problems Terence had in finding and, more importantly, keeping an audience (see p. xvi above), than in delivering a personal gripe about the nature of authorship and the criticism he has faced. The tone is peevish at best, concluding with the somewhat peremptory injunction, 'Please give your attention, listen in silence, and find out what *The Eunuch* has to say.' One thing Terence does admit is that he 'borrowed' the character of the soldier (Thraso) in *The Eunuch* from *The Flatterer* of Plautus.

What follows is certainly more subtle than either of the Plautus plays contained in this volume but offers similarities too. The play revolves around the rivalry of the young Phaedria and the soldier, Thraso, for the affections of a courtesan, Thais. A sub-plot, which becomes the central plot, involves Phaedria's younger brother disguising himself as a eunuch to gain access to a slave-girl called Pamphila. The setting is again a street in Athens with two adjacent houses but the play opens in the middle of an argument – the first line, 'What d'you want me to do, for heaven's sake?', introduces a young Athenian, Phaedria, and his clever and scheming slave, Parmeno. No surprises in this relationship. Phaedria is passionately in love with the courtesan Thais who also entertains an army officer called Thraso. Phaedria is upset because he has given Thais anything she wants and has now bought her a eunuch but she has refused to see him. Thraso seems to have trumped him by providing her with a beautiful young slave, Pamphila. The first confrontation between Phaedria and Thais reveals just how complicated this play is going to be, summed up neatly by Phaedria quoting Thais: '"Little girl ... pirates ... everyone thinks she's my own sister ... bring her back to Athens ... give her to her parents ..."' All you are saying is Thraso's back in favour, and I'm thrown out' (ll.155–9).

The twist to the plot occurs when Phaedria's brother Chaerea catches sight of this beautiful young girl, Pamphila, and instantly falls for her. His means of getting into Thais' house is by swapping clothes with the eunuch. No sooner is he alone with Pamphila than he rapes her and escapes. Further complications include Thraso trying to force his way into Thais' house with a private army and the arrival of the young men's father Laches. The resolution offers the revelation of Pamphila's citizen parentage. Chaerea, despite the rape, becomes betrothed to her. Phaedria ends up accepting a part-time relationship with the courtesan while the soldier, Thraso, pays all the bills. No wonder the Reverend Lucas had problems (see p. xxiii above)!

Though the contortions of the plot are complex, much more so than in Plautus, it is still in the characters that the main difference is to be found between Terence and Plautus. *The Eunuch* has fifteen speaking roles, more than *The Way of the World*, *She Stoops to Conquer* or *The Rivals*. Several of these characters are not highly developed, but those that are behave in a manner that is consistent and believable. The sour taste left by the callousness of Chaerea's assault on the young girl whom Thais is trying to protect is difficult for a modern audience to stomach, but its savagery is not glossed over. Her distress is matched by Thais' fury and the scene where Chaerea is called to account is barely rendered comic even with Chaerea still disguised as a eunuch. Ultimately he suffers both humiliation and ridicule, more perhaps than any of the other young men in New Comedy whose sexual attacks are, for the most part, excused as part of life.

The comedy in Terence is allowed to revolve around the discomfiture of those who lose their dignity from jealousy, greed, lust, envy, any or all, in fact, of the seven deadly sins. The initial transgressions are not condoned but where would comedy be without human frailty? This play, which is based on a Menander of the same name about which virtually nothing is known, takes its title from the disguise. Exactly what that disguise would have been in Terence's own time is unclear. There are a number of surviving illustrations which do show that eunuchs had a uniform. It may have been a yellow robe and/or a pointy hat. In the medieval manuscripts of Terence there are several possibilities, one of which was to dress the eunuch in this play as a friar: a solution which gives better evidence of a contemporary in-joke than any hint as to the original staging! A reading simply of the 'eunuch' scenes shows a highly developed sense of dramatic and theatrical structure.

Beyond that, what stands out here is a sense of consistency in character so that the complexity of the plot and all its ramifications are anchored in the nature of the people. In Menander for the first time in the history of drama the playwright created personalities who have a past and for whom you could believe there would also be a future. Julius Caesar wrote off Terence as 'dimidiate Menander', 'half-price Menander'. A direct comparison is denied to us and must await the fortuitous discovery of some of those manuscripts that Terence lost overboard. Nonetheless, there is in *The Eunuch* a Menandrian concern for people which is heartening. It can be no great surprise that it turned out to be Terence's greatest success.

Terence, *Brothers*

So far different is *Brothers* from any of the other plays in the present volume that it reads almost like a *pièce à thèse*, a thesis piece. This is the only play of the four which provides a simple answer to the question, 'What is it about?'. *Brothers* is about how to bring up children. Terence's last play before his untimely death, it was produced at the funeral games for Lucius Aemilius Paulus in 160 BC and seems to have been based on two comedies of Menander with the same name. The prologue has another of Terence's grumpy defences of his work, this time with reference to the last scene which he says he took straight from Diphilus because Plautus had decided not to use it. Of much greater interest is how Terence concludes the prologue where he says, 'Don't now expect the argument of the play. The old men who enter first will give some of the plot. The rest will become clear from the action.'

Unlike in *The Eunuch*, the background of *Brothers* is quickly told. Two brothers, Micio and Demea, live, one in Athens where the play is set, the other in the country. Micio is a bachelor. Demea, who appears not to have a wife any longer, at least none that features in the play, has given him his elder son, Aeschinus, to bring up. The two men have different outlooks, Micio easy-going and broad-minded, Demea hard-working but puritanical. The boys, brought up under different regimes, react accordingly, which leaves Demea permanently incensed about the dissipated life of the son he has relinquished.

The play is then crafted around a set of reversals, carefully devised and interwoven, the result of which is everyone coming to appreciate that they need to be more flexible. It is all so simple as to sound moralistic, which in a way it is. But, unlike anything that Plautus wrote, this is a thoughtful drama which sticks in the mind for what it is saying as much as for the way of saying it. It has that precious gift of the best of plays of becoming a kind of reference point against which facets of modern life may be measured. The comedy is very much the comedy of Menander, tarred only with the casual brutality that marks the Latin adaptations. It arises out of situation and character, and is seldom the result simply of the witty line or the horseplay which give Plautus his specific energy.

Unusually too for comedy of this time, the two younger brothers, Aeschinus and Ctesipho, are developed further than mere ciphers. Aeschinus, brought up in an atmosphere so lax that he can get away with anything, is thoroughly streetwise. When the more repressed Ctesipho starts to break out and finds himself in need of help, his elder brother comes to the rescue. So Aeschinus has carried off the girl with whom Ctesipho has fallen in love; and that is why his natural father is currently so upset. Misunderstandings become more complicated when news gets through of Aeschinus' exploits, apparently abducting this girl for himself, news which breaks while the girl he has promised to marry is actually in labour with his child.

The characters are not one-dimensional and, for all they represent contrary philosophies of child-rearing, they are not wholly predictable. The easy-going adoptive father, Micio, has an exchange with Aeschinus where Aeschinus shows his remorse:

AESCHINUS.
   . . . I shouldn't have done what I did and I apologise. I'm ashamed and upset.

MICIO.
   I believe you. Indeed I do. You've a good heart. But you can be so inconsiderate, I'm afraid. What sort of world do you think you live in? You seduce a girl, a virgin you

> had no right to lay hands on. That was a disgraceful way
> to behave ... did you never consider the consequences?
> Did you not give a moment's thought to what would
> happen and how it would happen? (ll. 681 ff.)

It is impossible to tell at this distance in time and with so
little corroborating evidence, but a speech like this from the
more liberal of the two fathers has the true ring of Menander
to it. Micio is an interesting character in another way. Much
of the comedy arises not so much from the contrast between
him and his repressed brother, Demea, the natural father of
the two boys, as from his pleasure in teasing him into
thinking that he, Micio, is more uncaring that he really is.
This is a clever platform for the play's big reversal when
Demea has his change of heart. Pushed to the limit by
circumstances that both are and are not Micio's fault, Demea
snaps:

> He suits himself how he lives and how he spends his
> money. Result. He's popular. Everyone loves him ...What
> about me ... They can't stand me ... They adore him as
> they avoid me ... Very well then. Time for a new
> approach. (ll. 865 ff.)

Demea's revenge has him freeing Micio's slaves, knocking
down the wall between his and the next-door house, giving
away part of Micio's estate and arranging this confirmed
bachelor's marriage with his son's future mother-in-law.

All this is great fun for an audience, the more manic and
frenetic it becomes – this is not intellectual comedy for all its
thoughtfulness. The sting in the tail is still to come when
Demea rounds on his son who has been applauding his every
liberal action and offers his ultimatum: accept my frugal way
of life or I disown you; if you do accept it I will always be
there for you. The comedy has only another three short
speeches to run. Aeschinus accepts on behalf of himself and
his absent brother in a single line. But the point is made. A
Roman audience would probably have loved such a decorous
ending, as much as did pre-Renaissance times when this and
other Terence plays were so popular. But again, the ending
has the ring of Menander, with the dissipated and the

thoughtless benefiting from their experience. Here is a comedy where all the main participants are more than mere stereotypes. Variations on what is expected of the stock characters free Terence, and, indeed, Plautus too, from the tedium of predictability. In *Brothers,* the central figures all go through their learning process and all emerge the better for it.

J. Michael Walton
Hull, 2002

A note from Michael Sargent

Kenneth McLeish made three translations of Roman plays (the two in this volume and Plautus' *The Rope*) for BBC radio in the 1960s. He did *The Eunuch* first and we have three versions, his original draft (dated 1965), a revision of this for radio (1967) and a new version intended for publication, which he had begun but only about one quarter completed at the time of his death in 1997. In preparing the text for this edition I have restored sections where Kenneth had cut or paraphrased the original but have used his words wherever possible. Kenneth's version of *The Haunted House* was translated directly for radio and is a much freer adaptation (for example, there are a number of cuts, several of the long speeches are replaced by songs, and the final scene is largely rewritten from the original). Again, wherever possible, I have used Kenneth's words, but more of the play has had to be translated afresh from the Latin. In the case of both plays, however, I hope these versions are very much what Kenneth himself would have wanted to see in print.

Line numbers alongside the text refer to the Latin originals rather than to these translations.

PLAUTUS

The Haunted House
(*Mostellaria*)

translated by Kenneth McLeish and Michael Sargent

Characters

GRUMIO, a country slave
TRANIO, a town slave
PHILOLACHES, their young master
PHILEMATIUM, beloved of Philolaches
SCAPHA, her attendant
CALLIDAMATES, a young friend of Philolaches
DELPHIUM, a girl companion of Callidamates
A SLAVE-BOY
THEOPROPIDES, an Athenian merchant, father of
  Philolaches
A MONEYLENDER
SIMO, Theopropides' elderly neighbour
PHANISCUS } slaves of Callidamates
PINACIUM }

An earlier version of this translation was first broadcast on the BBC Third Programme in September 1969. The cast included Peter Baldwin, John Bentley, Margot Boyd, Wilfrid Carter, Alaric Cotter, Jan Edwards, Leonard Fenton, John Gabriel, Madi Hedd, Nigel Lambert, Peter Pratt, Peter Tuddenham, Peter Williams and John Wyse, produced by Raymond Raikes.

The first stage production of this revised version was given by Xenia Theatre Company at the Old Red Lion Theatre, London, in December 2000. The cast included Bonny Ambrose, Joel Chalfen, Steve Dineen, Terry Jermyn, Gabrielle Kruger, Andrew Oliver and Lara Parmiani, directed by Michael Sargent.

The scene is a street in Athens, in front of the houses of THEOPROPIDES *and* SIMO. GRUMIO, *a country slave, is hammering on the door of* THEOPROPIDES' *house.*

GRUMIO.

Hey! Open up, Tranio! Let me in! ... I'll pay you back for this ... Come out of your kitchen, smart-arse! I'm warning you ... open this door!

The door opens and TRANIO, *a smart town slave, appears.*

TRANIO.

What is it now ... dungheap?

GRUMIO.

Dungheap? Say that again, you city scum you ... you kitchen-wrecker! You ought to be ashamed of yourself ... the way you've all been carrying on in that house while the master's been away ...

TRANIO.

Ah, clear off, can't you? You're fouling the footpaths of Athens! You're not in your farmyard now, you know: this is a sophisticated neighbourhood. Go back home ... you can howl as much as you like in your own farmyard ... with the other animals ...

GRUMIO.

Look, Tranio ...

TRANIO.

What're you waiting for. *This*? (*Slap.*)

GRUMIO.

Ow! What was that for?   10

TRANIO.

For living.

GRUMIO.

Well ... you wait till the old man gets back ... if there's anything left to come back to, by the time you've finished eating him out of house and home.

TRANIO.
Badly expressed and deficient in logic, cabbage-head! How can I be eating him out of house and home when he's not been here for three years!

GRUMIO.
Oh, very clever. Yes, you make the most of it while you've got the chance ... before you're carted off to join the chain-gang. Carry on with your all-night
20 parties, your *Greek* way of life. Buy up all the prostitutes in town and give them their freedom. You carry on ... that's what the master told you to do before he left. 'Look after the house for me, Tranio' – that's what he said – 'You're an honest servant, you know what's required.' Oh yes ... he'll be delighted when he comes back and sees what you've done to his only son!

TRANIO (*in a warning tone*).
Grumio ...

GRUMIO.
30 You've ruined that young man. The finest young gentleman in Athens he was once ... and now look at him! You must be really proud of yourself...

TRANIO.
That's enough, you sheep-wit! What's it got to do with you? Get back to the farm and lecture your cows! So I like drink and women ... what business is that of yours? It's my neck, isn't it?

GRUMIO.
Huh! Big talk...

TRANIO.
40 Big talk? (*With contempt.*) You stink, Grumio ... mud and dung, that's what you smell of ... mud and dung and goat and garlic...

GRUMIO.
So what? We can't all smell of Arabian perfumes like you. We don't all spend our lives lying on soft cushions, nibbling exotic delicacies. Some of us like

our honest country fare. You may think you're the
lucky one now ... but I know who'll be better off in   50
the end.

TRANIO.
You're jealous. That's what's wrong with you:
you're jealous because I'm doing well and you aren't.
I just have a talent for the high life: pigswill is all
you're fit for!

GRUMIO.
Maybe ... but it won't be me who'll end up on the
gallows when the master gets home ... it won't be
me they'll be driving through the streets with
skewers in his belly.

TRANIO (*nastily*).
What makes you so sure?

GRUMIO.
You've earned it, Tranio. You've worked hard for it
... and you deserve all you get!

TRANIO.
All right, that's enough. Clear off, or you'll get what   60
you deserve.

GRUMIO.
And what about the fodder?

TRANIO.
What fodder?

GRUMIO.
The cattle-fodder you're supposed to supply me
with ... unless you've eaten it yourself.

TRANIO.
Ugh!

GRUMIO.
Oh go to hell! Carry on with your drinking and your
fancy Greek food if that's what you want ...

TRANIO.
Shut up, and get back to your compost-heap. I'll

send some fodder over tomorrow. What are you
waiting for, jailbird?

GRUMIO.

70   That's what they'll be calling you before long.

TRANIO

'Before long' doesn't bother me; I'm too busy
enjoying 'now'.

GRUMIO.

Grr ... I know who'll get the last laugh ...

TRANIO.

Oh, clear off and leave me in peace! I've no more
time to waste. Goodbye! (*He goes off along the street.*)

GRUMIO (*shouts after him*).

Well don't say I didn't warn you ... My god, I hope
master gets home before long ... if he doesn't,
there'll be nothing left ... house, farm, fields, all
80   eaten up by that swarm of locusts. (*Going off in
opposite direction.*) I'll get back to the farm ... And
here comes the young master ... such a fine young lad
he was once, and now ... utterly gone to the bad! ...

He disappears. PHILOLACHES *enters from the
house. He sees the audience and addresses them.*

PHILOLACHES.

You know, there's a matter I've been giving a lot of
thought to lately ... arguing it through with myself
... a lot of heart-searching ... that's if I have
anything that can be called a heart. It's this: after
much pondering and cogitation, I've come to the
conclusion that MAN IS ... well, any man, that is,
whatever his station in life ... MAN IS RATHER LIKE ...
or, at least, IS NOT UNLIKE ... or, let's say, he
SOMEWHAT RESEMBLES ... at least I think I'll be able
90   to convince you of this ... when you've heard my
arguments ... MAN IS (when he's first born, that is)
LIKE A NEW HOUSE. Mmmm!

Now I dare say that you don't immediately notice
the similarity, but I hope ... in fact, I'm sure that

you'll agree with me ... when you've heard what I
have to say, that is. So listen carefully while I explain
... I don't want to keep this all to myself, I want you
all to share my great discovery.   100

So, A HOUSE. When a nice new house is built,
properly finished, constructed to a T, as they say ...
well, it may not actually be a T, it might be some
other shape, but you know what I mean ... everyone
likes it, they say the builders have done a splendid
job, everyone wants it, or rather wants one just like
it, and they start saving up so they can buy
something similar. But let's say the owner is some
idle, careless, good-for-nothing, lazy slob. What
happens? The house begins to suffer. There's a
storm ... wind and rain ... tiles fall off, roofs leak
(and the owner does nothing about it), rain comes   110
washing down the walls, drips through the ceilings,
the rafters start to rot, all the builder's work is
ruined. Things go from bad to worse ... it's not the
builder's fault, of course, a little bit of care and
money could have stopped the damage, but they put
it off and put it off and do nothing and ... CRASH!!!
... the whole house collapses ... and there's nothing
for it but to rebuild the whole thing from scratch.

Right! So that's a house. Now I want to go on and
explain why I think a MAN is like a HOUSE. Well, in
the first place, parents are the builders ... of their   120
children. They lay the foundations, raise the
structure up, guide its growth, spare no expense.
They want it to be a credit to them. They teach them
respect, what's right and wrong. They want their
neighbours to envy them and wish they had children
like that.

But sooner or later the boy leaves home ... military
service, perhaps ... the builder loses sight of him.
What happens to the building then?   130

Take me, for example. I was always a steady,
serious-minded chap, when I was in the builders'

hands. But left to my own devices ... well, it didn't take me long to undo all their work and make the house a ruin. Rainy weather ... that was idleness. Gales and hailstorms ... carelessness and indifference. I did nothing to repair the damage. And then came LOVE ... pouring into my heart and soul. I was flooded out. Goodbye to fortune, faith, my reputation, my honour! My house is beyond repair, nothing can stop it becoming a total ruin.

It makes me very sad to see what I am now, and what I was. I was a model child, top of the class in games and exercises, an example to all my friends; even the best of them said I could teach them something. Now ... I'm good for nothing. That's the one thing I have taught myself.

Noises off. The door of the house opens and PHILEMATIUM *and her attendant* SCAPHA *come out.* PHILOLACHES *keeps out of sight.*

PHILEMATIUM.
That *was* a nice bath, Scapha. I feel clean *all* over!

SCAPHA.
Then everything's fine, lady Philematium. And the barns are full too.

PHILEMATIUM.
Barns? What have barns to do with my bath?

SCAPHA.
Why, don't you know ... after the bath, the harvest!

PHILEMATIUM.
Oh, Scapha!

PHILOLACHES (*aside*).
I can hear her ... Venus herself ... the storm that stripped the roof from my house and soaked me to the skin with Love ...

PHILEMATIUM.
Scapha, you do like this dress, don't you? I want

everything to be perfect tonight for my dear lord
Philolaches...

SCAPHA.
I don't know why you bother. It's not clothes men
are interested in ... it's what's inside them.

PHILOLACHES (*aside*).
Old Scapha's got the right idea there ... she knows   170
exactly what a lover wants!

PHILEMATIUM (*posing*).
Well, now?

SCAPHA.
Well, what?

PHILEMATIUM.
Look, I'll turn round ... there ... does it suit me?

SCAPHA.
With a figure like yours, you'd look all right in
anything ...

PHILOLACHES (*aside*).
I'll give you something nice for saying that,
Scapha...

PHILEMATIUM.
Scapha, I don't want you to flatter me ... you
mustn't say what you think I want to hear ...

SCAPHA.
Don't you ever want to hear the truth? Silly girl! I'd
rather have compliments, even if they're not true!   180

PHILEMATIUM.
I like people to be sincere; I can't bear lying.

SCAPHA.
All right then, you're the most beautiful girl in the
whole of Greece, and I only hope your Philolaches
still loves you.

PHILOLACHES (*aside*).
What's that, you wretch? 'I only hope...'! And what

about *her* loving *me* ... No, after that remark I won't give you something nice after all!

SCAPHA.
But I do just hope that you're not making a fool of yourself, that's all.

PHILEMATIUM.
What do you mean?

SCAPHA.
Reserving yourself for one man alone ... a bit of variety never hurt anyone ... fidelity's for wives, not people like us!

190

PHILOLACHES (*aside*).
That old woman will ruin me ... I'll have to starve her to death!

PHILEMATIUM.
Scapha, I don't want to hear *that* sort of advice ...

SCAPHA.
It's all right now while he still says he loves you. But one day he'll grow tired of you, and then where will you be?

PHILEMATIUM.
My Philolaches won't ever grow tired of me. Why ...

SCAPHA.
That's what we all think, till it happens. It happened to me. I had one man ... but when my hair changed colour, he was gone ... it'll happen to you.

200

PHILOLACHES (*aside*).
I'll scratch her eyes out! The ...!

PHILEMATIUM.
But he *bought* me, Scapha ... you know he did ... bought me with his own money and gave me my freedom ...

SCAPHA.
So what?

PHILEMATIUM.
So I *must* be faithful.

PHILOLACHES (*aside*).
Gods! What a lovely, sweet girl she is! I'm glad I was
ruined for her sake...

SCAPHA.
You're just a fool...

PHILEMATIUM.
Why?

SCAPHA.
To care about whether he loves you or not.

PHILEMATIUM.
Why on earth shouldn't I care?

SCAPHA.
Because you're wasting your opportunities. You're a   210
free woman now ... you've got what you were
after...

PHILOLACHES (*aside*).
The old ... so and so ... I'll ... I'll...!

PHILEMATIUM.
I can't ever be grateful enough to him, never! I owe
him everything...

SCAPHA.
You've given him everything, you mean... Go on
your knees to one man while you're young and
beautiful, and you'll regret it bitterly when you're
old...

PHILOLACHES (*aside*).
Oh, the viper! I could choke her to death...

PHILEMATIUM.
And I ought to love him even more now I've got   220
what I wanted than when I had to coax and charm
him.

PHILOLACHES (*aside*).
Now I want to buy her her freedom all over again ...

and at the same time get rid of that wretched old
woman!

SCAPHA.

Well stick to him then ... even marry him if you
want ... but only if you can really be sure that he will
always love you and provide for you.

PHILEMATIUM.

If I can just keep my good name, that's all the wealth
I want.

PHILOLACHES (*aside*).

230   I'll see that you always have everything you need,
my darling ... I'll sell my own father if need be!

SCAPHA.

And what about your other lovers? What are they
supposed to do?

PHILEMATIUM.

I don't care about them any more.

SCAPHA.

He won't stick to you. Look at what goes on in this
house: drinking and parties night after night ...

PHILOLACHES (*aside*).

Not for you after this, Scapha ... no more parties for
you!

SCAPHA.

He'll soon forget you ...

PHILEMATIUM.

240   Scapha ... another word against Philolaches ... and
I'll have you whipped!

PHILOLACHES (*aside*).

Yes, that's the spirit! You can see she loves me with
all her soul! That money I paid for her is the best
investment I've ever made ... I certainly couldn't
have hired a better lawyer to plead my case for me!

SCAPHA.

I can see now that Philolaches is worth more to you
than all the men in the world put together. I

certainly don't want to be whipped on his account,
so I'd better agree with you...

PHILEMATIUM.
Now, hand me my mirror and my jewels, please.
Quick, Scapha... I want to be all ready for when my
darling Philolaches gets here.

SCAPHA.
I can't think what you want with this mirror.
Women only use mirrors to assure themselves   250
they're not as ugly as they think.

PHILEMATIUM.
Is my hair pretty enough, do you think?

SCAPHA.
When you're as pretty as you are, you don't need to
worry about your hair.

PHILOLACHES (*aside*).
What a sly creature! Now she's full of compliments...

PHILEMATIUM.
The rouge, please...   260

SCAPHA.
Why repaint a pretty picture ... Now you'd better
give me the mirror and wipe your hands.

PHILEMATIUM.
Why?

SCAPHA.
You've been holding this mirror and your hands may
smell of silver. We don't want your Philolaches to
think you've handled money...

PHILOLACHES (*aside*).
Crafty, clever old b...!   270

PHILEMATIUM.
Better still ... put scent on my hands...

SCAPHA.
No, no scent...

PHILEMATIUM.
Why not?

SCAPHA.
A woman smells sweetest when she smells of nothing
at all. The more make-up and perfume women use,
the more they've got to hide! You've seen those
hideous old creatures ... plastered with paint ...
scent and sweat all mixed together so they smell like
a stew when the cook's thrown in everything in sight
... horrible!

PHILOLACHES (*aside*).
She certainly knows it all ... she's quite right! (*To
the audience.*) I'm sure most of you can vouch for
280   that, too ... if you've got an old, rich wife at home!

PHILEMATIUM.
All right, Scapha ... do you think I'll do?

SCAPHA.
It's not my business to say.

PHILEMATIUM.
Then whose is it?

SCAPHA.
Philolaches, of course. He buys you things he thinks
will please you. But you don't need to show them off
to him. After all, a beautiful girl is more beautiful
290   naked than wrapped up in purple silks...

PHILOLACHES (*aside*).
My cue for an entrance. I can't wait any longer.
(*Steps forward.*) What have you been doing here?

PHILEMATIUM.
Making myself look nice to please you.

PHILOLACHES.
You can't help looking nice, my darling. (*To
SCAPHA.*) *You* can take this box ... and these
cosmetics ... and the mirror, Scapha, and...

SCAPHA.
Yes, sir?

PHILOLACHES.
Disappear!

SCAPHA *goes off with all the accessories.*

Now, Philematium, darling ... what I want from
you ...

PHILEMATIUM.
Whatever you want, my darling, I want too ...

PHILOLACHES.
I'd like to give you two thousand drachmas for that
pretty speech.

PHILEMATIUM.
One thousand will do ... I mustn't overcharge you.

PHILOLACHES.
Well that makes you one thousand to the good: I
paid three thousand for you ...

PHILEMATIUM.
But you're not sorry you bought me my freedom, are   300
you?

PHILOLACHES.
No money's ever been better spent ...

PHILEMATIUM.
And now I'll spend all that money ... in loving you!

PHILOLACHES.
Then we're quits ... you love me and I love you.
We're both satisfied.

PHILEMATIUM.
Come and sit down. (*Calling.*) Boy! Bring some
water for our hands, and set the table. It's time for
the party ...

Music offstage.

PHILOLACHES.
Listen, I can hear them coming! (*Looks offstage.*) It's   310
Callidamates, that lady-killer, with his girl-friend
Delphium. Come and look, darling ...

> *Enter along the street* CALLIDAMATES, *extremely drunk, supported by* DELPHIUM, *and attended by his slave* PHANISCUS.

CALLIDAMATES (*tipsily, to* PHANISCUS).
Listen carefully ... I want you to ... come back and get me ... later on ... at this house ... Philo-lo-lo-laches's house ... Got it? Those are your instr-str-structions.

> PHANISCUS *goes off down the street.*

CALLIDAMATES (*singing*).
O, the last place wasn't fun,
No fun for anyone...
I din' like it at all...

DELPHIUM (*as chorus*).
Not at all!

CALLIDAMATES.
I like a sober party,
Nothing posh or arty ...
I don' like that at all ...

DELPHIUM.
Not at all!

CALLIDAMATES.
At Philolucky's place
There's lots of drinking space
And fun for one and all ...

DELPHIUM.
One and all!

CALLIDAMATES.
We'll have a li'l drink
Get tipsy quick's a wink,
At Philolucky's house...

(*Breaking off.*) I say, Del-Delphin-inium ... you wouldn't say I was ... just a little bit in-ebri-ated?

DELPHIUM.
320   No more'n usual. Come along ... this is where we've got to go...

CALLIDAMATES.
  'S a good girl ... give's a kiss.

DELPHIUM.
  With the greatest of ... hic! ... pleasure.

CALLIDAMATES.
  Oh, darling, darling ... ooops! Where are you?

DELPHIUM.
  Over here. Careful! There you are...

CALLIDAMATES.
  Darling ... Let's have a little cuddle ... Mmmm,
  that's it...

DELPHIUM.
  No, no ... don't lie down in the street ... wait till we
  can find a nice soft couch...

CALLIDAMATES.
  Let's just lie here for a bit ... someone's sure to   330
  come and find us...

DELPHIUM.
  Darling, you're tipsy.

CALLIDAMATES.
  T-t-tipsy? Who says I'm tipsy?

DELPHIUM.
  Give me your hand ... you'll hurt yourself.

CALLIDAMATES.
  There.

DELPHIUM.
  Now, come on. I'll support you.

CALLIDAMATES.
  Where we going?

DELPHIUM.
  You know where we're going.

CALLIDAMATES.
  Do I? Oh yes ... home for a drink...

DELPHIUM (*trying to pull him along*).
No, no, we're going in *here*.

CALLIDAMATES.
Oh yes, that's right.

PHILOLACHES (*from his house*).
Oh, look, Philematium ... I'd better go and meet
them ... He *is* my best friend. I'll be back in no time
at all ...

PHILEMATIUM.
Even less if you can, darling ...

CALLIDAMATES.
Hello! Anyone at home?

PHILOLACHES.
Yes, we're here!

CALLIDAMATES.
340   Philolaches! Glad to see you ... best friend I've got
... in all the world! Glad to see ...

PHILOLACHES.
Callidamates, do come in. Sit yourself down. Where
have you come from?

CALLIDAMATES.
Where there were ... rather a lot of drunks ...

PHILEMATIUM.
Come in, Delphium. Sit next to me. Give your
friend a drink ...

CALLIDAMATES.
I think I'll just ... go to sleep ... (*He falls asleep on
the floor.*)

PHILOLACHES.
That's nothing new for him!

DELPHIUM.
What shall we do with him?

PHILEMATIUM.
Let him sleep, my dear. Come on, pass the cup
round ... you first, Delphium ...

*The party gets under way inside the house. After a
short pause,* TRANIO *rushes in along the street, out
of breath and in a state of panic.*

TRANIO (*sees audience and stops to explain to them*).
I expect you're wondering why I'm in such a panic?
Well, I'll tell you. (*Melodramatically.*) We're   350
doomed! It's all over!! There's no hope for us!!!
Why? I hear you ask. The master's come home from
his travels! I'm finished! Anyone here want to make
some easy money? Anybody would like to be
crucified in my place today? It's simple really . . . you
just jump on a cross . . . have some little nails
hammered through your hands and feet . . . and . . .
Any volunteers? No? When it's over you can come
and collect the money from me . . . cash on the nail!   360
Oh, you're all useless . . . what am I wasting my time
for? I'd better get home double-quick.

(*Rushes up to door and calls.*) Philolaches, sir! Quick,
come out here . . .

PHILOLACHES (*coming to door*).
What is it, Tranio?

TRANIO.
You and I . . . We're both . . .

PHILOLACHES.
Both what . . . ?

TRANIO.
We're done for!

PHILOLACHES.
What d'you mean?

TRANIO.
Your father's here!

PHILOLACHES.
What did you say?

TRANIO.
He's here . . . he's come back! We're done for!

PHILOLACHES.
But where is he?

TRANIO.
On his way here.

PHILOLACHES.
Who told you? Who saw him?

TRANIO.
I saw him, down at the harbour!

PHILOLACHES.
Oh my god! Now where am I?

TRANIO.
Where are you? You're sitting here drinking!

PHILOLACHES.
You actually saw him?

TRANIO.
Yes!

PHILOLACHES.
Are you sure?

TRANIO.
370   I'm sure I'm sure! What would I want to make it up for?

PHILOLACHES.
But what're we going to *do*?

TRANIO (*crossing to house*).
Do? Get rid of that lot in the house, for a start. (*Opens the door and looks in.*) Who's that asleep over there?

PHILOLACHES.
Callidamates! Oh my god! Quick, Delphium! Wake him up!

DELPHIUM.
Oh ... Callidamates! Callidamates!

CALLIDAMATES (*half-asleep, crawling out on his hands and knees*).
Wha ... wha ... ?

DELPHIUM
Get up! Quickly!

CALLIDAMATES.
Give's a drink...

DELPHIUM.
Never mind a drink ... hide before he gets here!

CALLIDAMATES.
Who?

DELPHIUM.
He's coming here ... Philolaches' father!

CALLIDAMATES.
Oh, Philo-lo-laches's father ... nice ol' man...

PHILOLACHES.
Nice old man? Wait till he sees what's going on here!
Get up, can't you! *My father's coming!*

CALLIDAMATES (*drowsily*).
Well, so wha'? Tell him to go 'way again. What's he
want to come back here for, anyway? (*Snores.*)

PHILOLACHES.
God, this is awful. My father will get here, find me
drunk, the house full of party-goers ... What the hell   380
can we do?

TRANIO.
Now look at him ... fallen asleep again!

PHILOLACHES.
Callidamates! For god's sake, wake up! *My father's
about to arrive!*

CALLIDAMATES (*suddenly awake*).
What's that? Your father? Get my armour ... we'll
fight to the death ... repel the invaders...

PHILOLACHES.
Shut up, you idiot, or we'll all be killed ...

DELPHIUM.
Do be quiet, darling.

TRANIO.
Just get him out of the way!

CALLIDAMATES (*suddenly*).
Help! Quick! I think I'm ... going to be s-s-s-s ...
(*He is dragged off.*)

PHILOLACHES.
We're finished!

TRANIO.
No we're not. Leave it to me ... I'll fix it so that
when your father does arrive, he won't come in ... in
390   fact, he'll run off in the opposite direction! But get
all this stuff inside, as quick as you can...

PHILOLACHES.
And where shall I be?

TRANIO.
Wherever you prefer ... this one, that one ...
(*Indicating the two girls.*)

DELPHIUM.
Hadn't we better go home?

TRANIO.
No, just carry on with the party inside, as if nothing
had happened...

PHILOLACHES.
But what'll we do ... I can't think straight...

TRANIO.
Just calm down, and do as I say. And you girls, get
inside.

DELPHIUM.
Whatever you say, Tranio.

   She and PHILEMATIUM *go inside.*

TRANIO.
Now, sir, listen very carefully ... this is what I want
400   you to do. First of all, go inside the house and bolt all
the doors.

PHILOLACHES.
Bolt all the ...?

TRANIO.
Don't argue ... just do it. Then keep everyone quiet
... there mustn't be a sound.

PHILOLACHES.
Not a sound. Right.

TRANIO.
Your father'll arrive any minute. He'll come up to
this door and knock.

PHILOLACHES.
Brrr!

TRANIO.
No, no, don't panic. Don't let anyone answer the
door, that's all.

PHILOLACHES.
Anything else?

TRANIO.
Er ... yes. Send someone out here with the main
door-key. I'll lock you all in from the outside.

PHILOLACHES.
Tranio, I haven't the slightest idea what you're
going to do, but I hope it works for all our sakes ...
(*He goes in.*)

TRANIO (*chuckling to himself*).
It's a masterly scheme ... masterly ... Yes, nothing
to choose between *master* and slave when it comes to
schemes like ... You see, anyone ... anyone at all can
do something off the cuff, if he has no choice. But it   410
takes a really intelligent man ... I don't think genius
is too strong a word ... to plan everything in
advance, so that it all goes without a hitch, from start
to finish. If he doesn't succeed, he's in dead
trouble ...

    A SLAVE-BOY *pops his head out of the door.*

What the hell are you doing out here?

SLAVE-BOY (*showing a key*).
I've got the ...

TRANIO.
420   Oh yes, that's right.

SLAVE-BOY.
And the master says, whatever you do, make sure his father is well and truly frightened away.

TRANIO.
Tell him not to worry. The old man won't even look at the house ... he'll cover his head and run for his life! Come on, give me the key.

SLAVE-BOY.
Here it is.

TRANIO.
Get inside and shut the door.

The SLAVE-BOY *goes in.*

Now, I'll lock it from the outside. (*Locks the door.*) There, that's done ... All right, father Theopropides, you can turn up whenever you like now. Everything's ready for you ... just a minute ... I'd better get away from this door (*Moving away.*) ... over here, where he can't see me ... I'll give him
430   something to come home for!

THEOPROPIDES *approaches along the street, followed by slaves carrying his luggage.*

THEOPROPIDES.
Home at last! Thanks be to Neptune for letting me out of his clutches to arrive here safe and dry ... but only just! That's the last time I'll go to sea! If you catch me putting as much as my big toe in sea-water again, Neptune can do ... whatever he planned for us all *this* time!

TRANIO (*aside*).
You made a big mistake there, Neptune ... losing a good chance like that!

THEOPROPIDES.
> Three years in Egypt, and then ... Never mind,
> we're here now. I'm sure everyone will be delighted 440
> to see me!

TRANIO (*aside*).
> They'd be more delighted just now to receive news
> of your death!

THEOPROPIDES (*going to door of house and trying to
open it*).
> That's odd! The door locked, in the middle of the
> day! I'll have to knock ... (*Knock.*) Hey! Anyone
> there? (*Knock.*) Open up! (*Knock! Knock! Knock!*)

TRANIO (*rushing forward as if he's just arrived*).
> Who's that hammering at our door?

THEOPROPIDES.
> Ah, it's Tranio. (*Effusively.*) Tranio ... my favourite
> slave...

TRANIO.
> Theopropides, my dear old master! Glad to see you
> back, sir! Quite well, are you, sir?

THEOPROPIDES.
> Perfectly well, thank you, Tranio ...

TRANIO.
> Marvellous!

THEOPROPIDES.
> But what's going on inside my house? Have my
> slaves all gone raving mad?

TRANIO.
> Eh?

THEOPROPIDES.
> I mean, there doesn't seem to be a living soul to open 450
> the door. And I've practically beaten it to
> splinters...

TRANIO.
> Oh my god! You haven't touched that door, have
> you sir?

THEOPROPIDES.
Touched it? Hammered it down, more like.

TRANIO.
Ohhh, Theopropides, sir ... you *have* touched it!

THEOPROPIDES.
Yes, of course, gave it a good hammering!

TRANIO.
Oh my god!

THEOPROPIDES.
What's the *matter* with you?

TRANIO.
You've done it now.

THEOPROPIDES.
What're you talking about?

TRANIO.
You couldn't have done anything worse...

THEOPROPIDES.
What?

TRANIO.
460   Fly, sir ... I beg you, fly with me from this *accursed* house! Fly ... over here, by me ... (*Drags him to the far side of the stage.*) You say you actually touched that door?

THEOPROPIDES.
How could I knock on it without touching it, idiot?

TRANIO.
We've had it ... all of us!

THEOPROPIDES.
What d'you mean, 'had it'? Now look here, Tranio...

TRANIO.
How will you ever atone?

THEOPROPIDES.
Atone? Atone for what? What's going on...?

TRANIO (*seeing that the slaves with the luggage are about to try the door*).
Stop! Tell those men to keep away from the house!

THEOPROPIDES.
Keep away!

TRANIO.
Don't touch the house! Touch the earth, all of you ...

The slaves run away, frightened.

THEOPROPIDES.
For god's sake, what's this all about?

TRANIO.
Seven months it's been shut up, locked and deserted   470
... we all had to leave ... no one's set foot in it
since...

THEOPROPIDES.
But *why*?

TRANIO.
Sshhh! ... Come over here! (*Moving to L.*) Anyone
about? Anyone 'listening in'?

THEOPROPIDES.
Not that I can see...

TRANIO (*moving to R*).
Quick! Over here, then ... anyone?

THEOPROPIDES.
Not a soul! So ... what's been going on?

TRANIO.
MURDER!

THEOPROPIDES.
Murder? I don't follow.

TRANIO.
Murder ... you know ... murder most foul.

THEOPROPIDES.
When?

TRANIO.
Years ago.

THEOPROPIDES.
Who?

TRANIO.
Ah! ... you may well ask ... (*Hoarse whisper.*) It seems that years ago ... a host ... took one of his guests by the throat, and ... (*Expressive noise.*)

THEOPROPIDES.
Good god! Who?

TRANIO.
SSHHH! ... They think it was ... the man you
480   bought the house from.

THEOPROPIDES.
What? He murdered a guest?

TRANIO.
Yes ... murdered him, robbed him, and ... (*Sibilantly.*) disposed of the evidence!

THEOPROPIDES.
Ugh! ... How did you find all this out?

TRANIO.
Ah! ... One night, your son Philolaches had gone out for the evening ... when he got back, we all went to bed ... fast asleep ... there was only one lamp burning, I'd forgotten to put out. Suddenly he uttered a terrible cry ...

THEOPROPIDES,
Who did? My son?

TRANIO.
Ssh! Don't interrupt. He said a dead man had
490   appeared to him in his sleep ...

THEOPROPIDES.
In his sleep? Really?

TRANIO.
  Yes, really. Listen. The dead man, so your son says,
  spoke to him as follows ...

THEOPROPIDES.
  In his sleep?

TRANIO.
  He couldn't very well speak to him awake, could he,
  since he was killed sixty years ago? Really,
  sometimes you are *so* stupid ...

THEOPROPIDES.
  All right, all right, I won't say a word. Go on.

TRANIO.
  And this is what the dead man said, to your son, in
  his sleep: 'Diapontus is my name ... Diapontus from
  across the water ... this is my dwelling place ... this
  is where I'm doomed to wander for evermore ... I
  was foully murdered, here in this house! I trusted,   500
  and I was deceived. My host murdered me, and
  buried me here ... under the floorboards. He was
  after my money ... Go! Leave this house of shame,
  this habitation of horror!' Those were his very
  words ...

  *Music and noise of party inside house becoming
  audible.*

THEOPROPIDES.
  Sshh! Sshh! What's that? ...

TRANIO.
  Yes, my god! What is it?

THEOPROPIDES.
  There's something going on inside.

TRANIO (*going up to the door and calling to the
supposed 'ghost'*).
  He did it! (*Pointing to* THEOPROPIDES.) He did
  the knocking!

THEOPROPIDES (*terrified*).
  Don't leave me, T-t-tranio ... my blood's turning to
  ice ... don't let them get me ... I'm too old to die.

TRANIO (*whispering urgently through closed door*).
  For heaven's sake, you fools, shut up in there! You'll
510 ruin everything! (*Music and noise fades; he moves
  back.*) Sorry, master, you were saying...?

THEOPROPIDES (*suspiciously*).
  Who were you talking to? Yourself?

TRANIO.
  Keep away from that door, sir! You must fly ... fly
  immediately!

THEOPROPIDES (*testily*).
  Fly? Where can I fly to? *You* fly!

TRANIO.
  No, no ... *I've* no need to fly ... I've no quarrel with
  the Dead.

CALLIDAMATES (*great drunken voice from within
the house*).
  Tranio! Tranee-oh!

TRANIO (*moving to door*).
  Rest, rest, perturb-ed spirit ... (*Aside.*) Shut up, for
  god's sake! (*Aloud.*) Begone, begone I say, and
  trouble us no more! 'Twas not I who knock-ed...

CALLIDAMATES (*from within*).
  We want to know...

TRANIO (*aside*).
  Shut up, all of you!

THEOPROPIDES (*calling to him*).
  Hey, Tranio!

TRANIO (*aloud*).
  Begone, begone!

THEOPROPIDES.
  Tranio! What's happening? Who were you talking
  to?

TRANIO (*moving back*).
Oh, it was you calling, master, sir ... I thought the   520
corpse had come out ... because you knocked at the
door. Please, sir, don't just stand there ... do as I
advise you.

THEOPROPIDES.
Do ... what?

TRANIO.
Fly! Cover your head and fly, while there's still
time...

THEOPROPIDES.
Why don't you fly?

TRANIO.
I told you ... they've no quarrel with me ...

THEOPROPIDES.
Why are you so scared, then?

TRANIO.
I'm scared for *you*, sir! If you don't fly soon ...
Listen! ... They're coming out!

THEOPROPIDES (*rushing away down the street*).
Good gracious, I'm off! ... Thank god I got away in
time ... (*Disappears from view.*)

TRANIO.
And thank god I managed to fool him! Ah, but that   530
was a good day's work ... (*Sees someone coming and
stands aside to listen.*)

MONEYLENDER (*coming along the street the other
way*).
Bad times for moneylenders! Never seen a worse
year in my life. I've spent whole days from dawn to
dusk in the forum and haven't been able to lend a
single penny to anyone...

TRANIO (*aside, to audience*).
Oh, god, more trouble! It's the moneylender who
lent us the cash to buy Philematium. We're done for

if the old man comes back... I'd better go and talk to
540   him ...

> *Before he can do so, he sees* THEOPROPIDES
> *coming back.*

Oh, hell, here's the master coming back already. I
wonder why ... I suppose I'll have to speak to him
first. (*As he crosses the stage.*) I'm not enjoying this
much; nothing's more wretched than a guilty
conscience, they say ... However, carry on regard-
less! ... (*Aloud.*) Yes, master? I thought you'd
decided to fly!

THEOPROPIDES (*grimly*).
So I had ... but I've just met the man who sold me
my house.

TRANIO.
Hahahaha! But you didn't mention anything to him
about ... what I've just been telling you?

THEOPROPIDES.
I certainly did. I told him everything.

TRANIO.
550   Everything ... *did* you?

THEOPROPIDES.
Yes ... just as you told me.

TRANIO.
Really. And ... did he, erm, admit that he was a
murderer?

THEOPROPIDES.
Denied every word.

TRANIO.
Denies it, does he?

THEOPROPIDES.
Yes. Now what's to be done?

TRANIO (*with sudden hope*).
Why, of course ... have him up in court ... (*Aside.*)
and for god's sake find a judge who believes me!

MONEYLENDER (*aside*).
Ah, there's Tranio, Philolaches' man. They owe me   560
money and I haven't had a penny back yet.

> TRANIO *sees the* MONEYLENDER *coming and*
> *edges towards him to keep him away from*
> THEOPROPIDES.

THEOPROPIDES.
Where are you going?

TRANIO.
Nowhere. (*Aside.*) Oh dear, this isn't my day! I'm
under fire from both of them. I'd better have a word
with *him*, I suppose.

MONEYLENDER.
Good, he's coming this way. Maybe I'll get my
money...

TRANIO (*aside*).
He looks very pleased with himself, worse luck!
(*Meeting him.*) Aha, Moneygrub ... lovely day it's
been...

MONEYLENDER.
Lovely for some, I dare say. Where's my money,
then, Tranio?

TRANIO.
Oh go away, you nasty little man. As soon as I see   570
you, you get your claws out.

MONEYLENDER (*aside*).
I don't think I'm going to get very far with him.

TRANIO (*aside*).
He's dead right.

MONEYLENDER.
Please stop messing me around.

TRANIO.
Well, please tell me what you want, then.

MONEYLENDER.
Where is Philolaches?

TRANIO.
Well, actually, you couldn't have come at a better time.

MONEYLENDER.
What d'you mean?

TRANIO (*trying to draw him further away*).
Just come over here.

MONEYLENDER.
Look here, I want my money! My money!

TRANIO.
Oh, very nice! Why not shout it to all the neighbourhood?

MONEYLENDER.
All right, I will.

TRANIO.
For heaven's sake ... can't you do me a favour?

MONEYLENDER.
Favour? Favours I don't do. What is it?

TRANIO.
Clear off.

MONEYLENDER.
Clear off?

TRANIO.
Yes, come back at twelve tomorrow.

MONEYLENDER.
580   You'll have the money then?

TRANIO.
You'll get it. Now go, for heaven's sake.

MONEYLENDER.
No! Why should I waste time and shoe-leather rushing backwards and forwards after you and your young master? I'll wait here ... all day, if need be!

TRANIO.
Oh no, you won't. Clear off, can't you?

MONEYLENDER.
No, I'm not budging till I get my interest.

TRANIO.
Clear off!

MONEYLENDER.
Look, I'll bloody well have him arrested, if he
doesn't...

TRANIO.
That's right. Shout your head off...

MONEYLENDER.
I'll have my rights! I'm fed up with you putting me   590
off day after day. If you want to get rid of me, give
me the money!

TRANIO.
You revolting creature! If you've come here for a
shouting match, hard luck! He's not paying you a
thing... he doesn't owe you anything!

MONEYLENDER.
Doesn't owe me...?

TRANIO.
Oh shut up. You're not getting it, so there. You're
not the only moneylender in the world, you know.   600

MONEYLENDER.
My interest! I want my interest! Are you going to
pay me my interest? *I can't wait any longer!*

TRANIO.
Interest, interest, interest ... It's the only bloody
word you know. *Now bugger off!*

MONEYLENDER.
You don't scare me, big mouth!

THEOPROPIDES (*aside*).
They seem to be getting a bit heated ... I can feel it
at this distance! (*Crossing to them.*) Er, Tranio ...
what's this interest he's asking for?   610

TRANIO.

There! Now you've disturbed this gentleman with your shouting. This is young Philolaches' father, just back from abroad. He'll give you your money . . . all of it . . .

MONEYLENDER.

Well let's have it then, if he's got it . . .

THEOPROPIDES.

What *is* going on, Tranio?

TRANIO.

Sir?

THEOPROPIDES.

Who is he? What's he want? What's he saying about Philolaches, and what's this debt?

TRANIO.

Oh, don't trouble yourself with all that, sir. Just give me the money . . . and let me rub his face in it!

THEOPROPIDES.

What?

TRANIO.

620   Rub his face in a handful of money.

MONEYLENDER.

Don't mind, as long as I get it . . .

THEOPROPIDES.

But what money is it?

TRANIO.

It's . . . er . . . a little debt your son owes him.

THEOPROPIDES.

How little?

TRANIO.

Oh . . . er . . . about four thousand drachmas.

MONEYLENDER.

Small change, really . . .

THEOPROPIDES.

What? How much does my son owe you?

MONEYLENDER.
Four thousand four hundred, to be exact.   630

TRANIO.
Oh, give him the money, and let's get rid of him.

THEOPROPIDES.
You want *me* to give him . . .

TRANIO.
No, no . . . just *say* you will . . .

THEOPROPIDES.
But what's happened to the money anyway?

TRANIO.
It's safe enough.

THEOPROPIDES.
Well, if it's safe enough, *you* pay him.

TRANIO.
Ah, well . . . you see, er . . . your son has just, er . . .
bought a house!

THEOPROPIDES.
A house?

TRANIO.
Yes, a house!

THEOPROPIDES.
Magnificent! Just like his father! My boy's got some
sense after all! . . . You did mean a house . . . a real
house?

TRANIO.
Yes.

THEOPROPIDES.
Mmm! What's it like?   640

TRANIO.
Well . . . it's. . . . erm . . .

THEOPROPIDES.
Yes?

TRANIO.
Words fail me.

THEOPROPIDES.
Well?

TRANIO.
Huge rooms ... sunny ... light and airy ... very
desirable!

THEOPROPIDES.
Excellent! And what did he pay for it?

TRANIO.
Twelve thousand drachmas. But he had to pay four
thousand deposit. So we borrowed ... from this...
this *thing*! You see, when your house here turned out
to be ... *you* know! ... your son went out and bought
another one.

THEOPROPIDES.
Good for him ...

MONEYLENDER.
650   Excuse me, it's getting rather late.

TRANIO.
Do pay him, sir, or he'll go on plaguing us.

THEOPROPIDES.
All right, fellow, I'll see you're paid ...

MONEYLENDER.
You will, sir?

THEOPROPIDES.
Yes, come and see me tomorrow. You'll get your
money then.

MONEYLENDER.
All right, then, I'll be off ... *provided* I get it
tomorrow ... (*Goes off.*)

TRANIO (*aside*).
I hope he meets some horrible fate tomorrow! He
very nearly ruined all my plans. Moneylenders ...

the most revolting and dishonest species known to
mankind!

THEOPROPIDES.
Well then, about this house my son has bought.
Where is it?

TRANIO.
Where is it? ... (*Aside.*) Aaaah, I'm done for now ...

THEOPROPIDES.
Are you going to answer me?   660

TRANIO.
Er, yes ... I'm just trying to remember the name of
the man he bought it from.

THEOPROPIDES.
Well try and remember more quickly.

TRANIO (*aside*).
Now what shall I do? I might as well say it's the
house next door ... they say the best lie is a big one
... Here goes ... I'll say what just came into my head.

THEOPROPIDES.
Have you remembered yet?

TRANIO (*aside*).
I wish he'd drop dead! (*Aloud.*) It was ... er ... oh
yes, of course ... that one there, right next door to
yours.

THEOPROPIDES.
Really? No joking?   670

TRANIO (*aside*).
It'll be no joke if you don't give us the money ...
(*Aloud.*) Yes, and it's in a very good neighbourhood,
isn't it?

THEOPROPIDES.
Yes, highly desirable! Well, don't let's waste any
more time. Let's have a look at it.

TRANIO.
What?

THEOPROPIDES.
Knock at the door, Tranio, there's a good chap, and call someone out.

TRANIO (*aside*).
Aaah! Floored again! What the hell can I say?

THEOPROPIDES.
Come on, get them to show me round.

TRANIO.
But ... but ... you can't do that!

THEOPROPIDES.
Why not?

TRANIO (*with sudden inspiration*).
680   The ladies!

THEOPROPIDES.
What ladies?

TRANIO.
The ladies inside that house next door ... they might not like it, without warning ...

THEOPROPIDES.
Yes, you're quite right. Go and find out if they mind. I'll wait along here at the end of the street ... (*He walks away out of sight.*)

TRANIO (*to audience*).
Now what am I going to do? Damn you, old man ... when everything was going so well!

Door of SIMO'*s house opens.*

Hey, here's a bit of luck. There's Simo himself coming out of his house. (*Moving out of sight.*) I'll listen to see if he's in a good mood, then step in to get him to ...

SIMO (*coming out of his house; to audience*).
690   That was the best meal I've had this year! I don't know when I've enjoyed my food so much! My wife has just given me a splendid lunch, and told me to go and have a nap. Huh! I don't think! There's more to

it than that! She wants to get me into bed, the randy old ... Yes!! I don't like doing it straight after lunch. No really. It's not very ... Mmmm, I can see you agree, sir. That's why I've slipped out quietly, to go for a little walk, and left her there all ... erm ... you know...

TRANIO (*aside*).

Oh, dear, there'll be trouble for him when he gets 700 back ... He's in for a bad dinner and a rough night!

SIMO.

It's the worst kind of torture, having a randy old wife. Yes, I can see you know all about that, sir ... do anything to avoid going to bed, do you? Mmmm ... Well, that's why I've decided to go off to town, keep out of the way until she's simmered down. At least it'll postpone the torture for a bit ... 710

TRANIO (*aside*).

Mmm, the old boy's going to get really punished for playing truant! Well, I suppose I'd better have a word with him, and ... That's it! I've got it! I know how to get myself out of this mess ... (*Approaching* SIMO.) The gods bless you, Simo.

SIMO.

And you, Tranio.

TRANIO.

How are you, sir?

SIMO.

Not bad. What are you doing here?

TRANIO.

Talking to a charming old gentleman.

SIMO.

Nice of you to say so. Pity that I'm talking to a rascal 720 of a slave! Well, is something the matter?

TRANIO.

The matter? Oh, er...

SIMO.

Something gone wrong with all your goings-on next
door?

TRANIO.

What goings-on?

SIMO.

730   You know perfectly well ... living it up in style ...
wine, women and song, eh?

TRANIO.

Oh, *yesterday*, you mean!

SIMO.

Yesterday? Oh yes, and the day before, and the day
before that ...

TRANIO.

But ... (*Melodramatically*.) never again!

SIMO.

Oh? Why not?

TRANIO.

We're done for!

SIMO.

Nonsense! You seem to have had it all your own way
up to now ...

TRANIO.

We're shipwrecked! A storm's blown up and
wrecked our chances!

SIMO.

Storm? What sort of storm?

TRANIO.

The worst possible!

SIMO.

What d'you mean? I thought you were safe
enough ...

TRANIO.

740   Oh ... it's all over ... we're completely wrecked!

SIMO.
  Sorry to hear it, Tranio. So what's happened?

TRANIO.
  My master's back!!

SIMO.
  Ah, that's bad ... for you, I mean. Flogging ...
  imprisonment ... the gallows ...

TRANIO.
  Please, please, Simo! You won't breathe a word, will
  you?

SIMO.
  No, no ... silent as the grave, don't worry. (*Laughs.*)
  You've got what's coming to you!

TRANIO (*on his knees*).
  I appeal to you!

SIMO.
  No, you don't. You don't appeal to me at all. In fact,
  if you were my slave, I'd give you your freedom just
  to get rid of you!

TRANIO.
  Please, Simo, this is serious. He sent me to see you.

SIMO.
  Who, Theopropides?

TRANIO.
  That's right.

SIMO.
  So, he doesn't suspect...

TRANIO.
  No, no.

SIMO.
  Quarrelled with his son, has he?   750

TRANIO.
  No, no ... calm seas, fine weather ... but he told me
  to come and ask you a special favour.

SIMO.
What?

TRANIO.
He'd like to look over your house.

SIMO.
It's not for sale.

TRANIO.
I know that ... but he's planning to have some
additions built on to his ... you know, women's
quarters, baths, a garden-walk and a portico ...

SIMO.
He's gone raving mad?

TRANIO.
No, it's for his son ...

SIMO.
Oh?

TRANIO.
Yes, the old man wants to get him married off.
Someone told him the man who designed your house
760   was a genius ... So, he wants to have a look round,
copy some of it, if that's all right with you. It's the
shade, you see ...

SIMO.
Pardon?

TRANIO.
The shade ... he's heard your house is cool and
shaded all day long ...

SIMO.
He's heard wrong ... there isn't an inch of shade
anywhere; and the sun's like my wife's relatives ...
can't get it out of the house! The only bit of shade
you'd find is down in the cellar!

TRANIO.
770   So, your house isn't as shady as I thought it was!

SIMO.
  Don't be impertinent. I'm telling you the facts.

TRANIO.
  Well, he'd like to see over it, anyway.

SIMO.
  He's welcome ... and if he finds *anything* he wants to
  copy, he's welcome to that, too!

TRANIO.
  Shall I go and fetch him?

SIMO.
  By all means. (*He remains at the door of his house.*)

TRANIO (*to audience, as he crosses the stage*).
  Brilliant! I knew my genius would find a way.
  Alexander the Great ... Agathocles ... they'll have
  to add *my* name to the list of champion wonder-
  workers of the world. Ladies and gentlemen, for my
  next trick I will take two old asses and load them up   780
  to breaking point without them even noticing!
  They're a bit slow on the uptake, these elderly pack-
  animals. (*Seeing* THEOPROPIDES *approaching.*)
  I'd better have a word with this one now ...
  Theopropides, sir!

THEOPROPIDES.
  Eh? Who's that?

TRANIO.
  Your ever-faithful slave, master.

THEOPROPIDES.
  Where have you been all this time?

TRANIO.
  Where you sent me ... the old gentleman was busy, I
  had to wait for him.

THEOPROPIDES.
  Trust you to take your time!

TRANIO.
  Oh sir! You know what they say: 'One cannot whistle

790 and eat at the same time.' I can't be in two places at once, can I?

THEOPROPIDES.
Well, well ... what did Simo say?

TRANIO.
The house is yours ... look over it whenever you like.

THEOPROPIDES.
Right away, then.

TRANIO.
Would you like me to take you in?

THEOPROPIDES.
'Take me in'? ... Oh, I see what you mean ...

TRANIO.
This way, then ... he's at the door. But, just a word, sir ... I'm afraid he's bitterly regretting having sold it.

THEOPROPIDES.
Oh, why?

TRANIO.
He wants me to persuade Philolaches to let him have it back.

THEOPROPIDES.
No way! It belongs to us now. You know what they say: 'Reap as you sow' ... 'What's done cannot be
800 undone' ... 'Finder's keepers' ... 'All's fair in love and business.'

TRANIO.
Yes, thank you, sir. Shall we go?

They approach SIMO's *house.*

SIMO.
Good day, Theopropides.

THEOPROPIDES.
Good day.

SIMO.
  Glad to see you safely back from abroad. I
  understand you want to look over my house ...

THEOPROPIDES.
  If it's not inconvenient.

SIMO.
  Not in the least. Come in and look round...

THEOPROPIDES.
  But the ladies ... ?

SIMO.
  Don't mind them! Walk about, wherever you like ...
  just as if the house belonged to you!

THEOPROPIDES.
  As *if* it ...   810

TRANIO (*aside, to him*).
  Ssh, master, he's not very well. Better not remind
  him you've bought it. You can see how ill he looks.

THEOPROPIDES (*aside*).
  Oh yes.

TRANIO (*aside*).
  Don't act as if you've got the better of him, or seem
  too pleased with the house ... in fact, don't say a
  word about the sale at all.

THEOPROPIDES (*aside*).
  Very thoughtful of you, Tranio, an excellent idea ...
  (*Aloud.*) Well now, Simo...

SIMO.
  Come in, come in ... (*Showing them round.*) Now
  this is the entrance-hall, and the main portico...

TRANIO.
  How d'you like it, sir?

THEOPROPIDES.
  Magnificent! Quite superb...

TRANIO.
  Look at these two old Roman pillars. (*Indicates to the*

audience that he means the two old men.) Really solid, and very thick!

THEOPROPIDES.

820   I don't think I've ever seen more handsome ones ...

SIMO.

They *ought* to be good ... I paid enough for them, and a long time ago now, too!

TRANIO (*aside, to* THEOPROPIDES).

Did you hear that, sir? He's almost in tears...

THEOPROPIDES.

And how much did you pay for them?

SIMO.

Three hundred drachmas for the pair, plus carriage.

THEOPROPIDES.

But wait a minute ... are you sure they're still in good condition? They're crumbling away a bit at the bottom...

TRANIO (*to audience*).

Mmmm, definitely past their prime, I'd say. (*To* THEOPROPIDES.) No, they'll be all right with a good coat of paint. Good native workmanship there, none of your foreign rubbish!

THEOPROPIDES.

830   I must say, the more I see of it, the more I like this house.

TRANIO.

Look at that picture, sir, of the crow...

THEOPROPIDES.

Which one do you mean?

TRANIO.

That one there ... a crow standing between two vultures and plucking at them. (*He is standing between the two of them.*)

THEOPROPIDES.

Where? I don't see the one you mean...

SIMO.
Nor do I ...

TRANIO.
Don't you? Look over there ... (*Business with both of them.*) Ah well, your eyesight isn't what it used to be! 840

THEOPROPIDES.
I'm very pleased with everything I *can* see, that's sure.

SIMO.
You ought to see the rest of the house ...

THEOPROPIDES.
Yes, indeed.

SIMO.
I'll call my slave-boy. I'd take you round myself, only I have business in town ...

THEOPROPIDES.
No, no, I don't need an escort. I can find my own way round.

SIMO.
Go ahead then.

TRANIO (*in the doorway*).
Wow! Sir, mind the dog ...

THEOPROPIDES.
Oh yes, Tranio ... please can you ...

TRANIO.
Brr! Get out, dog! Go away, dog! Brr! Go to hell! 850
Are you still there? Brrrrr! Get out!

SIMO.
She's quite harmless ... You don't need to worry about going in there ... Well, I'll be off.

THEOPROPIDES.
Have a pleasant walk!

SIMO *goes off along the street.*

Make a note, Tranio: that dog will have to go for a start!

TRANIO.
Oh, look, sir, she's lying down quite peacefully now.
Don't make a fuss sir ... you don't want to be
thought a coward.

THEOPROPIDES.
Just as you say. Let's go in.

TRANIO.
Yes, sir. You keep close to me...

THEOPROPIDES *and* TRANIO *continue into
the house.*

PHANISCUS *enters along the street, goes up to*
THEOPROPIDES' *house and listens, and then
turns to address the audience.*

PHANISCUS.
Y'know, if you want to be a really useful slave, you
have to be afraid of trouble even if you've done
860   nothing wrong. The ones who couldn't care less,
even when they *have* earned a thrashing ... they're
just stupid. So, they think of running away ... doing
a bunk? They're just saving up trouble for
themselves ... they'll get caught and have to pay up
in beatings much more than they could ever earn in
tips. Me? I aim to keep out of trouble. I like my skin
the way it is ... in one piece! If I can just keep a
watch on myself, I'll always have a roof over my
870   head ... other people can get soaked if they want to.
You see, I think that slaves get the masters they
deserve. Good slaves, good masters; bad slaves, bad
masters. In our house, now, they're really quite an
awful lot, wasteful, terribly rude and, of course,
always getting beaten. When they're called on to
attend the master, it's 'Oh, go to hell ... I'm not
going ... what's the hurry?' *I'm* not like that, I do
my duty. That's why I'm here ... the only one
880   who'd see the master home. Tomorrow when he
finds out, *they'll* all get a good thrashing ... as if I
care about them!

He is about to knock on the door when PINACIUM
rushes in – presumably not wanting to be left out.

PINACIUM.
'Ere, Phaniscus, wait! Stop there! Eh, wait, will yer?

PHANISCUS.
You let me alone.

PINACIUM.
Saucy bugger! Stop there, yer nasty parasite!

PHANISCUS.
What d'you mean?

PINACIUM.
I mean you'd do anythin' in return for a few scraps
of food!

PHANISCUS.
Mind your own business. I like to choose how I
live...

PINACIUM.
Bold as brass, ain't yer, just because you're the   890
master's little darling!

PHANISCUS.
Oh, you *do* go on, don't you?

PINACIUM.
Aw, shut up, you two-faced...

PHANISCUS.
There's no need to be *vicious*, Pinacium. I shall rise
above it ... I'm cultured ... ask young Master
Callidamates.

PINACIUM.
Hah! Master Callidamates knows 'is own favourite
cushion!

PHANISCUS.
Ooh! That was *cruel*, really cruel! You wouldn't talk
like that if you were sober...

PINACIUM.
I'm not taking orders from you, you bugger.

PHANISCUS.
Don't say another word. I've more to do than talk to you, heaven knows. (*Crossing to door.*) I'm here to fetch young Master Callidamates and help him home.

He knocks. No answer.

PINACIUM.
900 No answer? 'Ere, let me 'ave a go. (*Knocks loudly.*) I don't want to 'ave to knock the door down! (*He knocks more heavily. Still no answer.*) They're not going to answer. 'Ere, we'd better watch out ... we don't want 'em to rush out and mug us!

They creep cautiously round the side of the house to investigate.

THEOPROPIDES *and* TRANIO *emerge from* SIMO's *house.*

TRANIO.
Well, sir, what do you think of old Simo's house?

THEOPROPIDES.
Magnificent ... a real bargain. Yes, my son and you, Tranio, between you have certainly got a bargain ...

TRANIO.
You like the women's rooms? And the portico?

THEOPROPIDES
It's a wonderful portico. I doubt if there's a bigger one anywhere in the city.

TRANIO.
910 Absolutely true. In fact, Philolaches and I went round and measured all the porticos in the city.

THEOPROPIDES.
And ... ?

TRANIO.
It's easily the largest one.

THEOPROPIDES.

Yes, we've got an excellent bargain there ... a good investment!

TRANIO.

And of course, sir, it was entirely due to my advice and persuasion. I made Philolaches borrow the money to pay the deposit.

THEOPROPIDES.

A job well done! So, I'll let Simo have the balance of the money today.

TRANIO.

That's right, so he can't change his mind. Better   920
still, sir, you could let me have it, and I'll give it to him.

THEOPROPIDES.

Let you have it? Can I trust you?

TRANIO.

Oh, sir! D'you think I'd ever deceive you in any way, even as a joke?

THEOPROPIDES.

D'you think I'd not be extremely cautious about trusting you with anything important?

TRANIO.

Sir, in all the years I've been with you, have I ever tried to cheat you?

THEOPROPIDES.

I've taken good care that you never had the opportunity. Provided I keep my eyes on *you*, I'll be all right.

TRANIO (*aside*).

He's right there!

THEOPROPIDES.

Now then, off you go to the farm and tell my son I've arrived.

TRANIO.

Yes, sir.

THEOPROPIDES.
And bring him back here as quick as you can.

TRANIO.
930   Very good, sir ... (*Aside as he goes.*) Now all I've got to do is to nip round through the back garden, tell 'em that things have calmed down and fetch 'em out that way! ... (*Disappears.*)

PINACIUM *and* PHANISCUS *come round from the other side of the house.*

PHANISCUS (*back at the house door*).
Very odd! There's supposed to be a party going on in here ... flutes, glasses clinking, singing ...

THEOPROPIDES (*aside*).
What are those two doing outside my house? Don't they know it's haunted?

PHANISCUS.
I shall go on knocking. Hey, open up! Tranio! Open the door! We've come to fetch our master, Callidamates.

THEOPROPIDES (*approaching them*).
I say, you two ... what's happening? Why are you banging at that door?

PINACIUM.
940   What business it is of yours, old man?

THEOPROPIDES.
What business of ... ?

PINACIUM.
You're not by any chance a police inspector, are you ... nosing around in other people's business?

THEOPROPIDES.
You've come to the wrong house.

PINACIUM.
Wrong house, is it? I suppose young Philolaches 'as just sold it, 'as he? ... You pay no attention to this old man, Phaniscus ... 'es playing some sort of trick ...

PHANISCUS.
  You see, sir, our young master's at a party inside.

THEOPROPIDES.
  At a party?

PHANISCUS.
  'S right.

PINACIUM.
  And we've come to fetch 'im 'ome.

THEOPROPIDES.
  Fetch him home?

PHANISCUS.
  Our young master.

THEOPROPIDES.
  Your young master?

PINACIUM.
  He's just like a bleedin' parrot, this one!

THEOPROPIDES.
  You've come to the wrong house ... no one lives
  here any more. (*To* PHANISCUS.) Well, don't *you*
  believe me?

PHANISCUS.
  Me, sir? .

THEOPROPIDES.
  Yes, you. You seem to have more sense than him.

PHANISCUS.
  Doesn't young Philolaches live here, then?   950

THEOPROPIDES.
  He used to ... but he moved out a long time ago.

PHANISCUS.
  I'm sorry, sir, but unless he moved some time
  yesterday or today, he's certainly still living here.

THEOPROPIDES.
  No one's lived here for six months now.

PINACIUM.
You're dreamin', grandad.

THEOPROPIDES.
Me?

PINACIUM.
Yeah, you.

THEOPROPIDES.
Don't interrupt. I'm talking to your friend.

PHANISCUS (*to* PINACIUM).
See!

THEOPROPIDES.
I tell you that house is empty. No one lives there.

PHANISCUS.
Young Philolaches does. I can tell you that for sure.
He was here today ... and yesterday ... and the day
before ... Ever since his father left to go abroad, he's
had a party here, every single day ...

THEOPROPIDES.
What?

PHANISCUS.
Ooh yes ... three days some of them went on ...
960   women, drink, music ... living it up like Greeks!

THEOPROPIDES.
Who?

PHANISCUS.
Philolaches. I keep telling you.

THEOPROPIDES.
Which Philolaches?

PHANISCUS.
You mean there's more than one? His father's
name's Theopropides, I think.

THEOPROPIDES (*aside*).
God help me, if he's speaking the truth I'm a ruined

man. (*To* PHANISCUS.) You're talking complete
rubbish. You must be drunk!

PHANISCUS.
Who, me?

THEOPROPIDES.
Yes, you. You've got the wrong house.

PHANISCUS.
No I haven't. I brought my young master here this
evening, and this was where he told me to come and
fetch him after the party. Young Philolaches lives   970
here ... you know, the one that bought that girl and
gave her her freedom ... lucky thing!

THEOPROPIDES.
I don't believe it.

PHANISCUS.
Believe it or not, it's true. Philematium, her name
is ...

THEOPROPIDES.
What did he pay for her?

PHANISCUS.
Three thousand.

THEOPROPIDES.
What? Three thousand? And then he set her free?

PHANISCUS (*as though to a child*).
Yes. Three thousand drachmas ... and then he set
her free ... got it at last, have you?

THEOPROPIDES.
And you say that ever since his father went abroad
he's been having these drinking parties, with your
master?

PHANISCUS.
That's right.

THEOPROPIDES.
And then he bought this house next door?

PHANISCUS.
What? Simo's house? 'Course he didn't.

THEOPROPIDES.
Yes he did ... paid four thousand for it, too.

PHANISCUS.
No ... that *must* have been someone else ...

THEOPROPIDES.
I'm ruined!!

PHANISCUS.
No, not you. It's his father's ruined, not you ...

THEOPROPIDES.
980   You never said a truer word ...

PHANISCUS.
Ooh, you are getting upset. Are you a friend of his
father's or something?

THEOPROPIDES.
Three thousand! His father's ruined ...

PHANISCUS.
Three thousand ... that's nothing. You should see
what they spend on food and drink *alone*! That
Tranio ...

THEOPROPIDES (*sharply*).
Tranio? What about Tranio?

PHANISCUS.
He's a one. I've never seen a man spend money like
Tranio! He could win an Olympic medal for
spending money! But it's the old man I'm sorry for
really, the father ... he'll go up in a cloud of smoke
when he gets home, *I* can tell you ...

THEOPROPIDES.
He certainly will ... if what you've told me is true ...

PHANISCUS.
Of course it's true ...

PINACIUM (*at the door again*).
Hey! Is anyone going to open up?

PHANISCUS.
  'S no use banging at the door when there's no one
  inside ... they've probably gone off to drink
  somewhere else. Come on, let's go and look for
  them ...

PINACIUM.
  Coming.   990

THEOPROPIDES.
  D'you have to go already?

PHANISCUS.
  It's all right for some. I'm a slave ... if I don't do my
  master's bidding, I'll be in trouble ...

  PINACIUM *and* PHANISCUS *go off.*

THEOPROPIDES.
  This is the end! I'm done for! Or perhaps I'm
  dreaming and it will all ... Perhaps I didn't go to
  Egypt after all, but to some wonderland where
  everyone's crazy ... But here's reality coming back,
  the man my son bought the house from.

  SIMO *comes back from his walk.*

  Simo, what are you doing now?

SIMO.
  I'm coming home from town.

THEOPROPIDES.
  And did you see anything interesting in town?

SIMO.
  Yes.

THEOPROPIDES.
  What was it?

SIMO.
  A funeral procession.

THEOPROPIDES.
  Well?   1000

SIMO.
  Yes, it *was* interesting ... I saw this funeral ... of a

dead man ... and they said he'd died only recently, too.

THEOPROPIDES (*realising he is being made fun of*).
Oh, go to hell!

SIMO.
Well, if you will ask useless questions about what's been happening...

THEOPROPIDES.
I've only just got back today, from abroad...

SIMO.
Er ... I'm sorry, I'm busy this evening ... I can't invite you to dinner...

THEOPROPIDES.
No, no, I'm not expecting anything of that sort ...
Look, Simo, I need to ask you something.

SIMO.
Yes, what is it?

THEOPROPIDES.
1010   You've just had four thousand drachmas from my son, haven't you?

SIMO.
Me? No.

THEOPROPIDES.
Well from Tranio then?

SIMO.
Tranio? You must be joking...

THEOPROPIDES.
Yes, you have ... as a deposit.

SIMO.
Deposit? You're dreaming.

THEOPROPIDES.
Come on, don't play the fool. You know my son made a deal with you while I was away.

SIMO.
1020   What sort of deal? What was this for?

THEOPROPIDES.
I understand that I owe you eight thousand.

SIMO.
You certainly don't. But if you really want to give it to me, I won't object.

THEOPROPIDES.
Simo, please be serious. You admit that you've received four thousand drachmas already?

SIMO.
No. Why on earth would your son have given it to me?

THEOPROPIDES.
For your house, of course.

SIMO.
What're you talking about?

THEOPROPIDES.
You know perfectly well: my son bought your house, and gave you four thousand drachmas as a deposit.

SIMO.
No, no, you've got it all wrong. *You* want your son to get married, and you're building on to *your* house.

THEOPROPIDES.
What?

SIMO.
Or so Tranio told me.

THEOPROPIDES.
Tranio! I might have guessed . . . !

SIMO.
What's wrong?

THEOPROPIDES.
Simo, they've really done for me this time! I'm   1030
ruined!

SIMO.
How?

THEOPROPIDES.
Never mind how ... you can help me to get to the
bottom of all this ..

SIMO.
Me?

THEOPROPIDES.
Yes ... let me in to your house and I'll explain. And
lend me some of your toughest slaves ... and a whip
or two...

SIMO.
With pleasure. Step inside.

THEOPROPIDES (*as he goes into* SIMO's *house*).
1040   You'll never believe the story Tranio told me...

They go into SIMO's *house. After a short pause,*
TRANIO *emerges cautiously from the door of the*
'*empty*' *house.*

TRANIO.
The coast's clear ... I think ... yes ... (*Confidently,
to the audience*.) A man who's not able to show a bit
of bravado when he's in a tight spot isn't worth two
pins! Actually, I don't know how much two pins *are*
worth ... do you? Anyway, when the master sent me
off to the country to find his son, I slipped round the
back way, through the garden, and managed to get
them all out of the house without anyone seeing.
Having successfully completed this ... brilliant
manoeuvre, I called a council of war. And what did
1050   they say? 'Thank you very much, Tranio, we can
manage without you now.' Huh!! So what do I do
now? Just what any other genius would do on finding
himself in a dangerous and complicated situation ...
make everything even more complicated, so that
nobody can sort it out! But let's face it ... there's no
real hope of keeping the old man in the dark
1060   indefinitely. Perhaps I'd better take the risk, face up
to him and negotiate my own peace treaty ... and the
sooner the better...

Door of SIMO'*s house opens ... noise from inside.*

Hello! Someone's coming out of Simo's house ...
It's the master himself! I'd better listen to what he's
saying ... (*He steps aside.*)

THEOPROPIDES (*in doorway*).
Wait here, slaves, till I call, then come out and get
the chains on him! I'll give that joker something to
laugh about!

TRANIO (*aside*).
Oo-er ... the cat's out of the bag! It's up to me
now ...

THEOPROPIDES.
I shall play this very cleverly. I'll pretend at first that   1070
I don't know what's really happened.

TRANIO (*aside, sarcastically*).
Oh, he's a crafty devil! No one's going to fool him
easily! (*Approaching* THEOPROPIDES.) Were you
looking for me, sir? Here, at your service, master!

THEOPROPIDES.
Ah, Tranio. How did you get on?

TRANIO.
Fine, fine ... they're all back from the country. Your
son will be here directly.

THEOPROPIDES.
Excellent. I'm very glad you're here, Tranio.

TRANIO.
G-g-glad?

THEOPROPIDES.
Yes, I need your help.

TRANIO.
Eh?

THEOPROPIDES.
It's our neighbour here, Simo ... says he's never had
anything to do with you.

TRANIO.
No!

THEOPROPIDES.
And that he's never had a drachma from you.

TRANIO.
1080 He's joking! He can't deny it ...

THEOPROPIDES.
He does. Says he never sold his house to my son!

TRANIO.
Hah! And never accepted any deposit, either?

THEOPROPIDES.
Exactly. Says he'll swear to it in court if he has to.

TRANIO.
Er ... er ...

THEOPROPIDES.
Just what *I* said to *him*!

TRANIO.
What did he say then?

THEOPROPIDES (*advancing towards* TRANIO).
He said he'd call his slaves to witness...

TRANIO (*edging away*).
Oh, let's not bother with that, sir ... let me go and
have it out with him. (*He tries to get away.*)

THEOPROPIDES.
No, wait! I think I *should* try the slaves first...

TRANIO.
1090 Very well ... or perhaps we could just take him to
court and sue him?

THEOPROPIDES.
Erm ... No, I'll have these witnesses brought out for
questioning.

TRANIO.
You do that ... and I'll just sit here ... on this altar!

THEOPROPIDES.
What are you sitting on that altar for?

TRANIO.
Well, you see ... (*Sudden inspiration.*) If the slaves
don't want to give evidence, they might try to take
sanctuary here. I'll just keep guard for you from
here, so nothing can go wrong with your cross-
examination.

THEOPROPIDES.
Get up!

TRANIO.
Er ... no.

THEOPROPIDES.
I forbid you to sit on that altar.

TRANIO.
Why?

THEOPROPIDES.
Er ... (*Sudden inspiration.*) Don't you see? That's
exactly what I want ... that they should *try* to take
sanctuary there! It will make it easier for me to
persuade the judge to award me damages.

TRANIO.
No, you follow your first plan, sir. These judges can 1100
be very unpredictable.

THEOPROPIDES.
Get down and come here then. I want your advice on
one point.

TRANIO.
I'll give my advice from here ... I can think better
when I'm sitting down.

THEOPROPIDES (*getting angry*).
Oh, stop fooling around. Look here, Tranio...

TRANIO.
I'm looking...

THEOPROPIDES.
Look at me.

TRANIO.
I can see you. If there were anyone between us, he'd die of starvation.

THEOPROPIDES.
What d'you mean?

TRANIO.
Because he wouldn't get any pickings out of us ... we're neither of us going to give in!

THEOPROPIDES.
Tranio, this is the end!

TRANIO.
What's the matter?

THEOPROPIDES.
You've fooled me...

TRANIO.
How, sir?

THEOPROPIDES.
You've cleaned me out! You've wiped my nose...

TRANIO.
And done it properly, I hope. Not still dribbling, are you?

THEOPROPIDES.
1110 I know everything, you rogue. There isn't one of your tricks I haven't discovered this last half-hour.

TRANIO.
What tricks? I haven't done anything...

THEOPROPIDES.
Hah! It's fire and the rack for you, my lad ... and then the gallows!

TRANIO.
But what have I...?

THEOPROPIDES.
By god, I'll make an example of you!

TRANIO.
Thank you, sir, I'm so pleased that you want others
to copy me...

THEOPROPIDES.
Shut up and listen. What sort of son did I leave
when I went abroad?

TRANIO.
No different from anyone else... two feet, two
hands, ears, nose, mouth...

THEOPROPIDES.
That's not what I'm asking.

TRANIO.
It's what I'm answering.

THEOPROPIDES.
Tranio! I warn you...

TRANIO (*with relief*).
Hey!... Look! Someone's coming. It's   1120
Callidamates, your son's best friend. He can be a
witness ... if you've got any more to say, that is.

CALLIDAMATES (*aside, to audience, as he enters*).
I've had a good sleep, and woken up ... well,
reasonably sober. Philolaches has told me all about
his father coming back from abroad and the practical
jokes played by Tranio. He's afraid to come and face
up to his old man, so I've been designated
spokesman. (*Sees* THEOPROPIDES.) Ah, there he
is! ... Theopropides, I'm delighted to see you home
safe and sound from your travels. You must come
and have dinner with me this evening.

THEOPROPIDES.
Thank you, Callidamates, but I must decline your   1130
invitation.

CALLIDAMATES.
You're sure you won't come?

TRANIO.
Go on, sir. But if you don't want to, I'll go instead.

THEOPROPIDES.
That's enough of your mockery, you scoundrel!

TRANIO.
Oh, sir ... can't I even accept an invitation to go to dinner ...

THEOPROPIDES.
You're not going anywhere ... except to the gallows ... that's what *you* deserve!

CALLIDAMATES.
Oh, never mind him, Theopropides. Shall we say dinner tonight?

TRANIO (*to* THEOPROPIDES).
Go on, sir; don't be ungracious.

CALLIDAMATES (*to* TRANIO).
And what are you doing sitting on that altar anyway?

TRANIO.
I got scared because some rather ignorant man who'd just arrived here and didn't know the facts started to threaten me. (*To* THEOPROPIDES.) Look, sir ... we've got an arbitrator here now. Why don't you present the case for the prosecution?

THEOPROPIDES.
Very well. I accuse you of having completely corrupted my son.

TRANIO.
Oh, is that all? I admit he's had a few parties ... bought a girl and set her free ... borrowed money, and managed to spend it all. Just the same, in fact, as any other well-brought-up young man.

THEOPROPIDES.
Very persuasive! You'd make a fine attorney!

CALLIDAMATES.
Can I express my view, please?

THEOPROPIDES.
Yes, yes, let us have your learned opinion.

1140

CALLIDAMATES (*to* TRANIO).

Get up, and let me sit there.

TRANIO.

Only if you can promise me that I've got nothing to
be afraid of ... you take my place and you can be
afraid for me!

THEOPROPIDES.

What makes me really angry is how I've been made
to look a fool.

TRANIO.

A good thing too ... old men like you need to have
some sense knocked into 'em.

THEOPROPIDES.

Watch it, you! I'm just planning what to do with ...

TRANIO.

Tell you what ... if you know any writers of comedy,
like Diphilus or Philemon, tell them all about how   1150
your slave tricked you. It'd make a fine plot for a
play!

CALLIDAMATES.

Just keep quiet, Tranio. It's my turn to speak.
Listen.

THEOPROPIDES.

Go on.

CALLIDAMATES.

As you know, sir, I am your son's best friend. He
asked me for help, because he was ashamed to meet
you, after the things he's done ... the things he
knows you know he's done. Please sir, forgive him
... he *is* your son, and ... boys will be boys. And it
isn't just him ... we've all aided and abetted ...
we're all to blame. As for the money he owes, the   1160
money he spent on the girl ... we're all going to club
together and pay it back, at our expense, not yours.

THEOPROPIDES.

I must say you plead for him very eloquently. Well, I

won't be hard on him ... I'm not angry any more. In
fact, let him carry on ... loving, drinking, whatever
he wants ... just like when I was away. Provided he's
sorry ... for having wasted all that money.

CALLIDAMATES.
Oh, he is very sorry, sir.

TRANIO.
So, *he*'s forgiven. What about *me*?

THEOPROPIDES.
You? Whips and the gallows ... that's what's waiting
for you.

TRANIO.
Suppose *I* say I'm sorry too?

THEOPROPIDES.
I'll see you dead first, you rogue!

CALLIDAMATES.
Oh no, sir; make it a general pardon. Forgive Tranio
for what he's done ... for my sake!

THEOPROPIDES.
1170   Let that scoundrel off? Look at him ... impudent to
the last!

CALLIDAMATES.
Tranio! Stop it, if you've any sense!

THEOPROPIDES (*to* CALLIDAMATES).
And *you* stop asking me favours.

CALLIDAMATES.
Come on, let me persuade you ...

THEOPROPIDES.
No, I don't want to hear another word.

CALLIDAMATES.
Please forgive him ... just this once ... as a favour to
me.

TRANIO.
Don't worry, sir. Let me off this time ... I'm bound

to do something really wicked tomorrow ... then you
can punish me for both crimes at once!

CALLIDAMATES.
Won't you say yes, sir?

THEOPROPIDES.
All right, get out, get out! I'll let you off! And this is
the man (*Indicating* CALLIDAMATES.) you have
to thank for it!   1180

(*To the audience.*) That's the end of our play ...
please don't forget to applaud!

   They all go out.

PLAUTUS

Casina, or A Funny Thing Happened on the Way to the Wedding

translated by Richard Beacham

Characters

OLYMPIO, slave and country foreman of Lysidamus
CHALINUS, city slave of Lysidamus and his absent son
CLEOSTRATA, wife of Lysidamus
PARDALISCA, maid to Cleostrata
MYRRHINA, wife of Alcesimus, neighbour to Cleostrata
and Lysidamus
LYSIDAMUS, an elderly Athenian
ALCESIMUS, friend and neighbour of Lysidamus
COOK and ASSISTANTS

A street in Athens. The setting consists of an open stage backed by a scenic façade. This has two doorways, each of which has a small porch in front of it, with steps descending to the stage. The door to the left represents the house of LYSIDAMUS; *that to the right belongs to* ALCESIMUS. *The actor – or possibly two actors – representing the* PROLOGUE, *enter.*

PROLOGUE.
Warm welcome, folks, you faithful jovial crew.
You trust in me, I'll place my trust in you.
If that seems fair, then give a little sign
To show you'll hear me with an open mind.

   Waits for applause.

Now wise men – men of taste, refined –
Favour old farces, just like a vintage wine.
They love the works and wisdom of the good old days,
And fail to see the merit of these modern plays,
So faulty, feeble, flaccid, and fickle,
With less real value than a wooden nickel.   10

Now rumour has it – as people have their say,
You're longing to applaud a play by Plautus here
  today.
A titillating tale, to charm, amuse, and move;
The sort of stuff the older crowd approve.
You younger folks who don't remember Plautus,
We'll also do our best to win your plaudits
With such a play! The greatest glory of its age,
Once more before you on a modern stage!
Those dedicated, decorated, dear-departed souls,
Those ancient comic playwrights shall inspire our   20
  roles.

Now let me *earnest-nestly* urge you pay us close
  attention.
Away with sorrowing, thoughts about your
  borrowing, not to mention
Work! It's fun and games, so put your cares away.
Why even bankers get a holiday!

Now all is peaceful, quiet, sunken in repose,
The shops are shuttered, and the banks are closed.
They're calculating, bankers – no need to hinder us –
For while we take a break, they're taking interest!
So lend your ears and I'll your loan repay

30   By telling you the plot and title of our play!
Once known as *Clerumenoe* by the Greeks,
'Twas titled *Sortientes* in Latin speech
(Or, let's see now, that's *Lot-Drawers* to you)
When funny, punning Plautus fashioned it anew.

> *During the following passage, the characters appear
> 'on cue' in dumb-show behind the* PROLOGUE.

A married gentleman, somewhat past his prime,
His son, and slave, live here, and once upon a time –
Some sixteen years ago to be exact –
This slave, no knave, performed a kindly act.
A baby girl, abandoned by her mother – that's a
    fact! –

40   He saved, and gave her to the old man's wife,
Begging that the baby spend its life
Within this very house, the newfound foundling's
    home.
His mistress readily agreed and raised it as her own.

Now when the girl had reached that certain age,
When men begin to notice and to gauge
Their chance for romance and to 'have their way',
The young man fell in love with her – he has it bad –
And strange to say, so does his dad. How *sad!*

Now each prepares his forces; summoning all hands,
50   While knowing nothing of his rival's plans!
The father told a slave, a rustic chap,
His farmyard foreman (something of a sap),
To make the girl his own,
So, later, his foreman having wed her, unbeknownst
To Mother, Dad himself can bed her.

Meanwhile, the son has told his slave and right-hand
    man
To act for him, and seek the lady's hand

In marriage, knowing if the slave would keep his
  head
He'll bow to master: and so to bed.

The old man's wife has stumbled on the plot.   60
To thwart her husband, she would throw her lot
In with the son, but then, the secret's out!
Dad learns of son's infatuation, and – the lout! –
Sends him abroad while wily Mother, still party to
  the plan,
Determines to assist her son in every way she can.

Oh, a minor point and rather sad to say,
That son who went abroad won't make it back today.
Plautus changed his mind and dropped him from our
  play,
By washing out a bridge that lay upon his way.

Now some may mutter 'mongst themselves, no   70
  doubt,
'By Hercules! But what's all this about?
Since when can slaves propose, or marriages take
  place?
Nowhere in all the world, can such things be the
  case.'

And yet, *it is*, in Carthage, and Apulia – and the
  Greeks
Are prone and have been known to celebrate for
  weeks
When slaves get wed. Who dares to disagree?
I'll bet a drink, but let the referee
Be Carthaginian, Apulian, or Greek.
Well, now's your chance. No takers? Come on, speak
Up! Not got the nerve to bet or anything to say?   80
On second thoughts, I'll bet ... you've drunk
  enough today!

Now don't forget that foundling pet,
The girl I told you of.
The sweet young thing, whom, with a ring,
The men all long to love.
In fact she's free.

Well, don't blame me!
And, please, don't worry,
For she's in no hurry, to lose her ... 'way' –
90   Not in our play at any rate. But just you wait,
Till afterwards, to date her.
For a little money, she's anyone's honey,
And the marriage can wait till later!

That's all I know, enjoy the show,
Be healthy, wise, and strong
To obtain what through valour you gain:
Great victories, as ever.

> *Exit* PROLOGUE.

> *Enter* OLYMPIO *from the right, followed closely
> by* CHALINUS. *The scene between them should be
> played with a good deal of slapstick, including
> physical bullying of* CHALINUS *by* OLYMPIO.

OLYMPIO.
100   Can't I talk as I walk, or use my mind to mind my
own business without being overheard, *gallows bird*,
by you? Why are you following me?

CHALINUS.
You might as well know: I'm resolved to go
wherever you go. Just like your shadow, I'll follow.
Even if you're strung up on the cross, I'll string
along. So just decide for yourself, whether as bride
for yourself, you'd descend to taking my intended
Casina – by tricking me!

OLYMPIO.
Why bother with my business?

CHALINUS.
What's that, you creep? Why are you creeping
around the town, you oversized overseer?

OLYMPIO.
110   I feel like it.

CHALINUS.
Why aren't you back on the farm, on your own turf?

Why not mind your own business, there, and leave
city affairs to city folks? You've come to carry off
Casina, you cur! Get back to the outback,
clodhopper!

OLYMPIO.

I am perfectly mindful of my duties, Chalinus;
someone's looking after the farm. And when I've got
what I came for, and marry that girl you swoon over,
that fellow slave of yours – that pretty, sweet, little
Casina – when I've got her back with me on the
farm, you can bet I'll bed down with my bride, on
my 'own turf'!

CHALINUS.

You have her, you! Hang me, by Hercules, I'd
sooner die than let you get her!   120

OLYMPIO.

Hang on! She's mine, my booty, baby! So your
neck's for the noose.

CHALINUS.

You, *d-d-dug* from a *d-d-dungheap!* She's your
booty, booby?!

OLYMPIO.

You said it; you'll see it.

CHALINUS.

Damn you!

OLYMPIO.

Oh, how I'll needle you at my nuptials! As sure as I
breathe.

CHALINUS.

What'll you do to me?   130

OLYMPIO.

What'll I do to you? First, I'll make you carry the
torch for my new bride. Then, you'll go back to
being your usual good-for-nothing nobody. And
later, when you visit the villa, I'll give you one
pitcher, one path, one well, and eight enormous

casks to fill. And fill you will, or you'll be well full of welts! I'll bend you double with trouble, till you look like a yoke – no joke! And further, when you fancy some fodder, you'll eat dirt like a worm, compliments of the compost heap. By Pollux, you'll eat up less than nothing; you'll famish on the farm. And then ... at the end of the day, when you're

140   hungry and hurting, I'll see that you spend the night, just right.

CHALINUS.
What'll you do?

OLYMPIO.
I'll fasten you firmly in the frame of the window, where you can listen and *stew*, while I kiss and ... '*hug*' Casina. And when she murmurs to me, 'Oh, sweetie-pie! O Olympio, my darling, my little honey pot, my joy, let me kiss those cute little eyes of yours, my precious! Oh please, please, let me *love* you, light of my life, my little dickey bird, my lovey-dovey, my bunny-wunny! Well then, when she's cooing these things to me, you'll flutter, gallows bird, you'll

150   shudder like a mouse shut up in the wall. And you can shut up now. I'm going in. I'm tired of talking to you.

CHALINUS.
I'll follow you. By Pollox, you won't get away with anything! Not while *I'm* around!

> *They exit into* LYSIDAMUS's *house. Pause, then enter* CLEOSTRATA *from the same house, speaking within to* PARDALISCA.

CLEOSTRATA.
Lock up the pantry, and bring me the key. I'm going next door to the neighbour's. If my husband wants me, come and get me.

PARDALISCA.
'Sir' is asking for his dinner.

CLEOSTRATA.

Hush! Go away! Be quiet and be quick; I'll not do
his dinner today! Not when he turns against his own
dear son, and *me!* in order to appease his appetite,
that monster of a man! I'll wrack that rake with
hunger and thirst, curses and worse. By Pollux, I'll   160
torture him with torment from my tongue! I'll give
him the life he deserves, that dungheap dandy, the
haughty debauchee, that sink of sin! Oh, how
wretched I am! I think I'll just go and tell my
neighbour. Ah! I hear her door creaking, and there
she is herself, coming out. Dear me, I think I've
timed this visit badly.

Enter MYRRHINA *from* ALCESIMUS's *house.*

MYRRHINA.

Follow me next door, girls! Hey! You! Do you hear
what I say? I shall be there if my husband or anyone
wants me. Somehow alone at home, I'm so drowsy I
just keep drifting off. Didn't I tell you to fetch me
my distaff?   170

CLEOSTRATA.

Oh, *Myrrhina!*

MYRRHINA.

Why, hello! But why so miserable, love?

CLEOSTRATA.

It's the same with all unhappily married women.
Indoors or out, we're always down in the dumps. I
was just coming over for a visit.

MYRRHINA.

How about that! I was on my way over to you! But
what's on your mind? When you're troubled, it
troubles me too.

CLEOSTRATA.

By Castor, but I believe it does! There's none of my
neighbours I like more than you; you're always such   180
a comfort to me.

MYRRHINA.

I like you likewise, and I'm longing to know what's
the matter.

CLEOSTRATA.

It's simply a scandal how I'm abused in my own
home!

MYRRHINA.

Goodness, how's that again? I don't quite get it.

CLEOSTRATA.

My husband! It's perfectly scandalous how he treats
me, and as for justice, well, I can just forget about
that.

MYRRHINA.

If that's the case, it's very odd, since usually it's the
men who don't get what they deserve from their wives.

CLEOSTRATA.

190   Here he is, to spite me, intending to give my maid to
his foreman on the farm – the maid whom I've
reared myself – because *he* fancies her!

MYRRHINA.

Hush your mouth!

CLEOSTRATA.

I'll say what I like; we're by ourselves.

MYRRHINA.

So we are. Now how can she be yours? After all, a
proper wife ought not to have any property apart
from her husband. And if she does have things, in
my opinion she got them improperly; she's guilty
either of stealing or stealth, or ... *hanky-panky!* In
my opinion *all* that you have is your husband's.

CLEOSTRATA.

200   Now there you go! Accusing and abusing your own
dear friend.

MYRRHINA.

Oh, do be still, you silly-billy, and listen to me! Now
don't oppose your husband! Let him have his fling,

and do what he wants, just so long as he looks after
you properly at home.

CLEOSTRATA.
Are you out of your mind? There you go again,
speaking against me and your *own* interests!

MYRRHINA.
You stupid woman! There's one thing you must
always prevent your husband from saying.

CLEOSTRATA.
What's that, then?

MYRRHINA.
'Shove off, woman!'   210

CLEOSTRATA.
Shh-h! Be quiet!

MYRRHINA.
What's the matter?

CLEOSTRATA.
Look over there! My old man's coming! Go inside
quickly! Hurry, love!

MYRRHINA.
All right, already, I'm going!

CLEOSTRATA.
Soon as we've got a moment I want to have a proper
chat with you. But bye for now.

MYRRHINA.
Ciao!

> *Exit* MYRRHINA *into her house;*
> CLEOSTRATA *withdraws; enter* LYSIDAMUS,
> *garlanded, pleased with himself and more than a*
> *little inebriated as he sings his love song.*

LYSIDAMUS.
You can take it from me: not on land or at sea
Is there anything finer than love.   220
Nothing half so entrancing, everyday life-enhancing,
Not on earth nor in heaven above.

And I do think it odd, when a cook's at his job
Giving dishes the very best flavour,
He can't use for a spice, what is *ever* so nice,
Just a sprinkling of *Love* to add savour!

Why, what more could you wish, a mouth-watering
   dish,
Neither salty nor cloying? How handy!
Love would transform it all, making honey from gall,
230   (*Aside.*) And a dirty old man to a dandy!

Now, I didn't just hear this; I speak from
   experience,
For since Casina captured my heart,
Quite overpowered, I have utterly flowered:
I've turned nattiness into an art!

To become more alluring, I'm even procuring
The very best scent that's available.
Just a touch of perfume, to help her love bloom,
For I do think her virtue's assailable!

   Seeing his wife, glowering in the doorway.

Yet ... I *am* at a loss. There's that old rugged cross,
240   That I bear, while she lives, called my *wife!*
And she's looking quite vile – soothing words –
   mustn't rile.
Ah, how goes it, sweet light of my life?

CLEOSTRATA.
   Buzz off, and don't touch me!

LYSIDAMUS.
   Ah, now my Juno shouldn't be cross with her Jove.
   Where are you going?

CLEOSTRATA.
   Let me go!

LYSIDAMUS.
   But stay!

CLEOSTRATA.
   I won't stay!

LYSIDAMUS.
Well, then, by Pollux, I'll follow you.

CLEOSTRATA.
Good lord, is the man mad?   250

LYSIDAMUS.
Yes! I'm madly in love with you.

CLEOSTRATA.
I don't want any of your love.

LYSIDAMUS.
You can't avoid it!

CLEOSTRATA.
You will be the death of me!

LYSIDAMUS (*aside*).
If only it were true!

CLEOSTRATA (*hearing*).
Ah, now *that* I believe!

LYSIDAMUS.
Please look at me, O darling, mine!

CLEOSTRATA.
Right! Just like you're mine. Excuse me, love, but
where is that smell coming from?

LYSIDAMUS (*aside*).
Damnation! I'm afraid she's got me red-handed! I'd   260
better wipe it off on my cloak. (*Looking up.*)
Mercury, be a good chap and destroy that perfumer
who gave me this stuff.

CLEOSTRATA.
Why, you lecherous old louse! I'm almost ashamed
to tell you what I think of you. At your age, going
about town all perfumed up, you worm!

LYSIDAMUS.
Gosh, I was only assisting a certain friend of mine in
choosing a scent.

CLEOSTRATA.
Always ready with a smart answer! Have you no
shame?

LYSIDAMUS (*humbly*).
270   All you could want.

CLEOSTRATA.
What fleshpots have you been stewing in lately?

LYSIDAMUS. *I*, in a *fleshpot?*

CLEOSTRATA.
I know a lot more than you think I do.

LYSIDAMUS.
How's that? What exactly do you know?

CLEOSTRATA.
Of all the worthless old men, you're the worst of the
worthless. Well, where were you, thick-head? Where
have you been wallowing about? And, soaking it up?
By Castor, you're crocked! Here, just look at the
state of your cloak.

LYSIDAMUS.
May the gods not love me (*Aside.*) – or you either – if
280   a single drop of wine has passed my lips today.

CLEOSTRATA.
Never mind! Please yourself! Go right ahead: eat,
drink, waste your life!

LYSIDAMUS.
Oh now, dear wife, *please*, that's enough. Come on,
get hold of yourself. And that tongue of yours. Save
a bit of abuse for tomorrow's row. Now, how about
it? Instead of opposing him, can't you curb your
temper long enough to do a little something nice for
your husband? Hmmmm?

CLEOSTRATA.
Like what?

LYSIDAMUS.
Need you ask? Why, Casina of course. Don't you
think we ought to marry her off to that fine fellow of

a foreman of ours, Olympio, where she'll not want   290
for food, fuel, warm water, or nice clothes and where
she can bring up her babies? Instead of flinging her
at that good-for-nothing slave, that worthless rascal,
Chalinus, who hasn't got two pennies to rub
together?

CLEOSTRATA.
By Castor, you *disaster* of a man, you do amaze me!
At your time of life, forgetting how to behave.

LYSIDAMUS.
What now?

CLEOSTRATA.
Well, if you acted properly and with propriety, you'd
leave the maids to me; after all, they're my
responsibility.

LYSIDAMUS.
But, blast it, why do you want to give her to that
lack-lustre lackey?   300

CLEOSTRATA.
Because we ought to do something nice for our only
son.

LYSIDAMUS.
Only son be damned! He's no more my only son,
than I'm his only father! (*Realising his slip of the
tongue as* CLEOSTRATA *glares.*) I mean I'm as
much his only father, as he's my only son, of course!
He ought to want to do something nice for me.

CLEOSTRATA.
By Castor, dear boy, you're pushing your luck!

LYSIDAMUS (*aside*).
I think she's on to me! (*To* CLEOSTRATA.) *M-m-
m-m-eee?*

CLEOSTRATA.
Yes, you. Why are you stuttering? And why are you
so mad about this match?   310

LYSIDAMUS.
Why, I'd like to see her go to a worthy servant instead of to a rascal.

CLEOSTRATA.
Supposing I persuade Olympio as a personal favour to let Chalinus have her?

LYSIDAMUS.
And supposing I persuade Chalinus to give her to Olympio? (*Aside.*) Which, I believe, I *may* just be able to do.

CLEOSTRATA.
It's a deal. Shall I call out Chalinus for you? You work on him, while I deal with Olympio.

LYSIDAMUS.
320   Good idea!

CLEOSTRATA.
He's on his way. Then we'll see which of us is more persuasive.

Exit inside.

LYSIDAMUS.
By Hercules, I wish the gods would do something nasty to that woman! Is that too much to ask? Here I am, aching with love, while she's doing her worst to oppose me. She's definitely got wind of what I'm up to; that's why she's so keen on helping Chalinus. May the gods do their worst to him!

Enter CHALINUS *from* LYSIDAMUS's *house.*

CHALINUS (*sullenly*).
Your wife says you sent for me.

LYSIDAMUS.
That's right.

CHALINUS.
330   Well, go on, tell me what you want.

LYSIDAMUS.
Well, for starters, put on a happy face when you

speak with me; it's ridiculous for you to scowl like
that when I'm the master and you're the slave!
(*Winsomely.*) For some time now, I've considered
you an honest and upright fellow.

CHALINUS.
Oh, I quite agree. In that case, how about setting me
free?

LYSIDAMUS.
Oh, I'd really like to. But my wishes don't count
much, unless you do your part.

CHALINUS.
Well then, let me know what you have in mind.

LYSIDAMUS.
Listen, I'll speak frankly. I've given my word to
marry Casina off to Olympio.   340

CHALINUS.
Yes, but your wife and son gave me their words,
both of them: *two* words!

LYSIDAMUS (*patiently*).
I know. But now, which would you really prefer? To
be single and *free*; or married, with you and your
kids in slavery for ever and ever? The choice is
yours; choose whatever you prefer!

CHALINUS.
If I were free, I'd have to look after myself; as it is, I
live off you. As for Casina, I'm quite determined not
to give her up to any man alive.   350

LYSIDAMUS (*furious*).
Go right inside and summon my wife out here at
once. And bring out an urn of water and some lots.

CHALINUS.
That's okay with me.

LYSIDAMUS.
By Pollux, I'll soon foil your little plot. If I can't win
by persuasion, we'll draw lots. That's the way to
confound you and your confederates!

CHALINUS.

Fine. Except that the lots will go my way.

LYSIDAMUS.

The only way you're going, by Pollux, is toward titanic torture.

CHALINUS (*teasingly*).

360   You can curse and do your worst; the girl will marry *me!!*

LYSIDAMUS.

Will you get out of my sight?

CHALINUS.

Upset are we? Never mind! I'll live.

Exit inside.

LYSIDAMUS.

Was ever anyone more wretched than I? Now all things do conspire against me. Now I'm worried that my wife may have talked Olympio out of marrying Casina. If so, she's made an old man very unhappy. If not, there's still hope for me in the lots. If I lose the lots, I'll just lay down my life on my sword, and so, good night! But look! here comes Olympio. There's hope!

Enter OLYMPIO, *speaking to* CLEOSTRATA *within.*

OLYMPIO.

By Pollux, madam, you could put me in the oven and
370   turn me till I'm turned to toast, before I'd agree to what you're asking!

LYSIDAMUS.

Ah! Salvation! While I hear, I hope!

OLYMPIO.

Why are you trying to frighten me with threats about my freedom? Neither you nor your son, whether together or on your own, can keep me from being freed – for nothing!

LYSIDAMUS.
Why, what's the matter, Olympio, who're you
arguing with?

OLYMPIO.
The same one you're always at it with.

LYSIDAMUS.
My old lady.

OLYMPIO.
Lady? Lady is it? You follow a real sporting life with
that wife of yours: day and night with a baying   380
bloodhound.

LYSIDAMUS.
What's she been going on about with you?

OLYMPIO.
Screeching and beseeching me not to marry Casina.

LYSIDAMUS.
What'd you say?

OLYMPIO.
I wouldn't give her up to Jove himself, not even if he
begged me!

LYSIDAMUS.
The gods preserve you! (*Aside*.) For my sake!

OLYMPIO.
She's really on the boil now – about to explode!

LYSIDAMUS.
By Pollux, if only she'd have split right down the
middle!   390

OLYMPIO (*leeringly*).
Well, golly, as a good husband, you ought to know!
But seriously, I've had it up to here with this love
affair of yours. Your wife's turned against me, your
son, the whole household's turned against me.

LYSIDAMUS.
So what's your worry? As long as old Jupiter here is

on your side, these lesser deities can go flog
themselves!

OLYMPIO.

That's a load of litter! Don't you know how suddenly
these mortal Jupiters can shuffle off? Tell me this: If
old Jupiter here snuffs it, and your kingdom falls to
the small fry, who's going to save my hide and cover
400   my backside?

LYSIDAMUS.

Oh, things will go better for you than you think. Just
you and I cooperate, so Casina and I can ... (*Softly.*)
copulate.

OLYMPIO.

But, by Hercules, I don't see how, with your wife
dead set against my getting her.

LYSIDAMUS.

Here's what I plan to do. I'll put the lots in the urn,
and you and Chalinus will draw. If it comes to it,
we'll draw swords as well, and settle it by force.

OLYMPIO.

And what if the lots don't go your way?

LYSIDAMUS.

Don't even think such a thing! I trust in the gods.
410   We'll just put our faith in heaven.

OLYMPIO.

I wouldn't invest a penny up there. Why everyone
alive trusts in heaven, but I've seen plenty of those
faithful foolish folks flummoxed.

LYSIDAMUS.

Shh! Just be quiet for a moment.

OLYMPIO.

What's up?

LYSIDAMUS.

Look over there! There's Chalinus coming out with
the urns and lots. Now's the time to close ranks and
fight!

Enter CHALINUS *with urns and lots*;
CLEOSTRATA *in the door.*

CLEOSTRATA.
Now, Chalinus, what is it my husband wants me to
do?

CHALINUS.
Gosh, what he'd *most* like is to see you going up in   420
smoke out by the crematorium!

CLEOSTRATA.
By Castor, I think you're right.

CHALINUS.
I don't think; I know!

LYSIDAMUS (*aside*).
It appears I have more servants than I thought: we
seem to have a mind-reader on the staff. Well, then,
shall we raise our standards and sally forth? Follow
me. What are you two up to?

CHALINUS.
Everything you commanded is here: wife, lots, urn,
and yours truly.

LYSIDAMUS.
I could do very well without that last item.   430

CHALINUS.
By Pollux, I guess you could. I must really needle
you. A right prick in your backside, as it were. I've
got you in a real sweat, you old reprobate.

LYSIDAMUS.
Shut up, Chalinus!

LYSIDAMUS *pushes* CHALINUS.

CHALINUS.
Hey! Get hold of this fellow!

OLYMPIO.
Oh, no! Get hold of him. He loves it!

LYSIDAMUS.
Put the urn there.

With the urn in the centre, LYSIDAMUS *and*
OLYMPIO *stand on one side, and*
CLEOSTRATA *and* CHALINUS *on the other.*

Give me the lots. Now concentrate, both of you.
Now, my dear, I did hope, and indeed, still do hope
440   to persuade you, my wife, to make Casina my wife.

CLEOSTRATA.
Give her to *you!?*

LYSIDAMUS.
Oh, yes, please. To me ... (*Realising his 'Freudian
slip'*.) No! I take that back! What I *meant* to say was
me, when I said *him*. No, that's wrong. What I
wanted was for me ... Oh dear, I seem to have
become all muddled up.

CLEOSTRATA.
Yes, indeed! You certainly are!

LYSIDAMUS.
Let him ... No, that is, on the contrary, let ... Well
now ... uhmmm. I think I'm on the right path at
last.

CLEOSTRATA.
By Pollux, you're always straying from it!

LYSIDAMUS.
Well, now, that's just the way it is, when one wants
450   something bad – uhh – *badly* enough! But, anyway,
both of us – Olympio and I, recognising your rights
in the matter, appeal to you.

CLEOSTRATA.
For what?

LYSIDAMUS.
Just this, honey-pot. To do a little favour for our
foreman here in this Casina affair.

CLEOSTRATA.
By Pollux, I won't! I wouldn't dream of it.

LYSIDAMUS.
I see. Well, in that case I think we should have them both draw lots at once.

CLEOSTRATA.
What's stopping you?   460

LYSIDAMUS.
That is, after all, in my considered opinion, the best and fairest thing to do. Later, if things go as we would wish, we'll celebrate; if not, we'll bear it with a tranquil mind. Take this lot. What's written on it?

OLYMPIO.
One.

CHALINUS.
Hey! It's not fair he should get his before me!

LYSIDAMUS.
And you may take that one.

CHALINUS.
Let's have it!

OLYMPIO.
Wait a minute. I just thought of something. Make sure there isn't another one in there, underwater.   470

CHALINUS.
You rascal! Do you think I'm like you?

CLEOSTRATA.
No, there isn't. Now calm down, everyone.

OLYMPIO.
May good fortune attend my lot!

CHALINUS.
Misfortune will be your lot.

OLYMPIO.
By Pollux! I know all about your pious ways! Just wait a second. Your lot isn't made of wood, is it?

CHALINUS.
What's it to you?

OLYMPIO.
I just don't want it floating on top of the water.

LYSIDAMUS.
That's right! Be careful. Now both of you throw
480   your lots in here. There we go. Check them, dear.

OLYMPIO.
Never trust a wife!

LYSIDAMUS.
Keep your pecker up!

OLYMPIO.
By Hercules, I'm afraid if she touches them, she'll
put a spell on them!

LYSIDAMUS.
Be quiet.

OLYMPIO.
I'm quiet. I pray the gods ...

CHALINUS.
... will fit you with a ball and chain ...

OLYMPIO.
... that the lots will let me ...

CHALINUS.
... be hung up by your heels, by Hercules!

OLYMPIO.
No! Will have you blow your brains out through
490   your nose!

CHALINUS.
What are you worried about? The noose is all ready
and waiting for you!

OLYMPIO.
You're a dead man!

They square off to fight, but are restrained.

LYSIDAMUS.
Now pay attention, both of you!

OLYMPIO.
I'll not say another word.

LYSIDAMUS.
Now, Cleostrata, so you won't be suspicious or think
I've tricked you, I'll let you draw the lots yourself.

OLYMPIO.
You're killing me!

CHALINUS.
He'll be better off for that.   500

CLEOSTRATA.
Very well.

CHALINUS.
I beg the gods – let your lot slip out of the urn!

OLYMPIO.
You do, do you? Since you're so slippery yourself,
you want everything to imitate you?

CHALINUS.
Oh, if only your lot would dissolve, you dissolute
cur!

OLYMPIO.
And here's hoping you melt away yourself, soon.
Warmed up with a whipping!

LYSIDAMUS.
Pay attention, please, Olympio.

OLYMPIO.
If only this outlaw would allow me!

LYSIDAMUS.
May good fortune be with me!   510

OLYMPIO.
Hear hear! And with me too!

CHALINUS.
No!

OLYMPIO.
Oh, yes! With *me*, by Hercules!

CHALINUS.
Oh, no! By Hercules, *me!*

CLEOSTRATA (*to* OLYMPIO).
He's going to win, and you'll always be a loser!

LYSIDAMUS.
Shut that man's mouth this minute! Go on, what are you waiting for?

CLEOSTRATA.
Don't you dare raise a hand!

OLYMPIO.
520   Shall I sock him or slap him, sir?

LYSIDAMUS.
Whichever you prefer.

OLYMPIO.
Take that!!

    Hits CHALINUS.

CLEOSTRATA.
How dare you strike that man!?

OLYMPIO.
My Jupiter here gave orders.

CLEOSTRATA (*to* CHALINUS).
Well, you hit him right back!

    He does so.

OLYMPIO.
Owwwwww! He's pounding me to a pulp, Jupiter!

LYSIDAMUS.
How dare you strike that man!?

CHALINUS.
My Juno here gave orders.

LYSIDAMUS.
We'll just have to put up with it. My wife's already
530   giving the orders even though I'm still alive.

CLEOSTRATA.
Chalinus is just as much entitled to talk as Olympio!

OLYMPIO (*whining*).
Why did he have to go and spoil my omen?

LYSIDAMUS.
I warn you, Chalinus. Keep an eye out for trouble!

CHALINUS.
Oh, that's kind of you! After my eye's been
blackened!

LYSIDAMUS.
Get on with it, wife. Draw the lots. Both of you pay
attention. Dear me, I'm so worried, I hardly know
where I am! I'm afraid I've got palpitations. My
heart's pumping so it's pounding me to pieces!

CLEOSTRATA.
Oh, I've got a lot!

LYSIDAMUS.
Pull it out!   540

CHALINUS (*seeing the lot first*).
Oh, I'm a goner!

OLYMPIO.
Hold it up. Ah!! It's *mine!*

CHALINUS.
Hell and damnation!

CLEOSTRATA.
You've lost, Chalinus.

LYSIDAMUS.
The gods are smiling on us, Olympio. Rejoice!

OLYMPIO.
It's all due to the piety of me and my forefathers.

LYSIDAMUS.
Go right inside, woman, and make way for the
wedding!

CLEOSTRATA.
Just as you say.

LYSIDAMUS.
You do understand it's a long journey out to that
550 country villa where he's taking her.

CLEOSTRATA.
I know.

LYSIDAMUS.
Well, go on in, even though you're upset, and start
getting things prepared.

CLEOSTRATA.
As you wish.

Exit.

LYSIDAMUS.
Let's us go inside, too, and make sure things hurry
along.

OLYMPIO.
Who's delaying?

LYSIDAMUS.
I don't wish to say anything more in present
company. (*Indicating* CHALINUS.)

They exit to LYSIDAMUS's *house, leaving*
CHALINUS *alone on stage.*

CHALINUS.
560 If I hanged myself now from a noose
The effort would serve little use.
Why pay out for a rope,
And thus give my foes hope,
When I'm already dead from abuse?
That I've lost the lots can't be denied.
And Olympio's taken my bride.
But what rankles me so, and I'd most like to know –
Why was Master so keen on his side?

How it worried and wracked the old boy!
570 When he won, how he capered with joy!
Wait! They're coming outside;
From my *kind* friends I'll hide,
And learn what I can of their ploy.

Withdraws. Enter OLYMPIO *and* LYSIDAMUS
from the house.

OLYMPIO.
   Just wait till he comes to the farm! I'll return him to
   you bent double like a coalman.

LYSIDAMUS.
   Just as you should!

OLYMPIO.
   I'll make certain of that!

LYSIDAMUS.
   If Chalinus were here now, I'd send him off
   shopping with you – to give our fallen foe even more
   misery and woe!   580

CHALINUS.
   I'll just creep back against this wall like a crab, and
   listen to what they're saying. (*Conceals himself along
   the wall of the scenic façade.*) While one of them flails
   me, the other one nails me! Just look at how he struts
   about all dressed in white. That thing with horns!
   That thicket of thorns! That settles it. I'll postpone
   my passing: I won't perish till I've posted that pest
   off to purgatory!

OLYMPIO.
   I've certainly been a sensationally servile surrogate,
   helping you to help yourself to your lady love,
   without your spouse suspecting!

LYSIDAMUS.
   Be quiet!

   Seeing CHALINUS, *they feign the following
   homoerotic scene to put him off the track.
   Alternatively, since such an interpretation is not
   actually suggested by the text,* LYSIDAMUS's
   sudden passion for OLYMPIO *may simply be an
   expression of his overheated state.*

May the gods not love me, if on account of it I'm
able to keep myself from giving you a great big kiss,
590   my dear!

CHALINUS.
What's this!? 'A great big kiss'? How's that again?
'My dear'? Good Lord, I think Master intends to
f-f-f-fondle the f-f-foreman!

OLYMPIO.
You're just a little bit fond of *me* now, are you?

LYSIDAMUS.
Oh, *no!* Far fonder than I am of myself. Won't you
let me hug you?

CHALINUS.
What!? 'Hug' him?

OLYMPIO.
Oh, I suppose so.

LYSIDAMUS.
600   Oh, when I touch you it's like sucking sugar!

> OLYMPIO *pulls away and* LYSIDAMUS *is left
> clutching him from behind.*

OLYMPIO.
Hey there, lover boy! Get off my back!

CHALINUS.
There you have it! That's why he made that fellow
his foreman! I remember now once when I was with
him he offered to make me his '*butler*', on the spot.

OLYMPIO.
Ah, how I've pampered and pleased you today!

LYSIDAMUS.
Ah, what a friend I'll be to you all my life – even
more than I am to myself!

CHALINUS.
I'm afraid, by Pollux, those two will soon be head
over bollocks in bed! Actually the old boy always did
610   go for anything with a beard!

Starts to leave.

LYSIDAMUS (*possibly having seen* CHALINUS
earlier, and now believing him to have left).
Ah, how I'll kiss and cuddle Casina today! What a
life, what a lark! And my wife in the dark!

CHALINUS (*hearing this*).
Ah ha! Now, by Pollux, I'm on the right path at last!
He craves Casina for himself! I've got 'em!

LYSIDAMUS.
By Hercules, I'm dying to kiss and caress her right
now!

OLYMPIO.
Not before *I've* got her! What's the rush, damn it?

LYSIDAMUS.
I'm in *love*.

OLYMPIO.
Well, I don't think you can bring it off today.

LYSIDAMUS.
Oh, yes, I can. That is, if you'd like to be off
tomorrow: a *free* man.   620

CHALINUS (*still concealed*).
Now's the time to prick up my ears. What fun to
capture two boars in one bush!

LYSIDAMUS.
There's a place ready for me over there at the home
of my good friend and neighbour. I've told him
everything about my little love affair, and he's
promised to let me use his place.

OLYMPIO.
What about his wife? Where'll she be?

LYSIDAMUS.
It's neatly and completely arranged. My wife will
invite Myrrhina over for the wedding where she can
hang about, make herself useful, and stay the night.
I've told my wife to do it, and she's agreed. So
Myrrhina will sleep there, (*Indicating his house.*) and

I can *promise* you, her husband won't be here!
630 (*Indicating the other house.*) You'll take your bride off to the farm, but the farm will be right here where Casina and I will enjoy our wedding night.
Tomorrow, before dawn, you'll take her away to the country. Pretty clever, huh?

OLYMPIO.
Brilliant!

CHALINUS (*concealed*).
Go right ahead and plot a lot! By Hercules, you two will be screwed for being so shrewd.

LYSIDAMUS.
Do you know what to do now?

OLYMPIO.
640 Tell me.

LYSIDAMUS.
Take this purse and go shopping for the wedding feast. Be quick, but get something sumptuous since she's so scrumptious.

OLYMPIO.
Right!

LYSIDAMUS.
Get some cockles; some cuddly cuttlefish, some little octopussies, and maybe a nice piece of ass.

CHALINUS (*concealed*).
You mean a bit of bass, you ass!

LYSIDAMUS.
And some sole.

CHALINUS.
Sole? Why not get the whole damn shoe to smash
650 your face with, you odious old man?!

OLYMPIO.
How about a little snapper?

LYSIDAMUS.
Who needs a little snapper when we've got 'Jaws',

that wife of mine at home who never closes her
mouth?

OLYMPIO.
Once I'm there I can decide what to buy from the
fishmonger's stock.

LYSIDAMUS.
Okay. Get on with it. But buy plenty; don't be selfish
with the shellfish! Right now, I've got to meet with
my neighbour to make sure he does what I've asked.

OLYMPIO.
Can I go now?

LYSIDAMUS.
You bet!   660

They exit separately, leaving CHALINUS *on
stage.*

CHALINUS.
You could offer me freedom, nay offer it thrice,
But you couldn't dissuade me, whatever your price,
From cooking those two in a stew – and how?
By spilling the beans to my mistress right now.

Our rivals are cornered, and caught in the act.
If she does her part, then we've won – that's a fact!
We'll trap them but good; they won't get away.
We victims are victors – it's our lucky day!

How shameless our chef has cooked up his plan.
It's flavoured and simmering inside, in the pan.   670
But I'll lend a hand, and give it a stir;
The seasoning I use won't satisfy, sir!

The tables are turned, so ready or not,
He'll eat what *I* serve: thus thickens the plot!

Exit.

Enter LYSIDAMUS *and* ALCESIMUS *from the
latter's house.*

LYSIDAMUS.
Now we'll see whether you'll play the friend or foe, Alcesimus. The truth revealed, signed, and sealed! As for delivering lectures on my love life, you can dispense with 'a man of your age!' and 'with your grey hair!' – you can cut that, too. And as for 'and you a married man!' – you can most certainly take
680   that and shove it!

ALCESIMUS.
I've never seen anyone more lovesick than you!

LYSIDAMUS.
Get everyone out of the house.

ALCESIMUS.
All right, by Pollux. I'm sending all the servants over to your house.

LYSIDAMUS.
What a genuine genius you are! But make certain your servants bring their own provisions. Just like in the birdie's song, 'to eat! to eat! to eat! to eat! to eat!'

ALCESIMUS.
I'll keep that in mind.

LYSIDAMUS.
That's right. There never was a more generous,
690   ingenious genius than you. Keep an eye on things. I'm off to the forum; be back soon!

ALCESIMUS.
Have a nice day.

LYSIDAMUS.
And see that you teach your house some manners.

ALCESIMUS.
How's that?

LYSIDAMUS.
So when I return it puts out a welcome (*Spelling.*) *M-A-T* for me, alone. Get it? '*Em-pty!*' for me!

ALCESIMUS.

Yeaccch! You really ought to be suppressed – you
and your witticisms.

LYSIDAMUS.

What's the use of being in love, if I'm not allowed to
be wise and witty? Now make sure I don't have to go
looking for you.   700

ALCESIMUS.

I'll be here at home.

> *They exit, separately. Enter* CLEOSTRATA *from
> her house.*

CLEOSTRATA.

By Castor, now I know the reason why
My husband's been so keen to have the neighbours
   by.
With them all here, the house next door'd be free,
Where he could cuddle Casina, while conning me!
Well now, I shan't invite them, or provide a spot
For amorous rams to rut, however hot
They are. But wait! My neighbour's coming out.
Here comes that *bast*ion of the state, the lout
Who panders to my husband's fatal fault.
Such men as he aren't worth a pinch of salt!   710

> *Enter* ALCESIMUS.

ALCESIMUS.

I'm surprised no one's come to invite my wife over
to next door. She's been waiting ages, here, all
decked out, to be asked over. Ah! There's Cleostrata,
coming to invite her now, I suppose. Good day,
Cleostrata!

CLEOSTRATA.

And to you, Alcesimus! Where's your wife?

ALCESIMUS.

Right inside, waiting for your invitation. Your
husband beseeched me to send her over to help you
out. Shall I call her?

CLEOSTRATA.
No, not if she's busy.

ALCESIMUS.
720   Oh, she's not!

CLEOSTRATA.
Never mind! I don't want to bother her. I'll catch her later.

ALCESIMUS.
Aren't you arranging a wedding over there?

CLEOSTRATA.
That's right.

ALCESIMUS.
Well, couldn't you use a hand?

CLEOSTRATA.
There's plenty at home. I'll come and see her after the wedding. Well, *ciao* for now! And give her my regards.

Moves out of sight, in her doorway.

ALCESIMUS.
So what do I do now? What a dastardly deed I did! On account of that ruthless, toothless old goat, I'm offering my wife's services around like some sort of scullery maid. What a lying lout he is! Saying his
730   wife's inviting her over, and then *she* says she doesn't want her! By Pollux, I wonder if the woman's got wind of what's in the works? On the other hand, on second thoughts, if that were the case, she'd have questioned me about it. I suppose I'd better go inside and tow the old barge back to her berth.

Exit into his house.

CLEOSTRATA (*in doorway*).
Well, he's finely flummoxed! What a flutter the old fools are in! Now if only that worthless, washed-out wimp of a husband of mine would happen along, I could fix him just like I fooled the other one. I'd just love to stir up a quarrel between them! And here he

comes, right on cue! Goodness! Look at that solemn   740
face. You'd almost think he was an honest man.

Withdraws. Enter LYSIDAMUS, *returning from
the forum.*

LYSIDAMUS.
Now it seems to my mind really quite asinine
When a lover's in service to Cupid,
With a sweetheart so pretty, to spend time in the
    city,
Like I've done; why it's perfectly stupid!

For I've wasted my time on a kinsman of mine
Who used *me* as a character witness.
But I'm pleased to report, he was beaten in court.
Serves him right, bothering me with his business!

Now between me and you, it is patently true,   750
When a man asks a friend to bear witness,
It behoves him to find, if his friend's of sound mind;
Send him home if the witness is witless!

(*Seeing* CLEOSTRATA.) But I'm worried I'm
    screwed –
There's the wife, looking shrewd,
And she's heard all I said, I've a hunch.

CLEOSTRATA (*aside*).
Indeed, I did hear – it'll cost the rogue dear.

LYSIDAMUS (*aside*).
I'll approach. (*To her.*) Well, what's up, honey
bunch?

CLEOSTRATA.
I've been waiting for you, by Castor!   760

LYSIDAMUS.
Is everything prepared? Have you invited our
neighbour over to give you a hand?

CLEOSTRATA.
Well, yes, I did invite her over as you suggested. But
that good buddy and friend of yours, Alcesimus, was

fuming with her about something or other. He
refused to let her come over when I asked.

LYSIDAMUS.
That's your worst fault! You don't know how to ask
nicely.

CLEOSTRATA.
It's not the job of a wife, but the chore of a whore, to
give pleasure, *treasure*, to another wife's husband!
770   Go invite her yourself; I've got things to do inside
that need looking after – *darling!*

LYSIDAMUS.
Well, get a move on then!

CLEOSTRATA (*aside*).
By Pollux, I'll give him a fright, all right. I'll soon
make this lover suffer!

Exit. Enter ALCESIMUS *from his house.*

ALCESIMUS.
I'll just have a look to see if lover boy has come home
from the forum. Fancy that old ghoul making a fool
of my wife and me! Why, there he is, right in front of
the house! (*To him.*) By Hercules, I was just on my
way to see you!

LYSIDAMUS.
780   Same here, by Hercules! Listen, lunch-meat! – Just
what was it I asked you – nay – *begged* you to do?

ALCESIMUS.
Well, what?

LYSIDAMUS.
Fine job you did of emptying your house for me!
Fine job of getting your wife over to our place!
Because of you, me and my affair are finished!

ALCESIMUS.
Why don't you go hang yourself? Didn't you tell me
your very self, that your wife would invite my wife
over? *Uhmmmmmm?*

LYSIDAMUS.
Why, she says she *did* invite her, but that you said
you wouldn't let her come.   790

ALCESIMUS.
Why, she told me herself that she didn't *want* any
help!

LYSIDAMUS.
Why, she just told me herself to come and *get* her!

ALCESIMUS.
Why, I don't give a damn ...

LYSIDAMUS.
Why are you ruining me?

ALCESIMUS.
Why, that's a blessing!

LYSIDAMUS.
Why, I'll just linger a little longer.

ALCESIMUS.
Why, I'd like to ...

LYSIDAMUS.
Why ...

ALCESIMUS.
Why, to do something *nasty!*

LYSIDAMUS.
Why? I'll do the same. I'm going to have the last   800
'why' today, or know the reason why!

ALCESIMUS.
But ...

LYSIDAMUS.
That's better!

ALCESIMUS.
Why?

LYSIDAMUS (*striking him*).
That's why!!

ALCESIMUS.
> Well ... in that ... case ... (*Shouting.*) *why the hell
> don't you just go hang yourself once and for all!!!*

LYSIDAMUS.
> Now, how about it? Will you send your wife over to
> my place?

ALCESIMUS.
> Go on! Take her, and give yourself a fabulous
> flogging along with her, your own wife, and that girl
> of yours too!! (*Cooling off.*) Go away and leave it to
> me. I'll send my wife along to yours right away –
> through the back garden.

810

LYSIDAMUS.
> Now there's a real friend!

> *Exit* ALCESIMUS.

> I wonder what omen I omitted when I began this
> love affair. Or how I offended the goddess of Love.
> It's a clear case of *Venus-envy!* Here I am longing to
> get laid, and all I get is *de*-layed! Now what's all this
> unholy hubbub in the house?

> *Enter* MYRRHINA *from* LYSIDAMUS's *house.*

MYRRHINA.
> I'm lost! Totally done for and dead!
> My heart has stopped, my limbs are trembling with
> dread!
> Help! Safety! Shelter! Oh, where to turn for aid?
> Such things I saw inside, can scarcely be conveyed.
> Bold and brazen badness! Turmoil and alarm!
> (*Calling inside.*) Be careful, Cleostrata! Lest she do
> you harm!
> The woman's lost her senses – her mind has gone
> astray!
> For goodness' sake avoid her, but snatch the sword
> away!

820

LYSIDAMUS.
> Now what do you suppose has frightened our

neighbour half to death, and sent her scurrying
outside? (*Calls in.*) *Pardalisca!*

> *Enter* PARDALISCA *onto the porch.**

PARDALISCA.
Oh! I'm lost! What is this sound I hear?

LYSIDAMUS.
Look over here, will you?   830

PARDALISCA.
Oh, dear Master!

LYSIDAMUS.
What's wrong with you? Why are you so frightened?

PARDALISCA.
I'm dead!

LYSIDAMUS.
Really? Dead?

MYRRHINA.
Dead, indeed! And you're dead, too!

LYSIDAMUS (*checking himself*).
I'm dead? How come?

PARDALISCA.
Oh, woe is you!

LYSIDAMUS.
Woe is me? No, make that, 'woe is you'!

PARDALISCA.
That's just what I said!

MYRRHINA.
Please help me! I ... I ... feel faint!   840

LYSIDAMUS.
Look, what's going on? Tell me right now!

* The following passage, which in the Latin text is between
Pardalisca and Lysidamus, has been altered to include Myrrhina, in
the interest of making for a more lively and effective scene. The lines
have therefore been given to two foils for Lysidamus, instead of only
one, with plural forms used as necessary.

PARDALISCA.

Please hold me – by the waist – fan me – with your
cloak!

LYSIDAMUS.

You know, I'm worried about all this. Unless the two
of them have been knocking it back with Bacchus.

MYRRHINA.

Oh! Hold my head!

LYSIDAMUS.

Oh, get hanged, and stop hanging on me! Go flog
yourselves, waist, head, the lot! Unless you tell me
this instant what's going on, I'll bash both your
brains in, you silly sluts. You've played with me long
850   enough!

PARDALISCA.

Dear Master!

LYSIDAMUS.

What now, dear servant?

PARDALISCA.

You're too hard on us.

LYSIDAMUS (*aside*).

You ain't seen nothing yet! (*To* MYRRHINA.) Now
out with it! What the hell's going on inside? Make it
snappy!

MYRRHINA.

I'll tell you, just listen. (*Melodramatically.*) Oh! It
was absolutely horrible inside, just now! Your
servant girl ran completely amok, and began
carrying on in the most awful, most appalling, most
un-Athenian manner!

LYSIDAMUS.

860   What!? *Anti-Attic-antics?!*

PARDALISCA.

I'm so frightened, I can't speak properly ... either.

LYSIDAMUS.

Will you *please* tell me what happened?

MYRRHINA.
I'll tell you. That serving girl that you wanted to
marry off to your foreman ...

LYSIDAMUS.
Yes??

MYRRHINA.
Well, inside there, she ...

LYSIDAMUS.
What happened inside?

PARDALISCA.
She's acting like a really nasty ... wife.

LYSIDAMUS (*relieved*).
Oh.

PARDALISCA.
Threatening to *kill* her husband!   870

LYSIDAMUS.
What the *hell!?*

MYRRHINA.
AAAHHhhh!

    Faints.

LYSIDAMUS.
What now?

PARDALISCA.
She says she wants to kill him. She's in there with a
sword.

LYSIDAMUS.
A *what?*

MYRRHINA (*revives*).
A *sword!*

LYSIDAMUS.
What about this sword?

PARDALISCA.
She's got one!

LYSIDAMUS.

880   *Mamma mia!* Why's she got that?

MYRRHINA.
She's chasing everyone all over the house and won't
let a soul come near her! They're all hiding under
tables and beds – struck dumb with fear!

LYSIDAMUS.
I'm dead and done for! But what the hell's got into
her?

MYRRHINA.
She's insane!

LYSIDAMUS.
If I'm not the wretchedest wretch alive!

PARDALISCA.
You should have heard what she was saying just
now!

LYSIDAMUS.
Yes, indeed? What did she say?

MYRRHINA.
Just listen. She swore by all the gods and goddesses
890   that the man she sleeps with tonight ... she'll
murder!

LYSIDAMUS.
Murder *me?*

PARDALISCA (*innocently*).
What's it got to do with you, sir?

LYSIDAMUS (*aside*).
Damn!

MYRRHINA.
Why should you be concerned about that?

LYSIDAMUS.
Why, I misspoke myself. I meant to say Olympio.

MYRRHINA (*aside*).
He's good under pressure!

LYSIDAMUS.
   She's not threatening *me*, is she?

PARDALISCA.
   Why, you're the one she hates the very most of all!

LYSIDAMUS.
   What for?

MYRRHINA.
   Because you want to marry her to Olympio. She's   900
   sworn that neither he, nor she, nor you will make it
   to tomorrow.

PARDALISCA.
   I was sent out here to tell you. So you can keep away
   from her.

LYSIDAMUS.
   By Hercules, I'm a goner!

MYRRHINA (*aside*).
   You deserve it!

LYSIDAMUS (*aside*).
   No old lover ever lived, or lives less lucky than I!

PARDALISCA (*aside*).
   What fabulous foolery! It's all fantasy from first to
   finish! Mistress and her neighbour here set the trap,
   and I've been sent to spring it on him!   910

LYSIDAMUS.
   Hey, Pardalisca!

PARDALISCA.
   Yes sir?

LYSIDAMUS.
   There's ...

PARDALISCA.
   What?

LYSIDAMUS.
   Something I'd like to ask you.

PARDALISCA.
   Well, make it snappy!

LYSIDAMUS (*aside*).
I'm so unhappy! (*To her.*) Look, has Casina still got
the sword?

PARDALISCA.
No sir.

LYSIDAMUS.
920   Whewww!

MYRRHINA.
She's got *two* of them.

LYSIDAMUS.
Two?! Why two?

PARDALISCA.
She says one's to kill Olympio with; the other's for
you. This very day!

LYSIDAMUS.
I'm the dead-deader-deadest man alive!
To try and save my life, I'll put on armour!
But what about my wife, couldn't *she* disarm her?

PARDALISCA.
Well, she had to be very evasive.

LYSIDAMUS.
The old girl can be awfully persuasive!

PARDALISCA.
930   That's undoubtedly true, but I'm still telling you,
How our Casina's sworn with an oath,
That she won't let them go, until given to know,
That she won't have to marry that oaf!

LYSIDAMUS.
Well, like it or not, the ungrateful slut
Will be given in marriage today.
I won't change what's planned:
She'll give me her hand ...
(*Catching himself.*) To my *foreman*, I meant to say!

MYRRHINA.
Seems you stumble a lot.

LYSIDAMUS.

I'm so frightened, I'm not   940
Giving thought to the words that I say.
(*To* PARDALISCA.) But please beg my wife, if she
   values my life,
To get Casina out of the way!
(*To* MYRRHINA.) And you beg her too.

PARDALISCA.

And I'll beg with you!

LYSIDAMUS.

Do your best, as you know how to do.
If you hush up these scandals, I'll buy you some
   sandals,
A gold ring (and some other treats too!).

PARDALISCA.

Well, I'll do what I may, sir.   950

LYSIDAMUS.

Oh, please try to persuade her!

MYRRHINA.

We'll go now, without further delay.

LYSIDAMUS.

Yes, go right in my dear.

> *They exit into the house;* OLYMPIO *enters with a*
> COOK *and* ASSISTANTS.

Oh! Olympio's here!
And he's gathered a crowd on his way.

OLYMPIO (*to* COOK).

Now see to it, you crooked cook, that you keep these
brambles (*Indicating the assistants.*) of yours under
tight control.

COOK.

Why, pray, do you term them 'brambles'?

OLYMPIO.

Because they cling to whatever they touch; try and   960
get it back and it's gone. Coming, going, or standing
still, they're double-trouble.

COOK.
> Oh dear, oh dear!

OLYMPIO.
> Aha! Now to dress myself in a fancy-pants patrician sort of way, and meet my master.

LYSIDAMUS.
> Ah, hello, my good man!

OLYMPIO.
> I admit it!

LYSIDAMUS.
> What's the latest?

OLYMPIO.
> You're still in love, and I'm hungry and thirsty.

LYSIDAMUS.
970   You've come well-equipped!

OLYMPIO.
> Ah, yes! Today I intend to gorge myself on 'sweet delights'!

LYSIDAMUS.
> Now just a minute! Don't get so uppity!

OLYMPIO.
> Oh, save your breath! It offends me.

LYSIDAMUS.
> What's this?

OLYMPIO.
> Standing around like this is a chore, and you're a bore!

> *Starts to go inside.*

LYSIDAMUS (*restraining him*).
> Unless you stand still, I'll more than bore you – I'll whip you as well!

OLYMPIO (*shaking him off, and again starting to leave*).
> Leave me alone, for the gods' sake. Do you want to
980   make me retch, wretch?

LYSIDAMUS.
  Wait!

OLYMPIO.
  Just who do you think you are?

LYSIDAMUS.
  I'm the master here!

OLYMPIO.
  Master of what?

LYSIDAMUS.
  Of *you!*

OLYMPIO.
  I? A slave?

LYSIDAMUS.
  Yes, my slave.

OLYMPIO.
  Am I not a free man? You do remember, don't you?
  Don't you?

LYSIDAMUS.
  Wait! Stop!   990

OLYMPIO.
  Leave me alone!

LYSIDAMUS (*on his knees*).
  I'll be your slave!

OLYMPIO.
  That's more like it.

LYSIDAMUS.
  Dear, dear Olympio, my father, my patron, I beg ...

OLYMPIO.
  Now you're talking sense.

LYSIDAMUS.
  Yes, I'm yours. Indeed I am.

OLYMPIO.
  What do I want with such a knave of a slave?

LYSIDAMUS.
Well then, make me over. When do we start the *re-serection?*

OLYMPIO.
1000 As soon as supper's ready.

LYSIDAMUS (*indicating* COOK *and assistants*).
Well, let them get on with it then!

OLYMPIO (*haughtily*).
Get on inside and hurry things along! Move! I'll be in in a minute. And make sure it's a super supper, with lots to drink. An elegant and dandy dinner; none of your rotten Roman slop! Well? What are you waiting for? Be off!

They exit inside.

(*To* LYSIDAMUS, *who lingers.*) What's keeping you?

LYSIDAMUS.
They say Casina's waiting inside with a sword. Waiting to finish us both off!

OLYMPIO.
I see. Well, let her wait. What nonsense! I know how to deal with a bad bargain of a woman. Go on into
1010 the house ... (LYSIDAMUS *refuses to move.*) with *me.*

LYSIDAMUS.
By Pollux, I fear the worst! *You* go ahead and reconnoitre. See what's going on.

OLYMPIO (*thinking better of it*).
Look, I value my life as much as you do yours! So – *you* go in.

LYSIDAMUS.
Well, if you insist ... we'll go *together.*

They exit, each trying to get the other to go first.
After a short pause indicating a passage of time,
enter PARDALISCA *from* LYSIDAMUS's *house.*

PARDALISCA.
  They never have games at Nemea,
  Nor in the Olympian arena,
  Such sport of the sort as we're playing inside,
  With Master and foreman – taking them for a ride!   1020

  The whole house is in turmoil and all in a flurry,
  Since Master is mad to make the cooks hurry;
  'Don't fidget in the kitchen, but make haste now!
  Our *tempus fugits*, so give us the chow!'

  While Olympio struts in the room just outside,
  Clothed in white, wreathed and bright, as he grooms
    for his bride –
  In her bedroom the bride's being dressed by her
    minions.
  They're aware of a plot, but suppress their opinions!

  And the cooks in their cunning are conning their
    master
  By delaying his meal, and designing disaster: 1030
  Overturning the pots right into the fire,
  And contriving whatever the ladies desire!

  They would like, if they can, to deprive him of food,
  And consume it themselves, once he's gone – very
    rude!
  I confess that the ladies eat more than they should,
  They would bloat on a boatload of food if they could!

  But wait! I hear the door.

    She hides. Enter LYSIDAMUS.

LYSIDAMUS (*calling back inside*).
  If you're wise, my dear, you women should go right
  ahead and eat as soon as dinner's done. I'll
  consummate – *consume* – mine at the farm. I want to   1040
  escort our new bride and groom there – so no one
  will *way-lay* her – knowing as I do the sort of
  unsavoury characters there are around here. You two
  go right ahead and enjoy yourselves. (*Growing
  impatient.*) Just hurry up and send them out now, so

we can get there before dark. I'll be back tomorrow
and enjoy my piece of the party then, dear.

PARDALISCA (*aside*).
What did I tell you? The ladies are sending the old
boy off, unfed!

LYSIDAMUS (*seeing her*).
What are you doing here?

PARDALISCA.

1050   Going where Mistress sent me.

LYSIDAMUS.
Really?

PARDALISCA.
Yes sir!

LYSIDAMUS.
Then why are you spying here?

PARDALISCA.
I – spy? Not a bit of it!

LYSIDAMUS.
Well, be off! Here you are hanging about when
everyone else is rushing around inside.

PARDALISCA.
I'm off!

LYSIDAMUS.
On your way, triple-tramp! Is she gone yet? Now I
can say what I want! By Hercules! A fellow in love
feels full even when he's famished! (*Seeing*
OLYMPIO *approaching*.) Ah, here he comes now!
Garland on head, and torch in hand! My comrade,

1060   ally, co-husband, and foreman!

    Enter OLYMPIO.

OLYMPIO.
Come on, flautist! (*Indicating the onstage musician*.)
When they bring on the bride, make the whole street
sound with sweet music! (*Sings*.) 'Here comes the
bride! Here comes the bride!'

LYSIDAMUS.
How are you, my saviour?

OLYMPIO.
Hungry, by Hercules! And there's nothing around to savour.

LYSIDAMUS.
Yes, but I'm in love!   1070

OLYMPIO.
I don't give a flying flogging! You can feast on love – as for me, my guts have been rumbling for hours!

LYSIDAMUS.
What makes those laggards linger so long? The more I hurry them, the slower they go. It almost seems on purpose!

OLYMPIO.
Well, suppose I sing the wedding song again, and see if that gets them going?

LYSIDAMUS.
Good idea! And I'll sing too, since it's a twosome screwsome!

LYSIDAMUS *and* OLYMPIO.
'Here comes the bride! Here comes the bride!'   1080

LYSIDAMUS.
By Hercules! I'm beat! I could sing until I'm flat on my back, but I'd prefer her flat on her back in the sack!

OLYMPIO.
By Pollux, if you were a horse, you'd be a real champion!

LYSIDAMUS.
Why's that?

OLYMPIO.
Always champing at the bit!

LYSIDAMUS (*suggestively*).
Ever fancy trying a *bit* with me?

OLYMPIO.
The gods forbid! But the door's creaking – they're coming out!

LYSIDAMUS.
By Hercules! The gods are looking after me!

Music. Enter CHALINUS, *disguised as a bride,* PARDALISCA, CLEOSTRATA, *and* MYRRHINA.

PARDALISCA.

1090   Here we go, take it slow,
Step over the threshold with care.
By his side, blushing bride,
Keep the upper hand always and dare

To hold sway, night and day.
Make him pamper you as his task.
Never cease him to fleece.
Just treat him like dirt's all I ask!

OLYMPIO.
By Hercules, she'll get a whopping whipping if she's guilty of even any eany meany minimischief!

LYSIDAMUS.

1100   Shut up!

OLYMPIO.
I won't!

LYSIDAMUS.
Why not?

OLYMPIO.
That bawd is teaching the broad to be bad!

LYSIDAMUS.
You'll unsettle what I've set up! That's what they'd like: to undo what I've done.

PARDALISCA.
Go on, Olympio. If it's what you want, receive your bride from us.

OLYMPIO (*impatiently*).
  Well, go ahead and give her, if you intend doing it
  today!

LYSIDAMUS.
  Go back inside.   1110

PARDALISCA (*delaying*).
  Just be kind to this innocent, unspoiled girl.

OLYMPIO.
  I will be!

PARDALISCA.
  Farewell!

OLYMPIO.
  Go already!

LYSIDAMUS.
  Go!

PARDALISCA.
  Well, then, farewell.

  The women exit into LYSIDAMUS's *house.*

LYSIDAMUS.
  Has my wife gone?

OLYMPIO.
  Don't worry. She's in the house.

LYSIDAMUS.
  Hurrah! Now, by Pollux, I'm free at last! Oh, my
  little sweetkins, honeykins, spring chick-chickens!   1120

OLYMPIO.
  Hey, you! If you're wise, you'll keep your eyes open
  for trouble! The girl is mine!

LYSIDAMUS.
  I know, but the first fruits are mine!

OLYMPIO.
  Here! Hold this torch.

LYSIDAMUS.
  Oh, no! (*Caressing* CASINA.) I'd rather hold *this*

one! Almighty, mighty Aphrodite! What pleasure
you gave in giving me this treasure.

OLYMPIO (*holding her*).
Oh, your iddy, biddy, body, baby! – *What the hell!*

LYSIDAMUS.
1130   What's wrong?

OLYMPIO.
She just stamped on my foot like an elephant!

LYSIDAMUS.
Hush up! Never a cloud was softer than this breast!

OLYMPIO (*fondling her*).
By Pollux, what an iddy, bitty pretty titty!
Owwww! Good lord!

LYSIDAMUS.
What now?

OLYMPIO.
She hit me in the chest – it wasn't an elbow; it was a
battering ram!

LYSIDAMUS.
Well, why are you handling her so roughly, then?
Look at me. Just treat her kind and she doesn't
mind!

OLYMPIO.
1140   *Ouch!*

LYSIDAMUS.
What's the matter now?

OLYMPIO.
Damnation! What a pint-sized power-house she is!!
Her elbow almost laid me low!

LYSIDAMUS.
Maybe *she'd* like to be laid low – you know?

OLYMPIO.
Let's go!

LYSIDAMUS.
Look lively, little, lovely lady!

They exit into ALCESIMUS's *house. Music. Enter*
CLEOSTRATA, PARDALISCA, *and*
MYRRHINA *from the other house, somewhat*
inebriated.

MYRRHINA.
Nicely wined and dined, inside! Now we can come
out and watch the wedding games. By Castor, I've
never laughed so much, nor ever shall again!

PARDALISCA.
I'd like to know how Chalinus is getting along –   1150
(*Making a joke.*) the new *male* ordered *bride* and his
new husband!

MYRRHINA.
No playwright ever conceived a plot cleverer than
this masterpiece of ours!

CLEOSTRATA.
I'd like to see the old fool come out now with his face
smashed! He's the nastiest old man alive. Not even
that one of yours who procured the place for him is
worse. Pardalisca, I'd like you to stand watch here to
abuse and be amused by my husband when he
appears.

PARDALISCA.
Gladly. Just like always.

MYRRHINA.
You keep an eye on things here. Report to us inside   1160
what's happening.

PARDALISCA.
Get thee behind me, madam!

MYRRHINA.
And don't be afraid to speak up!

PARDALISCA.
Shh! Your door's creaking!

They withdraw. Enter OLYMPIO, *in great haste,*
from ALCESIMUS's *house.*

OLYMPIO.
    Oh, where to run to or to hide myself from shame!
    And oh, the *scandal* that it casts on Master's name,
    And *mine!* I tremble at the shame of it and how
    Ridiculous we've made ourselves appear just now.
    And this is something new for me to have to say –
1170   A *fool!* – I never felt such shame until today.

    (*To audience.*) So listen while I tell you all, and lend
      an ear.
    It's just as comical to narrate as to hear
    The quite appalling mess I've made of things inside.
    The moment that we went in there, I took my bride
    Straight to a little bedroom, which was dark as night.
    Before the old man had arrived, I said, 'All right,
    Get comfy on the couch.' Then helped to smooth the
      bed,
    And soon began to soothe her there, and said
    A few kind words and some sweet nothings to her,
1180   So prior to Master I could start to ... *woo* her.

    I start out slowly, but am filled with fear
    Lest turning round I find the old man there.
    To get things going and begin her bliss,
    I start by asking for a sloppy kiss.
    She wouldn't kiss me; pushed my hand away.
    That only stiffened my ... *resolve* ... which stayed
      that way.

    I longed to taste in haste chaste Casina's embrace,
    And let the old man come in second place!
    And so, I closed the door to try and minimise
1190   The chance that in the dark he'd take *me* by surprise.

MYRRHINA (*to the women*).
    All right now. Let's go up to him.

CLEOSTRATA (*approaching*).
    Where is your bride, for goodness' sake!

OLYMPIO (*aside*).
    Damn! (*Despairing.*) I'm done for! It's all out!

MYRRHINA.
In that case, you might as well tell all. What's going
on inside? How's Casina? Did you find her
sufficiently obliging?

OLYMPIO.
I'm embarrassed to say.

CLEOSTRATA.
Go right on with your story.

OLYMPIO.
By Hercules! I'm so *ashamed!*

PARDALISCA.
Stiff upper lip! That bit about the couch – I'd like to   1200
hear what happened next.

OLYMPIO.
It's shocking.

CLEOSTRATA.
It'll be a good lesson for our audience.

OLYMPIO.
It's such a scandal!

MYRRHINA.
Nonsense! Why don't you go on?

> *During the following sequence, the text of which is
> very fragmentary, the characters may huddle to
> confer closely among themselves, with only the
> occasional word uttered aloud.*

OLYMPIO.
When (*Whispers.*) ... then down below ...
(*Whispers.*)

CLEOSTRATA.
Well!

OLYMPIO.
... Wow! ... (*Whispers.*)

MYRRHINA.
What about it? (*Whispers.*)   1210

OLYMPIO.
Oh *my!*

PARDALISCA. Was it? ... (*Whispers.*)

OLYMPIO.
Oh, it was just *enormous!* I was afraid she must still
have a sword. So I started to investigate, and while
I'm searching for the sword, checking to see if she's
carrying one, I got hold of its hilt. On second
thoughts, though, she couldn't have had a sword; the
hilt would have felt cold ...

CLEOSTRATA (*intrigued*).
Go on.

OLYMPIO.
I'm so embarrassed!

PARDALISCA.
1220   Let's see ... was it a carrot?

She plays charades.

OLYMPIO.
No!

MYRRHINA (*also acting charades, and suddenly
thinking she has it*).
A cucumber!!

OLYMPIO.
No, it wasn't any sort of vegetable. Or at least, if it
was, it certainly was never nipped in the bud:
whatever it was, it was full-grown!

MYRRHINA.
What happened next? In detail!

OLYMPIO.
I appealed to her then by her name:
'Little wife, don't be spurning my claim!
By heaven above, though I crave all your love
1230   For myself, I'm not *really* to blame!'

Not a word does she say, but by turning away, \
Puts an end to that line of pursuit.

Since she's in that position, I ask her permission,
To attempt the alternative route!

PARDALISCA (*collapsing in laughter*).
What a marvellous tale!

OLYMPIO.
As I tried to prevail,
I leant over to smooch with my sweet.
But something was weird: she'd a bristly beard!
Then she kicked me with both of her feet!

I fell flat on the ground, and she started to pound   1240
And beat me just as you discern.
Without a word more, I ran straight out the door,
To let the old man have his turn!

CLEOSTRATA.
That's just *great!* But what happened to your cloak?

OLYMPIO.
I left it inside.

PARDALISCA.
Well, what do you think of our trick – pretty neat,
huh?

OLYMPIO.
We deserve it. But the door's creaking! She's not
coming for me again, is she?

They all withdraw. Enter LYSIDAMUS *from*
ALCESIMUS's *house.*

LYSIDAMUS.
Oh! I burn with disgrace, and I'm dreading to face   1250
The awful contempt of my wife.
The whole business is out – and this miserable lout
Apprehends it's the end of his life!

The best thing, I suppose, is to suffer the blows
That my wife will exact from my hide.
(*To the audience.*) Is there no one out there who'd be
    willing to share
The fate that awaits me inside?

Then I think I'll behave like a runaway slave,
Since my back's for the rack in these parts.
I get beat black and blue. You may laugh, but it's
1260   true!
It's my folly but, by *golly*, it smarts!
I think I'd better make a run for it now!

Enter CHALINUS *from* ALCESIMUS's *house.*

CHALINUS.
Hold it right there, lover boy!

LYSIDAMUS.
Damnation! Someone's calling. I'll go on as if I
    didn't hear.

CHALINUS.
Just where do you think you're going, you sneaky-
Greeky lover? If you want to debauch me, now's
your chance! Don't you yearn to return to the
bedroom? You're finished, by Hercules! Come right
this way! We don't need to go to court; I've a good,
1270   strong, honest judge right here! (*Brandishing a club.*)

LYSIDAMUS.
I'm sunk! That fellow's going to tenderise my
slender thighs with his club! It's either make tracks
this way, or break backs that way!

Starts to leave in the opposite direction.

CLEOSTRATA.
Greetings, lover boy!

LYSIDAMUS.
Egad!! There's the wife! Caught between the devil
and the deep blue sea! Wolves to the right of me,
bitches to the left! (*Indicating* CHALINUS.) Only
the wolf at *this* door has a club! I think I'd better
change the proverb, by Hercules, and hope to teach
this old dog a new trick.

Turns to face CLEOSTRATA.

MYRRHINA.
1280   How's the secondhand husband?

CLEOSTRATA (*sweetly*).
Why dear, why are you going about in this garb?
What did you do with your cane? Why, whatever's
become of your cloak?

PARDALISCA.
I think he lost them in lechery: *conjugating* with
Casina.

LYSIDAMUS (*aside*).
This is *murder!*

CHALINUS.
Don't you want to go back to bed again? (*Throwing
off his bridal attire.*) *I am Casina!*

LYSIDAMUS.
Go to blazes!!

CHALINUS.
Don't you love me?   1290

CLEOSTRATA.
Answer me now! What happened to your cloak?

LYSIDAMUS.
By Hercules, wife, some maenads ...

CLEOSTRATA.
Maenads?

LYSIDAMUS.
Lord yes, dear. Many maenads ...

CLEOSTRATA.
That's rubbish and you know it. There aren't any
maenads any more!

LYSIDAMUS.
I forgot. Well, there may not have been many
maenads, but there were *some!*

CLEOSTRATA.
No, there weren't.

LYSIDAMUS.
Well, if I'm not able to ...   1300

CLEOSTRATA.
By Castor, you seem nervous!

LYSIDAMUS.
I?

All three speaking together:

CLEOSTRATA.
Yes, by Hercules, you're lying!

MYRRHINA.
Why, how pale you look!

PARDALISCA.
Why, what's wrong with you?

LYSIDAMUS.
Who, *me?*

OLYMPIO (*joining in*).
Yes, *you!* Congratulations! You're the dirtiest old
man that ever was! And he's brought misery and
mockery on me because of his dastardly deeds.

LYSIDAMUS (*frantic*).
1310   Can't you be *quiet!?*

OLYMPIO.
No, by Hercules! I won't be quiet! Why, you begged
and egged me on to marry Casina – on account of
your love affair!

LYSIDAMUS (*innocently*).
I!! I did *that?*

OLYMPIO.
No, Hector of Troy did it!

LYSIDAMUS (*aside to him*).
At least he would have throttled you! You really
mean to say I did all these things?

CLEOSTRATA.
You dare to ask? (*Threatening to strike him.*)

LYSIDAMUS.
Wait, by Hercules! If I did it, then it was wrong.

CLEOSTRATA.
Just march yourself right inside. Mama will limber
and dismember your timber till you remember!   1320

   They all advance on him.

LYSIDAMUS.
Oh no, by Hercules!! I think I'd better just take your
word for everything! But, dear wife, please pardon
your husband this once. Myrrhina, beg Cleostrata!
If, after this, I make love to Casina – or even *appear
to want* to do so – let alone *do* it – if I ever again do
such a thing – well then, dear wife, you can just
suspend me and skin me alive.

MYRRHINA.
By Castor ... (*Pauses.*) I really think you ought ...
(*Pauses.*) to *forgive* him.

CLEOSTRATA (*after long hesitation*).
... Well ... if you say so ... I'll do it. And the other
reason I'm willing to indulge you with forgiveness –   1330
this time! – is to keep a long play from running any
longer.

LYSIDAMUS.
You're really not angry?

CLEOSTRATA.
No, I'm not really angry.

LYSIDAMUS.
Do you promise?

CLEOSTRATA.
I do.

LYSIDAMUS.
There's not a living soul with a more loving and
lovely wife than mine!

CLEOSTRATA (*to* CHALINUS).
Go and give him back his cloak and cane.   1340

CHALINUS (*doing so*).
If you wish, I'll surrender this booty.
But, by Pollux, I've suffered acutely

For I think it's a sin to be wed to *two* men,
With neither performing his duty!

Epilogue

ALCESIMUS.
But audience, *wait!* Learn Casina's fate.
We'll share what's discovered inside.

CLEOSTRATA.
A slave no more, she's the girl from next door!
And soon, our darling son's bride.

OLYMPIO.
And now it's your right with all of your might
1350   To applaud till you bring down the house!

PARDALISCA.
If you do your part, you'll get a sweetheart!

LYSIDAMUS.
To enjoy without telling *your* spouse!

MYRRHINA.
Yet listen, because – if you curb your applause –
You'll live to regret it, please note:

CHALINUS.
No nooky! Instead, we'll send you to bed.
With a sodden and smelly old goat!

TERENCE

The Eunuch

translated by Kenneth McLeish
(edited by Michael Sargent)

Characters

PHAEDRIA, a young Athenian, in love with Thais
PARMENO, his chief slave
THAIS, a courtesan
GNATHO, a parasite
PAMPHILA, a beautiful young girl*
CHAEREA, Phaedria's younger brother
THRASO, an army officer, in love with Thais
PYTHIAS, Thais's housekeeper
CHREMES, a young nobleman
DORIAS, Thais's maid
ANTIPHO, a friend of Chaerea's
DORUS, a eunuch
PRIVATE DONAX ⎫
PRIVATE SIMALIO* ⎪
PRIVATE SYRISCUS* ⎬ Thraso's army
CORPORAL SANGA ⎭
SOPHRONA, Pamphila's old nurse
LACHES, father to Phaedria and Chaerea

* non-speaking parts

An earlier version of this translation was first broadcast on the BBC Third Programme in January 1968. The cast included Christopher Bidmead, David Brierley, Sian Davies, Alan Dudley, Michael Harbour, Betty Hardy, Frank Henderson, Anthony Jackson, Alexander John, Harold Kasket, Leroy Lingwood, Victor Lucas, Margaret Robertson, Alexa Romanes, Ian Thompson, Lockwood West and John Wyse, produced by Raymond Raikes.

The first stage production of this revised version was given by Xenia Theatre Company, as a double-bill with a revival of *The Haunted House*, at the Courtyard Theatre, London, in February 2003. The cast for the double-bill included Maria de Caldas, Joel Chalfen, Steve Dineen, Terry Jermyn, Dan Skinner and Alex Woodhall, directed by Michael Sargent.

PROLOGUE.

Your playwright's aim is to please as many people as possible and to avoid giving offence. So if a certain critic thinks that something rather harsh has been said against him, let him please note: it was not an attack but an answer ... he started it! He may be a competent translator, but he has turned good Greek plays into bad Latin ones. It was he who ruined Menander's *The Ghost*, and in *The Treasure* he made   10
the defendant state his claim first, before the plaintiff had even explained how the treasure got into the tomb! He mustn't think this is the end of the matter. There are plenty of other things I am overlooking for the moment but will produce later if he persists in making these attacks.

The play we're presenting today is Menander's *The*   20
Eunuch. After the officials had bought it, that critic managed to get an opportunity to see it, and at the first rehearsal started shouting out, 'This is the work of a thief, not a playwright; he's stolen the characters of the sponger and the soldier from Naevius and Plautus's old play, *The Flatterer*.'

If in fact your playwright *is* at fault, it is through ignorance, not any intention to steal. You must judge for yourselves. It's true that in Menander's *Flatterer* there is a sponger and a boastful soldier, and he has   30
transferred these characters from the Greek original, but he was not aware that the play had already been translated into Latin. If your playwright is not allowed to use the same characters as other writers, how can he show you a running slave, good wives, dishonest courtesans, greedy spongers, boastful soldiers, a child being substituted, an old man being tricked by his slave, love or hate or jealousy? In fact,   40
nothing is ever said that has not been said before.

We hope that you recognise this, and forgive new playwrights if they do what earlier writers did repeatedly. Please give your attention, listen in silence, and find out what *The Eunuch* has to say.

The scene is a street in Athens, in front of the houses of LACHES *and* THAIS. PHAEDRIA *and* PARMENO *are in the middle of an argument.*

PHAEDRA.

What d'you want me to do, for heaven's sake? Surely you don't expect me to go and see her again just because she asks me? It's time I stood up for myself. Yesterday she slams the door in my face; today she sends me a loving invitation. Well, it's no use. Even if she goes down on her bended knees, I won't go back.

PARMENO.

50   Well said, sir. A firm decision, sir. But ... you'll never hold out: in a couple of days you'll be telling me you can't stand it any longer, your love won't give you any peace, you've got to see her whether she invites you round or not. Don't you see, sir? She's got you where she wants you. You're not just fighting her: you're fighting Love, and you can't win. So stop and think. This has to be carefully planned. The mistake people make is thinking love is a game, that can be played according to proper rules. It isn't a game. What game is played with insults, jealous
60   quarrels, arguments, making up, more arguments ...? It's lunacy! Look at you, now. What's going on in your mind at this moment? 'She can't ask me to ... not after she ... with him ... then with me ... then nothing ... I'll show her! ... I'll die before I ...' That's what your feelings are just now, sir: but you wait. All she has to do is rub her eyes till she squeezes out one tiny little tear, and you're done for! You'll go crawling back to her, and she'll have you right where she wants you!

PHAEDRIA.

70   I know, it's monstrous! But ... what can I do? I can't help being in love with her. She's eating me alive;

I'm walking on the edge of a precipice, with my eyes
wide open. There's no way out.

PARMENO.
The only thing to do is break away from her
completely. Try to forget her, and make a fresh start.

PHAEDRIA.
Forget her? You're joking.

PARMENO.
It's the only way, sir: a clean break. Love's bad
enough, without you adding to your own miseries.
Look: here she comes. Now's your chance. Make a
firm stand: tell her you're finished with her, and
you'll never see her again. (*Aside.*) And good
riddance, too: every penny we ought to have, he uses
for buying *her* presents!   80

THAIS *comes out of her house, but doesn't see the
others.* PHAEDRIA *starts trembling violently.*

THAIS.
Oh dear, I know Phaedria wasn't pleased yesterday.
But what else could I do? I simply had to tell them
not to let him in.

PHAEDRIA.
Brrr! You see, Parmeno: it's no use. As soon as I see
her, I start shivering all over.

PARMENO.
That's all right: as soon as you go near this little fire,
you'll warm up again.

THAIS.
Who's that? Ah, Phaedria, darling! You're here, are
you? But why are you waiting outside? Why don't
you come in?

PARMENO.
Convenient memory: it was a different story
yesterday.

THAIS.
Speak to me, darling. Say you're not angry.

PHAEDRIA (*sarcastically*).
90   Angry? Why should I be angry? I know you've eyes
for no one else, and I'm always welcome at your
house.

THAIS.
Please, no more.

PHAEDRIA.
Why 'no more'? Oh Thais, Thais, if only love meant
the same thing to you and to me! Then either you'd
be suffering as much as I am, or I simply wouldn't
mind what you're doing to me.

THAIS.
Oh please, my dear, don't torment me. I had to do
what I did yesterday. I swear to you, you're the only
man I've ever loved, or ever will love.

PARMENO.
Oh yes! Funny way to show how much you love him,
slamming the door in his face!

THAIS.
Parmeno! (*To* PHAEDRIA.) Darling, listen: the
100   reason I wouldn't let you in was ...

PARMENO.
Huh!

PHAEDRIA (*sulkily*).
Well?

THAIS.
I can't tell you if Parmeno keeps on interrupting.

PARMENO.
Oh, I won't say a word. I'll keep as quiet as the
grave, so long as you tell the truth. It's only lies that
make me interrupt. You tell the truth, and I'll keep
quiet.

THAIS.
My mother came from Samos, but we lived in
Rhodes.

PARMENO.
You see? No need to interrupt that bit.

THAIS.
While we lived there, a businessman lodged with us.
He gave my mother a present: a little girl stolen by
pirates who came raiding here in Athens.

PHAEDRIA.
An Athenian, you mean?   110

THAIS.
I think so. She told us her father's and mother's
name, but she was only a child: she didn't know what
town she came from, or anything else to identify her.
The businessman wasn't much help either: he said
the pirates told him she had been carried off from
Sunium. My mother adopted her, and brought her
up as her own daughter. In fact, everyone thought
she was my little sister. She stayed in Rhodes when I
moved here; I met a soldier, and he brought me to
Athens, and gave me everything I own.   120

PARMENO (*suddenly*).
That's not true! I'll have to interrupt that one!

THAIS.
What d'you mean?

PARMENO (*scornfully*).
Gave you everything you own! Hasn't my young
master, Phaedria here, been loading you with
presents ever since you arrived? Presents he couldn't
afford, either!

THAIS.
Oh, Parmeno, let me finish! That's not important!

PARMENO.
Hmmmph!

THAIS.
Almost as soon as we arrived, my soldier friend had
to leave to join his regiment. And that's when I met
you, my darling. You know that since then I've had

eyes only for you. I've shared all my secrets with
you, and no one else will ever be ...

PHAEDRIA.
Parmeno, quick! Interrupt her!

THAIS.
130   Shhh! Listen. My mother died not long ago. Her
brother inherited, and all he was interested in was
money. As soon as he saw the girl was beautiful, and
could sing, he realised how much he could get for
her, and sold her as a slave to the first person who
came along. Well, that was Thraso, my military
friend. It was so lucky! He bought her, and brought
her back here as a present for me. Of course, he
didn't know what I've told you; she was a complete
stranger, for all he knew. Now he's back in Athens,
but when he found you here on my doorstep, he
began making excuses not to give her to me. He said
he couldn't trust me and that as soon as he handed
140   her over, I'd leave him. He says he's going to keep
her for himself, if that happens. I'm certain that's
what he wants anyway ... he's much too affectionate
with her for my liking ...

PHAEDRIA (horrified).
Surely he hasn't ...

THAIS.
No, he hasn't: I've made enquiries. But you see, my
dear Phaedria, I've got to get the girl away from him.
After all, she's supposed to be my sister, but what I
want is to find her real parents, and give her back to
them. You see, I've got no friends here in Athens,
and if I can do someone a favour, I'll get to know *one*
150   family here at least. You can help me, Phaedria. All I
want you to do is stay away from Athens for a day or
two. Let Colonel Thraso think he's the only man I
love.

PHAEDRIA.
What? You're crazy! I'll do no such thing.

PARMENO.
  Well said, sir. You show her you're a man ...
  (*Aside*.) at last!

PHAEDRIA (*angrily*).
  D'you think I couldn't see it coming? 'Little girl ...
  pirates ... everyone thinks she's my own sister ...
  bring her back to Athens ... give her to her
  parents...' All you're really saying is, Thraso's back
  in favour, and I'm thrown out.

THAIS.
  Phaedria!

PHAEDRIA.
  Yes, that's it! You obviously love him more than me,   160
  and you don't want to lose him. You're afraid he's
  losing interest. You think he's found someone else,
  and you're jealous.

THAIS.
  It's not true!

PHAEDRIA.
  Not true? You don't want to lose all his presents ...
  that's the truth! Of course it is! Anyone would think
  he was the only one who ever gave you anything.
  What about me? When you told me you'd like a little
  negro slave-girl, didn't I drop everything and go
  looking for one? Then you said you wanted a
  eunuch, because only Arabian princesses had them.
  Well, I've got you one. And they cost ten gold
  pieces! I spend all my time and money trying to
  please you, and what do I get in return? The door   170
  slammed in my face!

THAIS.
  Phaedria, my darling, I'll do anything you want. I've
  got to get the girl away from the colonel, and I still
  think my plan is best ... but I'll give it up and do
  whatever you ask, just so long as you still say you
  love me.

PHAEDRIA (*weakening*).
'Still say you love me ...' If I thought you really meant that ...

PARMENO (*aside*).
I knew it: one word, and he's done for.

THAIS.
180   Of course I mean it! Have I ever refused you anything? And yet you still won't do as I ask, and give me two little days.

PHAEDRIA.
'Two little days ...' If I could be sure it won't turn into twenty ...

THAIS.
No, no, I promise, two days ... or at least...

PHAEDRIA.
'Or at least'? Never mind 'or at least'!

THAIS.
Only two, then ... Please, Phaedria, please!

PHAEDRIA (*reluctantly*).
Two days, then. All right.

THAIS.
Oh darling, I do love you! (*She throws her arms around his neck.*)

PHAEDRIA.
I'll spend them in the country: two days of pure hell. I'd do anything for you, Thais darling. Parmeno, bring the slave-girl and the eunuch here.

PARMENO (*glumly*).
Yes, sir. (*He goes inside.*)

PHAEDRIA.
190   For two days, then, Thais darling, goodbye ... (*Kiss.*)

THAIS.
Goodbye, my darling ... (*Kiss.*)

PHAEDRIA.
There's ... (*Kiss.*) ... just one thing ...

THAIS.
Yes, my love? (*Kiss.*)

PHAEDRIA.
When you're with this ... this colonel, act as though
you weren't there at all. All night, all day, think of
nothing but me. That's all I ask. Dream of me ...
(*Kiss.*) ... wait for me ... (*Kiss.*) ... think of me ...
(*Kiss.*) ... long for me ... (*Kiss.*) ... live for nothing
but me ... love me as much as I love you.

THAIS.
Oh darling!

> *After a long embrace,* PHAEDRIA *reluctantly
> breaks away.*

PHAEDRIA.
Goodbye. Ohhhhhh! (*He rushes into his house.*)

THAIS.
He doesn't trust me. He thinks I'm like other
women. But to tell the truth, no one in the world
means more to me than my dear Phaedria.   200
Everything I've done has been for the *girl's* sake.
Yesterday I found a man I think is her brother, and
I've arranged for him to visit me today. I must go
and get ready to see him.

> *She goes into her house. Almost at once* PHAEDRIA
> *comes out of his house, ready for departure, followed
> by* PARMENO.

PHAEDRIA.
I thought I told you to bring the slave-girl and the
eunuch here.

PARMENO.
Yes sir.

PHAEDRIA.
Well, hurry up, then.

PARMENO.
   Yes sir.

PHAEDRIA.
   Go on, can't you?

PARMENO.
   Yes sir.

PHAEDRIA.
   Don't you understand? Get on with it.

PARMENO.
   I understand. That's not the problem.

PHAEDRIA.
   What's wrong with you?

PARMENO.
210   I'm just wondering, sir, if you're going to get as
   much out of this, as you're going to lose by it.

PHAEDRIA.
   What's that supposed to mean?

PARMENO.
   Oh, nothing. Anything you say, sir. Anything you
   say.

PHAEDRIA.
   When you take her my ... eunuch, make him seem as
   ... magnificent as possible.

PARMENO.
   Yes sir.

PHAEDRIA.
   And do your best to keep that rival of mine away
   from her.

PARMENO.
   Yes sir.

PHAEDRIA (*bravely*).
   I shall be in the country for a couple of days.

PARMENO.
   Right, sir.

PHAEDRIA.
It's just that ...

PARMENO.
Yes sir?

PHAEDRIA.
I don't know ... d'you think I'll be able to stick it
out? Can I last two whole days?

PARMENO.
Two days? Never! You'll be back before you even
get there ... or at any rate, as soon as you've spent
one sleepless night, you will.

PHAEDRIA.
No, no. I'll work so hard I'll tire myself out, and be   220
sure of sleeping soundly.

PARMENO.
Tired out or not, you won't sleep.

PHAEDRIA.
That's ridiculous. I've made up my mind, and I
intend to stick to it. I won't give in. Two days, huh!
... if necessary I could do without her for ... *three*
days!

PARMENO.
Three days? Be careful, sir ... don't tempt fate!

PHAEDRIA.
I've made up my mind, and I know I can do it. I
know I can do it ... I know I can do it ... I know I
can do it...

He goes off, muttering.

PARMENO.
And very good luck, sir! I don't know ... love's a
very peculiar disease. Once you catch it, your whole
character changes. Look at my master: one minute
there's no one more sure of himself ... the next ...

He hears someone coming.

230

Just a minute who's this? Oh-oh, it's Gnatho, the colonel's horrible little friend. And he's got the girl. Things are beginning to move. Good heavens, she's not bad-looking! I'm not going to make much of an impression with my tattered old eunuch. This girl's prettier than Thais herself!

He steps aside as GNATHO *comes in, followed by* PAMPHILA. GNATHO *is in the middle of a lecture.*

GNATHO.

240

I hope you've realised by now the difference between me and ordinary mortals ... the difference between intelligence and stupidity. You saw what happened just now, when we met that beggar? He started life the same as I did: a gentleman, born into a wealthy family with high social standing. Then, just like me, as soon as he inherited he squandered all his money. We both ended up bankrupt. But that's where the resemblance ends. He ended up a beggar, covered in filthy rags and feeling his age, whereas I, on the other hand ... you heard our conversation. 'What are all those rags in aid of?' I asked him. 'I'm bankrupt,' he said, 'and all my friends have left me to die in misery.' 'Hah!' I said. 'Is that all? You fool! You've lost all your money and all your friends, but you haven't lost your brains as well, have you? Look at me, now: the same thing happened to me. But I'm well-dressed, I'm fit and healthy, everyone respects me. I own nothing, but I've got everything.' Then the fool had the cheek to say, 'Yes, but I'm not like you. I can't act the fool or stand by and let people thrash me without fighting back.' The idiot! As if that's how it's done! He was right out. That sort of thing died with my grandfather. 'No, no,' I told him ... you heard me ... 'Its very simple. I'll show you my method, the new way to make friends and influence people ... the Gnatho Way to Success. You pick your victim ... some fool who wants to be popular, well thought of,

the best of men ... you follow him around, you
praise him, you don't let him laugh at you, you laugh
at him. You tell him how clever he is, laugh at his   250
jokes, agree with whatever he says, and when he says
the opposite, agree with that too. He says "No", you
say "No", he says "Yes", you say "Yes" ... it's a
simple question of self-discipline.' That's what I
told him ... and that's the way to make money these
days, believe me.

PARMENO (*aside*).
This one needs watching. Give him a fool, and he'll
turn him into a grinning idiot.

GNATHO.
As we walked along, chatting in this delightful
manner, we came to the market-place. At once I'm
surrounded by all the stallholders ... bakers,
butchers, fishmongers, pastry-cooks, pie-makers,
eel-sellers ... all the people I patronised while I had
money, and still do now I've none. They shake my
hand, ask me to dinner, say how glad they are to see
me, as though I'm some rich nobleman. And what
does our beggar friend do then? You saw him: down   260
on his knees, begging me to take him on as my pupil,
and teach him the Gnatho Way to Success. I tell
you, I could make my fortune. Philosophers have
schools named after them ... Epicurus and the
Epicureans, Plato and the Platonists. I shall found a
school of parasites, and call them the Gnathonians.

PARMENO (*aside*).
All this without raising a finger to earn the food he
eats.

GNATHO.
But here we are, chattering away, and I'm forgetting
I'm supposed to deliver you to Thais, and give her
Thraso's invitation to dinner. Ah well.

PARMENO (*stepping into view*).
Oh dear!

GNATHO.

Look, there's Parmeno, our rival's slave. No wonder
he looks so miserable; they don't stand a chance.
Now, just watch this . . .

He goes up to greet PARMENO.

PARMENO (*aside*).

And he really thinks that it only takes a present to
make Thais all theirs!

GNATHO.

270   My dear Parmeno, how nice to see you . . . how very,
very nice . . . Tell me, how do we find you today?

PARMENO.

Easy. You just come over here.

GNATHO.

Come over . . . Ah, a joke! Hahahahaha! But what's
the matter? Is something upsetting you?

PARMENO.

Yes. You.

GNATHO.

Of course. Hahahahaha! Is that all?

PARMENO.

All?

GNATHO.

Yes. You look unhappy.

PARMENO.

Oh, I'm perfectly happy.

GNATHO.

Good, good. And how d'you like this for a slave-girl?

PARMENO.

Oh, not bad, not bad.

GNATHO (*aside*).

That annoyed him.

PARMENO (*aside*).

That's what he thinks.

GNATHO (*slyly*).
Tell me, d'you think Thais will like her?

PARMENO.
I suppose you're trying to tell me we've been thrown out, and you've won? Ah well, that's life.

GNATHO.
My *dear* Parmeno, I was only thinking of you. Once I deliver this little parcel, you won't have to run around any more, carting presents about, waiting up in the middle of the night while your master sings serenades under Thais's window. I was only thinking of you.

PARMENO.
How kind.

GNATHO.
I always aim to please.

PARMENO.
Good, good.

GNATHO.
Er, but don't let me take up any more of your time. 280
I'm sure you've plenty to do ... er, somewhere else.

PARMENO.
Me? No, no.

GNATHO.
Ah! Then perhaps you wouldn't mind doing me a little favour ...

PARMENO.
Eh?

GNATHO.
Help me get in to see her.

PARMENO.
Nothing easier, my dear fellow. You've only got to knock. Now you've got the girl, the door's wide open for you.

GNATHO.
Perfect.

> *He knocks.* THAIS's *door is opened by a welcoming slave.*

(*To* PARMENO, *with heavy sarcasm.*) Er, er, perhaps there's someone inside I can send out to speak with you.

> *He goes inside, taking* PAMPHILA.

PARMENO.
Hah! You wait! Two days, that's all. Now all you do is push the door with your little finger and it opens. But you won't be able to get in with a battering-ram, once Phaedria gets back.

> GNATHO *comes out again, beaming.*

GNATHO.
Oh, still here, Parmeno? I suppose your master leaves you here to intercept any secret messages Colonel Thraso sends to Thais?

PARMENO.
Oh, very good! You must keep Thraso in fits of giggles.

> GNATHO *goes out. There is the sound of running feet offstage.*

Now who's coming? Good heavens, it's Chaerea, Phaedria's young brother. What's *he* doing here? He's supposed to be on guard at the harbour today. Whatever's the matter with him? And what's he looking for?

> CHAEREA *hurries in. His attention is so much on what he's looking for that he doesn't see* PARMENO.

CHAEREA.
Hell and damnation! She's gone ... I'll never find her now! I don't even know where to start looking, let alone who to ask or where to go. There's one thing, though: wherever she is, she can't stay hidden

290

for long. She's beautiful. I've never seen a girl like
her. And I'll never look at anyone else now, either . . .

PARMENO (*aside*).
Another of 'em babbling of love! It's their poor old
father I'm sorry for, I really am. Once this one starts,   300
he'll make Phaedria's love look like some sort of
innocent game.

CHAEREA.
Damn the old fool who held me back. And damn me
too for letting him. Silly old twit. Oh, hello, Parmeno.

PARMENO.
What's the matter? What's wrong with you? And
where have you been, anyway?

CHAEREA.
Where have I been? No idea. I can't even remember
where I'm going.

PARMENO.
What's the matter?

CHAEREA.
I'm in love!!!

PARMENO.
Oh.

CHAEREA.
Now's your chance, Parmeno . . . your chance to
show me what sort of man you are. How many times
have you said to me, 'Chaerea, all you've got to do is
decide who you're going to love, I'll do the rest. I'll
show you how useful I can be.' Oh yes, you did. It
was in the days when I used to creep in to your
room, to bring you juicy bits from my father's   310
larder.

PARMENO.
You're joking.

CHAEREA.
Of course I'm not joking. I've found someone, and
your chance has come. And she's worth straining a

muscle for, too, let me tell you. Not like the rest of
the girls here. D'you know what their mothers make
them do? Hunch up their shoulders and walk round
flat-chested so as to be in the height of fashion. If
there's one who's slightly plump they say she looks
like a prize-fighter and put her on a diet, so she ends
up thin as a rake! It's revolting!

PARMENO.
And yours is different?

CHAEREA.
Quite different.

PARMENO
I guessed.

CHAEREA.
Natural complexion ... fantastic figure ... like a
juicy peach ...

PARMENO.
Age?

CHAEREA.
Sixteen.

PARMENO.
Huh! Ripe, too.

CHAEREA.
You must get her for me, Parmeno. Any way you
320   like, I don't care. I've got to have her.

PARMENO.
All right. Who does she belong to?

CHAEREA.
I've no idea.

PARMENO.
Where does she come from?

CHAEREA.
No idea.

PARMENO.
Where does she live?

CHAEREA.
No idea.

PARMENO.
Where did you see her, then?

CHAEREA.
In the street, of course.

PARMENO.
Well, that's something, at least.

CHAEREA.
Ah, but then I lost her.

PARMENO.
How?

CHAEREA.
That's what I've been moaning about all this time. I don't think anyone's ever had worse luck. It was really terrible. You won't believe me.

PARMENO.
What happened?

CHAEREA.
What happened? You know my father's old friend Archidemides?

PARMENO.
Yes, of course. Well?

CHAEREA.
I was following the girl, when I bumped into him.

PARMENO.
Awkward.

CHAEREA.
Awkward? It was a bloody catastrophe! I haven't   330
seen him for the last six months, and I had to bump into him at the worst possible moment. It's fate, that's what it is ... I'm doomed ...

PARMENO.
Oh, don't start again! Tell me what *happened*!

CHAEREA.

He comes panting up, behind me, slobbering and gasping for breath. 'Eh! Eh! Chaerea! Chaerea! I want to talk to you!' he says ... so I stop. 'You know what about, surely.' 'No.' 'I've got to go to court tomorrow.' '*So*?' 'Be sure and remind your father 340   he's been called as a witness.' He rambled on and on, took hours to come to the point. At last I said: 'Is that all?' 'Yes,' he said ... so at last I made my getaway. I looked around for the girl, and of course she'd disappeared.

PARMENO.

Which way did she go?

CHAEREA.

This way, as it happens. Down our own street.

PARMENO (*aside*).

You know what I think? It's Pamphila, the girl they've just brought for Thais.

CHAEREA.

When I got here, there was no sign of her.

PARMENO.

Was there anyone with her?

CHAEREA.

Oh yes. A little, greasy sort of man.

PARMENO (*aside*).

Told you! It's her! (*Aloud.*) You'd better give up, sir: you're wasting your time.

CHAEREA.

What?

PARMENO.

It's hopeless.

CHAEREA.

What d'you mean?

PARMENO.

I know who she is.

CHAEREA.
You know? You mean you've seen her?   350

PARMENO.
I've seen her. I know who she is. I know where she comes from.

CHAEREA.
But d'you know where she is now?

PARMENO.
Yes.

CHAEREA.
Where? Where?

PARMENO.
In Thais's house. She's just been given her as a present.

CHAEREA.
What? Who by? Some millionaire?

PARMENO.
Huh! Some millionaire! Colonel Thraso, Phaedria's rival.

CHAEREA.
Oh. Phaedria's had it, then?

PARMENO.
You can say that again ... especially considering the present *he*'s got her.

CHAEREA.
What present?

PARMENO.
A eunuch.

CHAEREA.
Oh god, not that revolting creature, that old woman of a man he bought yesterday?

PARMENO.
That's right.

CHAEREA.
She'll slam the door in his face.

PARMENO.
  You said it.

CHAEREA.
  But who is this Thais anyway? I didn't know we had
  a neighbour called Thais.

PARMENO.
  She only moved in a few days ago.

CHAEREA.
360 She must have. I've never seen her. They say she's
  ... quite a ...

PARMENO.
  Yes, she is. Quite a ...

CHAEREA.
  But not like *mine*?

PARMENO.
  Not in the same class.

CHAEREA.
  Oh, Parmeno, you must help me get that girl.

PARMENO.
  I'll do my best, I'll do what I can. (*Turning away.*)
  Anything else?

CHAEREA.
  Where are you going?

PARMENO.
  Home. I've got to get the slaves and give them to
  Thais.

CHAEREA.
  That eunuch doesn't know how lucky he is ... going
  into that household.

PARMENO.
  Why?

CHAEREA.
  Why? Every day he'll be able to look at the most
  beautiful slave-girl in the world; he'll be able to talk

with her, walk with her, eat with her, sleep ... under
the same roof.

PARMENO (*casually*).
  And suppose it was you?

CHAEREA.
  What d'you mean?

PARMENO.
  Why shouldn't it be you?

CHAEREA.
  How?

PARMENO.
  Change clothes with him ...   370

CHAEREA.
  Then what?

PARMENO.
  I'll pretend you're him, and give *you* to Thais.

CHAEREA.
  I get you ...

PARMENO.
  Then you can do all the things you've been on about.
  Eat with her, walk with her, touch her, fondle her,
  sleep ... near her.

CHAEREA.
  But ...

PARMENO.
  They all arrived only a few days ago. No one in the
  house has ever seen you before.

CHAEREA.
  But I'm not a eunuch.

PARMENO.
  At your age, who's to know?

CHAEREA (*ignoring this*).
  Splendid! It's a marvellous idea! Quick, come home
  at once, dress me up, take me round there. I'll do it!

PARMENO (*abruptly*).
Do it? Oh no, I was only pulling your leg.

CHAEREA.
Too bad.

PARMENO.
You don't mean you're going to?

CHAEREA.
Yes.

PARMENO.
380   Oh my god! We'll never get out of it alive. You
can't...

CHAEREA.
Oh yes I can ...

PARMENO.
Not really ...

CHAEREA.
Really ...

PARMENO (*aside*).
Oh god, I've done it this time. (*Aloud.*) But ... I'm
the one who'll get the blame ...

CHAEREA.
Huh!

PARMENO (*desperately*).
We'll be doing wrong.

CHAEREA.
Wrong? For me to be taken into a house like ... *that*,
and pay back those ... tormentors who ... entice
young men in to suffer all kinds of ... indignities.
Wrong for me to deceive them as they do us? Would
you rather I deceived my father? That'd be
wrong...

PARMENO (*resigned*).
All right, all right. But don't blame me if ...

CHAEREA.
I won't blame you.

PARMENO.
You're sure you want to go through with it?

CHAEREA.
Sure? I'm certain!

PARMENO.
But ...

CHAEREA.
Don't argue! Come on!

PARMENO (*gloomily*).
It'll never work ... it'll never work ... it'll never...   390

> CHAEREA *pushes* PARMENO *inside. There is a*
> *short pause, and then* GNATHO *comes back with*
> *his master* THRASO.

THRASO
Hah! Grateful, was she?

GNATHO.
Incredibly. It wasn't so much the present itself, as
because *you* gave it her. She says that's a real feather
in her cap.

PARMENO (*opening the door and looking out*).
I must watch for the right moment to take him
across. Oh, there's the colonel.

THRASO.
I've got this gift, d'you see: everything I do ...
bound to please.

GNATHO.
Don't think I haven't noticed.

THRASO.
The late king, you know, always thanked me
personally for services rendered. Singled me out,
you might say ...

GNATHO.
Indeed? Of course, a really intelligent man ... like
you ... will always get the credit even if others have
contributed with their hard work...   400

THRASO.
Absolutely true!

GNATHO.
So the king held you ... ?

THRASO.
Oh yes!

GNATHO.
... in high regard?

THRASO.
Absolutely! Entrusted me with his entire army.
Consulted me on every point of policy ...

GNATHO.
How wonderful!

THRASO.
And whenever he was bored with court business, or
needed to have a bit of ... you know ...

GNATHO.
Mental relaxation?

THRASO.
Exactly! He would make me his sole companion.

GNATHO.
410 He certainly picked the right man.

THRASO.
Of course, they were all jealous, calling me names
the whole time. Especially the chap who looked after
the Indian elephants ... damn nuisance, he was.
'Strato,' I used to say to him, 'What's the matter
with you, man? Just because you look after wild
animals, no need to act like one yourself!'

GNATHO.
Ah, brilliant! I bet that shut him up.

THRASO.
Hah! Didn't say another word.

GNATHO.
I can well believe it.

PARMENO (*aside*).
God, what a hopeless fool! And the other one's a
complete liar!

THRASO.
My dear Gnatho, did I tell you how I dealt with that   420
Rhodian at dinner the other night?

GNATHO.
No, never. Please tell me ... (*Aside.*) ... for the
thousandth time!

THRASO.
Well, I was at a party, d'you see, sitting opposite this
young feller from Rhodes. I was with a ... hem ...
lady, and he began making fun of me. 'Look, sonny,'
I said, 'I've heard of putting all your eggs in one
basket, but you seem to me to be crossing your
bridges before you come to 'em.'

GNATHO (*in a fit of false laughter*).
Hahahahahaha!

THRASO.
What's the matter?

GNATHO (*wiping his eyes*).
Brilliant! Magnificent! I've heard nothing better for
years! I bet the Rhodian had nothing to say.   430

THRASO.
He was done for ... completely stumped. Everyone
in the room crying with laughter. You know, after
that, no one dared say a word to me. They all gave
me a wide berth.

GNATHO.
I bet they did.

THRASO.
But look here: what about this gel ... Pamphila,
whatever her name is. D'you think I ought to try and
convince Thais I'm not in love with her?

GNATHO.

No no, quite the opposite. Make her think you can't
live without the girl.

THRASO.

Why?

GNATHO.

It's obvious. You know how *you* jump like a startled
rabbit every time *she* mentions Phaedria's name?

THRASO (*jumping about*).

Grrr! Yes!

GNATHO.

Well, here's your chance to put a stop to it.
Whenever she mentions Phaedria, you talk about
440   Pamphila. If she says, 'Phaedria's coming to dinner,'
you say, 'In that case, we must get Pamphila to sing.'
If she says how handsome Phaedria is, you start
praising Pamphila. Tit for tat. She'll soon give it up.

THRASO (*sighing*).

If she really loved me, Gnatho, that would be the
thing to do.

GNATHO.

Of course she loves you. She loves your presents,
doesn't she? And look how easily she gets upset
when she thinks you might go off in a huff and she'd
450   lose everything she gets from you.

THRASO.

H'm. I never thought of that.

GNATHO (*oilily*).

You've been far too busy! You could have thought of
a *far* better plan yourself, if you'd only had the time.

THRASO.

Look out: here she comes.

THAIS *comes out of her house.*

THAIS (*sweetly*).

I'm sure I heard my colonel's voice ... Ah, Thraso
darling, there you are.

THRASO.
Oh Thais, darling, does my present ... er ... make
you love me ... just a little?

PARMENO (*aside, with extreme sarcasm*).
Ah, what subtlety! What taste!

THAIS.
As much as you deserve ... (*Sweetly.*) my darling.

GNATHO.
All right, then ... to dinner! What are we waiting for?

PARMENO (*aside*).
And there's the other one. Hardly human, is he?   460

THAIS.
Whenever you wish; I won't keep you a moment.

  PARMENO *comes forward out of* LACHES's
  house.

PARMENO.
Ah, Thais! Are you going somewhere?

THAIS.
Yes, Parmeno, I'm just off to ...

PARMENO.
Oh, but you mustn't go yet. I'm bringing you
Phaedria's presents.

THRASO.
What's the delay? What are we waiting for?

PARMENO (*going humbly to him*).
Oh please, sir, if you don't mind ... Let me have a
word or two with the lady, and give her the presents
we've got for her.

THRASO.
Presents? Huh! They'll never be a match for mine.

PARMENO.
We'll see. (*Calling through the door of* LACHES's
house.) OK. Send them out now.   470

  The black SLAVE-GIRL *comes out.*

Over here, that's right. She's from Africa, you know.

THRASO (*scornfully to* GNATHO).

What d'you think they paid for *her*? Three gold pieces?

GNATHO.

At the most.

PARMENO.

Dorus! Where are you? Hurry up!

CHAEREA *comes out, dressed as a eunuch.*

Over here. There now. You don't see a eunuch like this every day, do you Thais?

THAIS.

No ... no ... he's very good-looking!

PARMENO.

Well, Gnatho? Any criticisms? What about you, Thraso? Hmmm, nothing to say? (*To* THAIS.) Ask him anything you like: music, literature, athletics, he's expert at them all. He's young, handsome, intelligent, a real bargain.

THRASO (*aside to* GNATHO).

He's certainly a bit more like it. I wouldn't mind ...

PARMENO.

480   The man who sends you these presents isn't like your other friends: *he* doesn't insist that you throw out everyone else, and live for him alone; *he* doesn't bore you by going over all his battles; *he* doesn't jump out at you and force you to admire his scars ... not like some people we know! He's happy to see you when it's convenient and when *you* have time for *him.*

THRASO (*to* GNATHO, *but not bothering to lower his voice*).

His master's obviously penniless, and pretty pathetic too!

GNATHO.

Mmmm, he wouldn't put up with *him* if he could afford something better!

PARMENO (*turning on* GNATHO).
Shut up, scum! I know your sort, always ready to
flatter and wheedle your way ... You'd steal from a   490
corpse.

THRASO.
Thais, how much longer are we to put up with this?

THAIS (*sweetly*).
I'll just take these two inside. I won't be long ...

> *She takes* CHAEREA *and the* SLAVE-GIRL *into
> her house.* PARMENO *walks round* THRASO,
> *mocking him.*

THRASO (*very crossly to* GNATHO).
I'm going. You can wait for her.

PARMENO (*sneering*).
That's right! The Lord High Commander shouldn't
be seen out in the street with its lady-friend!

THRASO.
Pah!!! You're beneath contempt ... like your master!

> PARMENO *goes out, laughing.* THRASO *turns
> angrily round, to find* GNATHO *shaking with
> laughter.*

THRASO.
What are *you* laughing at?

GNATHO.
Oh, er ... that story of yours, about the Rhodian.

THRASO (*not convinced*).
Oh.

GNATHO (*quickly*).
Look, here's Thais.

THRASO.
You go on ahead and get everything ready.   500

> GNATHO *goes off.* THAIS *comes out of the house
> with her housekeeper* PYTHIAS.

THAIS.
... and be sure and look after them. Oh, and if that

young man Chremes turns up ... the one I think is
Pamphila's brother ... ask him to call again. If that
isn't convenient, ask him to wait, and if all else fails,
bring him to see me at Thraso's.

PYTHIAS.
Yes, my lady.

THAIS.
Was there anything else? ... er, oh yes: make sure
Pamphila's looked after. No one's to leave the house
till I get back.

PYTHIAS.
I understand, madam.

THRASO (*impatiently*).
Aren't you ready yet?

THAIS.
Yes, let's go.

She takes his arm and they go off. PYTHIAS *goes
back into the house, just as* CHREMES, *looking lost
and bewildered, comes in. He speaks crossly to the
audience.*

CHREMES.
I don't like it ... I don't like it at all. The more I
think about it, the more certain I am that Thais is
510   playing some kind of trick. 'Chremes,' she says,
'come and see me right away. I've important
business to discuss with you.' (I'd never met the
woman, so was naturally a bit suspicious.) When I
did go, all she asked was when my father and mother
died. Years ago, I said. Then she asked me if I
owned any land at Sunium, and how far from the sea
it was. (I've a feeling that's what she's after: she
wants to get it away from me!) Next she wants to
520   know if I had a little sister, who was stolen from
there, and who was with her, and what she had when
she left, and was there anyone who could recognise
her. Why? Surely she's not trying to make out *she's*
my long-lost little sister? She's much too old ...

Pamphila would only be sixteen if she was still alive.
This morning I get another letter from Thais, telling
me to come round again at once. Well, I've had
enough of it. Either she tells me what she wants or
she leaves me alone. I'm not coming again.

He knocks. PYTHIAS *opens the door a chink.*

PYTHIAS (*suspiciously*).
Yes? What is it?

CHREMES.
Come on, open up. It's me, Chremes.   530

PYTHIAS (*flinging the door wide open*).
Ah, my dear Chremes! My mistress is expecting you.

CHREMES (*aside*).
There you are, it's some kind of trick.

PYTHIAS.
My mistress sends you her compliments, and will
you come back tomorrow?

CHREMES (*crossly*).
I will not. I'm going to the country.

PYTHIAS.
Well, will you come in and wait for her?

CHREMES.
Certainly not.

PYTHIAS.
Oh dear, oh dear. Well then, my mistress says you're
to go round to where she's having dinner in
Athens . . .

CHREMES (*very crossly*).
I suppose so.

PYTHIAS (*calling inside*).
Dorias! Dorias!

DORIAS (*entering from the house*).
Yes, madam?

PYTHIAS.
Show this gentleman the way to Colonel Thraso's.

DORIAS.

Yes, madam. Come on, sir. I'll show you the way.

They go off along the street; PYTHIAS goes back into the house. Almost at once ANTIPHO rushes in from the other side of the stage.

ANTIPHO.

540

Where on earth has he got to? We arranged a dinner-party for today ... those of us doing guard duty at the harbour, that is ... and we put Chaerea in charge of the food. We made quite definite arrangements ... the time, the place ... and all agreed to be there, but nothing seems to have been done, and there's no sign of *him*. The others have given me the job of looking for him, so I've come to see if he's come home, or something. Oops! Someone's coming out of next door ...

THAIS's door is opened and CHAEREA, still dressed as a eunuch, peers out.

Good lord, it can't be! No, surely ... yes, it is! What on earth's he playing at, dressed like that? I'd better keep out of the way and listen.

CHAEREA (*coming forward*).

550

Anyone here? Nobody. Anyone follow me out? No, it's all clear. (*Skipping about with excitement.*) Oh, what a glorious day! If only I could die now, before the gods have time to spoil my happiness! Thank god there's nobody here to pester me with questions ... 'Why are you so happy? Where are you going? Where've you come from? Where did you get those clothes? Have you gone raving mad?'

ANTIPHO (*aside*).

I'll go and do him the favour I see he wants! (*Calling.*) Chaerea!

CHAEREA (*startled*).

Oh!

ANTIPHO.

What are you doing? Why are you wearing those

clothes? Why are you so happy? Have you gone
raving mad? ... Can't you answer?

CHAEREA.
Oh, Antipho, my dear fellow! Today's the happiest
day of my life.   560

ANTIPHO.
Good: yes.

CHAEREA.
I must tell you everything that's happened.

ANTIPHO.
Please do.

CHAEREA.
Listen, then: you know my brother's girl-friend?

ANTIPHO.
Thais, you mean?

CHAEREA.
Yes. She was given a slave-girl today. But not just a
slave-girl, Antipho! What a face! What a figure!
She's fantastic! As soon as I saw her I fell in love
with her. She's the only girl for me.

ANTIPHO.
Oh yes? (*Aside.*) Again?

CHAEREA.
By an incredible piece of luck my brother had just
bought Thais a eunuch, but he hadn't been delivered
yet. Parmeno had a marvellous idea ...   570

ANTIPHO.
What was it?

CHAEREA.
Stop interrupting and I'll tell you. He got me to
change clothes with the eunuch, and go to Thais's
house.

ANTIPHO.
As a eunuch?

CHAEREA.
That's right.

ANTIPHO.
What good was that going to do?

CHAEREA.
What good? Don't you see? I could see her whenever
I wanted; talk to her, be with her ... Wasn't it
brilliant? Anyway, I was delivered to Thais, who was
very pleased to see me. She put the girl in my
charge ...

ANTIPHO.
Your charge?

CHAEREA.
That's right.

ANTIPHO.
I don't believe it.

CHAEREA.
She told me no one was to be allowed near the girl. I
was to stay by her side at all times, and make sure no
one entered her quarters. I stood meekly by, with my
eyes on the ground, and nodded ... like this ...

ANTIPHO.
580   Idiot!

CHAEREA.
'I,' she says, 'am going out to dinner.' And off she
goes, with her maid, leaving a few younger ones to
look after the girl.

ANTIPHO.
Yes? What happened?

CHAEREA.
They began getting her ready for her bath. I stood
by, telling them to get a move on.

ANTIPHO.
I bet you did!

CHAEREA.
She sat waiting in her room, looking at a picture on
the wall ... it was the story of Jupiter pouring the
shower of gold into Danaë's lap. I looked at it too,
and it got me all excited ... to think *he*'d played the
same game, disguising himself and coming down,
through the skylight, to seduce a woman! I thought
if he, a god, the greatest of the gods, could do that,   590
why shouldn't I ... Anyway, the girl went off and
had her bath, and then they brought her back and
put her to bed. I stood there in case she ... wanted
anything. One of the slave-girls came up and said,
'Hey Dorus, take this fan and fan her gently while
we have a bath; then, when we've finished, we'll take
over while you have a bath.' I nodded and looked
glum, like this ...

ANTIPHO.
You great fool! Standing there with your fan in your
hand like a half-witted windmill!

CHAEREA.
Wait and see. They all went off to have their bath,
giggling and chattering. Meanwhile the girl's gone   600
off to sleep. I peer over the top of the fan ... like this;
I look round, make sure everything's safe; bolt the
door ... and then ... !!!

ANTIPHO.
Yes? Then what?

CHAEREA.
What d'you mean, then what? What do *you* think?

ANTIPHO.
Oh.

CHAEREA.
Well, what would *you* have done? This was a chance
in a million, the moment I'd been waiting for. If I
hadn't ... I'd really have been what everyone
thought I was.

ANTIPHO.
Yes, true, true. But what about our dinner?

CHAEREA.
Eh, what dinner?

ANTIPHO.
The one we planned for tonight.

CHAEREA.
Oh, that. It's ready.

ANTIPHO.
Good man! Where? At your house?

CHAEREA.
No, no, at Discus's.

ANTIPHO.
Come on, then, we're going to be late. Get changed.

CHAEREA.
610   Where? I can't go home: Phaedria might be there.
And my father might have got back from the country
by now, too.

ANTIPHO.
Never mind. You can get changed at my place.

CHAEREA.
Come on, then. And on the way you can help me
work out the best way of marrying this girl ...

ANTIPHO.
All right ...

> *They go off.* DORIAS *comes in, very upset,*
> *carrying a box of jewellery.*

DORIAS (*to the audience*).
Oh dear, the man must be crazy. Fancy treating
Thais like that ... You should have seen him just
now, at the dinner party ... the one he's giving for
my mistress. Chremes turned up ... that's the young
man Thais thinks is Pamphila's brother. He turned
up, and Thais told Thraso to ask him in. You should
have seen his face ... He went purple with anger,

and started shouting and spluttering. But Thais
insisted, and he had no choice. You see, she had to
keep Chremes there, because it wasn't the right time   620
to tell him everything she wanted about his sister. Of
course Thraso thought he was some sort of rival, so
to pay Thais back he told a slave to go and fetch
Pamphila. 'To sing for us,' is what he said. Thais
was furious. 'You can't have that girl at a dinner
party,' she said. 'Oh yes I can,' said Thraso, and they
had a big argument. Then Thais took off all her
jewels ... I've got them here in this box. She always
does that when there's a fight coming, so she can slip
away from the party as soon as she can.

She is about to go into THAIS's *house when she sees*
PHAEDRIA *coming, she stands back to listen.*

PHAEDRIA (*to the audience*).
Huh! I set off for my break in the country, trudging
along, thinking of this and that ... as you do when   630
you're upset ... and ... well, to cut a long story
short, I went right past our farm without realising it.
So I turned back, even more fed up, but when I
reached the turning, I stopped and began thinking:
'Two days? Two whole days without Thais? Is it
really necessary? I know I can't actually be with her,
but at least I could see her ... you know, from a
distance ... surely that's allowed.' So this time I   640
passed the farm deliberately, and ...

Suddenly PYTHIAS *bursts out of* THAIS's *house,*
in a furious temper.

PYTHIAS.
Where is he? Where is that swine?

PHAEDRIA (*aside*).
Now what's the matter?

PYTHIAS.
Where is he? The beast! I'll kill him when I find
him!

PHAEDRIA (*aside*).
Oh dear, I don't like the sound of this!

PYTHIAS.
And to make things worse, after he'd had his way
with her, he ripped her dress and even tore her hair!

PHAEDRIA (*aside*).
What?

PYTHIAS.
Just let me get my hands on him ... I'll scratch his
eyes out, the wretch!

PHAEDRIA (*aside*).
What's been going on since I left? (*Aloud.*) Er,
650   Pythias ... ahem ... what's happened?

PYTHIAS (*angrily*).
Phaedria! Need you ask? Go to hell ... you and your
charming presents!

PHAEDRIA.
But what's *happened*?

PYTHIAS.
A fine question! That eunuch you gave us ... oh god,
what a mess! ... and the girl that soldier gave us ...
Well, he's ... (*Gesture*).

PHAEDRIA (*astounded*).
He hasn't!

PYTHIAS.
He has. It's a disaster!

PHAEDRIA.
Rubbish! You must be drunk!

PYTHIAS.
I only wish I was.

DORIAS.
But, Pythias ... I don't understand ... it's
unbelievable.

PHAEDRIA.
You're crazy. How *could* a eunuch ...?

PYTHIAS (*angrily*).
How do *I* know how? The fact remains, he has! The
girl won't stop crying, and the eunuch's gone.   660

PHAEDRIA.
What?

PYTHIAS.
Disappeared, nowhere to be seen. He's probably
stolen some of our valuables as well!

PHAEDRIA.
Well, there's one thing: he won't get far, a poor old
thing in his condition.

PYTHIAS (*astonished*).
What?

PHAEDRIA.
He's probably gone back to our house. Just a
minute...

He goes into LACHES's *house.*

DORIAS.
Heavens above! Whatever next? What a thing to do!

PYTHIAS.
I've always heard that they really fancy women, even
though they can't ... you know, actually do it ... I
never imagined ...

DORIAS.
How could anyone ...

PYTHIAS.
And to think I even locked him in alone with her!

PHAEDRIA *comes out again, dragging* DORUS,
the real eunuch, dressed in CHAEREA's *clothes.*

PHAEDRIA.
Come on, you swine! Come on, can't you? What a
thing to do!

DORUS (*plaintively*).
But sir ...

PHAEDRIA.

670
Never mind but sir! What d'you mean by it, going
straight back and dressing up in those ridiculous
clothes? If I hadn't come back when I did, I suppose
we'd never have seen you again.

PYTHIAS (*surprised*).
You've caught him, then?

PHAEDRIA.
Of course I've caught him.

PYTHIAS.
Oh, well done!

DORIAS.
Marvellous!

PYTHIAS.
Well, where is he?

PHAEDRIA.
Here, of course!

PYTHIAS.
Here?

PHAEDRIA.
Can't you see him?

PYTHIAS.
Who?

PHAEDRIA (*kicking* DORUS).
Him, of course.

DORUS.
Ow!

PYTHIAS.
But ... who's he?

PHAEDRIA.
Who's he? The man we want, of course.

PYTHIAS.
I've never seen him before in my life.

PHAEDRIA.
 What?

PYTHIAS.
 You're not trying to tell me *this* is the man you sent   680
 me?

PHAEDRIA.
 Of course it is. Who d'you think it is?

PYTHIAS.
 But ... they're completely different. The other one
 was good-looking ... quite a gentleman ...

PHAEDRIA.
 That was just because of his smart clothes. Now that
 he's changed, you don't ...

PYTHIAS.
 No, listen, they're not the same at all! The one you
 sent us was young and handsome. This one's old and
 wrinkled... and far too fat!

 They all look at DORUS, *who is very embarrassed.*

PHAEDRIA.
 Damn it, are you trying to make out I don't know
 what I've done myself. Hey, Dorus!   690

DORUS.
 Sir?

PHAEDRIA.
 Didn't I buy you yesterday?

DORUS.
 Oh yes, sir.

PYTHIAS.
 Can *I* ask him something?

PHAEDRIA.
 Go ahead.

PYTHIAS.
 Did you come round to our house today?

DORUS.
 Oh no, madam.

PYTHIAS.
> There you are! The one who came to us was young
> ... about sixteen. Parmeno brought him.

PHAEDRIA (*to* DORUS).
> All right, then: tell me what's been going on.
> (*Pause*). Come on, say something, can't you?

>> DORUS *shuffles his feet, but doesn't answer.*

> What the devil's the matter with you?

DORUS.
> Er ... your brother Chaerea came, with Parmeno ...

PHAEDRIA.
> When?

DORUS.
> Today.

PHAEDRIA.
> What time?

DORUS.
> An hour ago.

PHAEDRIA.
> You'd met him before?

DORUS.
> No ... I'd never even heard of him.

PHAEDRIA.
700   Well, how did you know who he was?

DORUS.
> Parmeno told me. They gave me these clothes ...

PHAEDRIA.
> Good lord!

DORUS.
> ... and your brother took mine. Then they both left.

PYTHIAS (*triumphantly*).
> There you are! Now d'you believe the girl was ...?

PHAEDRIA.
> You don't mean you believe this ... *creature*?

PYTHIAS.
No need; the facts speak for themselves.

PHAEDRIA (*aside, to* DORUS).
Here, Dorus, come over here. Tell me again, slowly.
Chaerea took your clothes ...?

DORUS.
Yes.

PHAEDRIA.
And put them on himself?

DORUS.
Yes.

PHAEDRIA.
And went round there instead of you?

DORUS.
Yes.

PHAEDRIA (*aloud, in pretended anger*).
Good god, what a lying bastard!

PYTHIAS.
You see? Oh, I'll never get over it!   710

PHAEDRIA.
You still insist on believing him? (*Aside.*) How am I
going to get out of this one? (*To* DORUS.) Psst!

DORUS.
Sir?

PHAEDRIA (*in a low voice*).
Answer 'No' this time, whatever I say.

DORUS.
Eh? Oh.

PHAEDRIA (*loudly*).
I'll get the truth out of him, even if it kills him! Did
you really see my brother Chaerea?

DORUS.
Er ... no!

PHAEDRIA.
You see! One minute he says he did, the next he
denies it. There's only one way to get the truth out of
him ... torture! (*To* DORUS.) Beg for mercy.

DORUS (*in pretend terror*).
Sir, sir ... Phaedria!

PHAEDRIA.
Get into the house!

DORUS.
Oh! Ooh! Ah! Ouch!

PHAEDRIA (*kicking him into the house*).
You'll be sorry you ever lied to me! (*Aside.*) My god,
I hope it works! (*Aloud.*) I'll teach you, you swine!

He storms in and slams the door.

PYTHIAS.
Parmeno's at the bottom of this.

DORIAS.
Certain to be.

PYTHIAS.
I'll pay him back when I catch him. But what d'you
720   think I ought to do?

DORIAS.
About the girl, d'you mean?

PYTHIAS.
Yes. Do we tell Thais, or keep it quiet?

DORIAS.
Well, if you've got any sense, you don't know
anything ... either about the eunuch or what
happened to the girl. That'll keep you out of trouble.
Just say that Dorus ran away.

PYTHIAS.
Right, I'll do that.

DORIAS.
Look, there's Chremes coming. That means Thais'll
be here soon.

PYTHIAS.
How d'you know?

DORIAS.
Because when I left they'd just started quarrelling.

PYTHIAS.
You go in and put those jewels away. I'll find out from him what's happened.

DORIAS *goes into the house.* CHREMES *comes along the street, rather drunk.*

CHREMES.
I dunno ... hic! I think I must be drunk. Legs all right when I was sitting down... now don't seem to know where they're going. Oops! (*He staggers across towards the house.*)

PYTHIAS.
Chremes!   730

CHREMES.
Whosat? Pythias! God, you look jolly attractive. Give us a kiss.

PYTHIAS.
You're drunk!

CHREMES.
'S true, 's true. Know what they say? 'A bite to eat, a spot to drink, Gets it up, quick's a wink!' Hic! Where's Thais?

PYTHIAS.
She's left Thraso's, has she?

CHREMES.
Hours ago ... years ago. They had a terrible quarrel ...

PYTHIAS.
Didn't she tell you to come back with her?

CHREMES.
No. She just gave me ... a bit of a nod ... as she left.

PYTHIAS.
Wasn't that enough?

CHREMES.
Didn't know what she meant ... until Thraso put me right, by throwing me out in the street! (*Sees her in the distance.*) Oh, there she is! Woo-hoo, Thais! (*To himself.*) I wonder how I got here first?

THAIS *comes in.*

THAIS.
Quick: Thraso and his gang will be here any minute to take back the girl. He'll be lucky! If he so much as
740   lays a finger on her, I'll scratch his eyes out. I can put up with his stupidity as long as he sticks to words, but if he tries actions, I'll have him whipped!

CHREMES (*lurching forward*).
Thais ... I been waiting ... ages ...

THAIS.
Ah, Chremes. I was looking for you. This is all your fault, you know.

CHREMES.
Eh?

THAIS (*clearly*).
It's ... all ... your ... fault.

CHREMES.
My fault? Whysat?

THAIS.
It's all because of your sister.

CHREMES.
Sister?

THAIS (*patiently*).
I've got your sister in the house ... your long-lost sister. I'd have given her back ages ago, if all this hadn't happened ...

CHREMES *is so surprised he starts to sober up.*

CHREMES.
My sister, Pamphila ...

THAIS.
Pamphila, yes.

CHREMES.
Where is she?

THAIS.
Inside.

CHREMES.
But ...

THAIS.
Don't worry: she's safe and sound. All I want is to
give her back to you ...

CHREMES (*making an effort to be formal*).
Thais, I shall be eternally grateful to you and hope   750
to ...

THAIS.
Shhh! We've got to hurry, or we'll lose her. Thraso's
coming to try and get her back by force. Quick,
Pythias, go in and fetch the little box with the
tokens ...

  The sound of marching feet is heard offstage.

CHREMES.
Look, he's coming ...

PYTHIAS (*to* THAIS).
Where is it?

THAIS.
In the cabinet. Do hurry!!!

  PYTHIAS *goes inside.*

CHREMES (*looking along the street*).
Heavens, look at the army he's got with him!

THAIS.
You're not afraid of him, are you?

CHREMES.
Afraid, me? N-n-no, of course not. N-n-n-nobody
on earth can f-f-frighten me.

THAIS.
That's the spirit! Just remember that he's a
foreigner, not as influential as you, and without as
760   many friends in Athens ...

CHREMES.
Yes, I know. But it's better to avoid violence if you
can. Tell you what, you go inside and bolt the door,
and I'll run along to the market-place and see if I can
whip up some support ...

THAIS.
Stop!

CHREMES.
I think I'd rather ...

THAIS.
Forget it!

CHREMES.
I'll be back in a moment ...

THAIS.
We don't *need* help, Chremes. All you have to do is
tell him she's your sister, and you're taking her back.
You lost her when she was a little girl, but now
you've recognised her. (*To* PYTHIAS, *who has come
out with the casket.*) Show him the tokens.

PYTHIAS.
Here they are.

CHREMES.
But suppose he tries force?

THAIS.
You can sue him for assault and battery.

CHREMES.
Oh, charming!

THAIS.
Pull yourself together. Put your tunic straight.
(*Aside.*) I don't know ... he's not the man I'd *choose*
in a crisis.   770

> *They all go into the house. A sort of army marches
> on: four broken-down soldiers led by Corporal
> SANGA. GNATHO and THRASO are at their
> head.*

THRASO.
Right you are, men, stand easy. Now, you all know
why we're here. Insults to avenge! Better death than
dishonour!! Lieutenant Gnatho ...

GNATHO (*springing to attention*).
Sir!

THRASO.
First we'll storm the house.

GNATHO.
Right, sir!

THRASO.
Then we'll take back the gel.

GNATHO.
Very good, sir!

THRASO.
Then we'll see about Thais.

GNATHO.
Splendid!

THRASO.
Private Donax!

DONAX.
Sir!

THRASO.
You've got your crowbar? Good man. Keep to the
centre, then. Private Simalio, the left wing. Private
Syriscus, on the right. Corporal Sanga, you take

command of the rest ... Good heavens, man, what
have you got there?

SANGA (*with a lisp*).
A sponge, sir.

THRASO.
A sponge? You horrible little man, are you expecting
to fight a battle with a sponge?

SANGA.
Sir? I thought to myself, sir, 'The colonel's a brave
man,' sir, 'bound to be blood spilled ... need a
sponge to clean the wounds!', sir.

THRASO.
I see. All right, carry on. Where are the others?

GNATHO.
What others, damn it? There's only Sannio left to
780   keep guard at home.

THRASO.
Right, Gnatho, get them lined up. I'll lead ... er ...
from behind ... where I can see clearly to give my
orders.

GNATHO.
Sound tactics, sir! (*Aside.*) Strategic self-
preservation!

THAIS *and* CHREMES *appear at a window.*

CHREMES.
You see, Thais, he's crazy. I was right about bolting
the door.

THAIS.
Huh! You don't need to be afraid of him. He's
nothing but a bag of wind.

GNATHO.
Sir ...

THRASO.
What is it?

GNATHO.
We ought to get one of those big siege-catapults;
that'd soon bring them out.

THRASO.
I say, look: they *are* out! There's Thais.

GNATHO.
Good lord, yes. Shall we attack?

THRASO.
Er, no. Not for a moment. Diplomacy, y'know ...
sign of a wise man. Never fight till you have to ...
might get off without a battle.   790

GNATHO.
Good heavens, you're right, sir! What a brain! I
learn something from you every day!

  THRASO *braces himself, then steps forward.*

THRASO.
Now then, Thais.

THAIS (*coldly*).
Well?

THRASO.
One question: when I gave you the gel, didn't you
say you'd keep the next few days free for me alone?

THAIS.
Yes. What of it?

THRASO.
What of it? Didn't you invite your lover to dinner in
my house, under my very nose?

THAIS.
What if I did?

THRASO.
And slipped away with him when I wasn't looking?

THAIS.
Well, I wanted to.

THRASO.

What? Then give me Pamphila back ... unless you
want me to take her by force!

CHREMES.

If you lay one finger on Pamphila ...

GNATHO.

Shut up, you ...

THRASO.

What? You mean I'm not allowed to handle my own
property now?

CHREMES.

What d'you mean, *your* property, scum?

GNATHO.

Be careful: you don't realise who you're insulting.

CHREMES (*to* GNATHO).

You clear off! (*To* THRASO.) Do you know what
you're letting yourself in for? I warn you, if you
800   cause any more trouble, I'll make you regret this
time and this place ... and me... for ever!

GNATHO.

You don't know the sort of enemy you're making.

CHREMES.

Look, you: shut up or I'll knock your head in.

GNATHO.

Charming!

THRASO.

Who are you, anyway? What's it got to do with you?

CHREMES.

Never mind. The first thing you don't seem to know
is, the girl isn't a slave.

THRASO.

What?

CHREMES.

She's a freeborn Athenian citizen.

THRASO.
What?

CHREMES.
And my sister.

THRASO.
WH-A-AT?

CHREMES.
So I warn you, just leave her alone. Thais, I'm going
to get Pamphila's old nurse, and show her the
tokens.

THRASO.
Just a minute, just a minute. Are you forbidding me
to take back my own property?

CHREMES.
Exactly ... scum! (*He disappears from the window.*)

THRASO.
Now what?

GNATHO.
Clear case of theft. This time you've really got them.   810

THRASO.
What d'you say to that, Thais?

THAIS.
Find someone else to answer you.

    She slams the window shut.

THRASO.
Now what?

GNATHO.
Go home.

THRASO.
What?

GNATHO.
She'll be round, crawling on bended knees ...

THRASO.
You're joking.

GNATHO.
No, no. Women are all the same. When you want something, they refuse; when you don't, they can't leave you alone.

THRASO (*doubtfully*).
If you really think so ... All right, then.

GNATHO.
Platoon, atten-*shun*! Corporal ...

SANGA.
Sir!

GNATHO.
The time has come to think of home again.

SANGA.
I've been thinking of my pots and pans for the last half hour.

GNATHO.
Good man. Platoon, right turn! Quick march! Left right, left right, left right, left ... left ... left... left ...

THRASO.
Follow me, men ...

> *They march off. There is a short pause.* THAIS *and* PYTHIAS *come out of the house.* THAIS *is furious.*

THAIS.
For goodness' sake, woman, tell me what's the matter! 'I know ... I don't know ... he ran away ... I was told ... I wasn't there ...' Can't you speak
820   plainly? The girl's sobbing in the bedroom, the eunuch's disappeared. What's been going on?

PYTHIAS (*fearfully*).
I don't know how to start. Er ... they say he wasn't a eunuch at all.

THAIS.
Well, who was he?

PYTHIAS.
That Chaerea ...

THAIS.
What Chaerea?

PYTHIAS.
Phaedria's little brother.

THAIS.
You're joking.

PYTHIAS.
No no, it's true.

THAIS.
But ... what on earth was he doing, coming to my
house?

PYTHIAS.
I think he's in love with Pamphila.

THAIS.
My god! I'll die of shame, you wretch, if what you
say is true ... Is *that* what she's crying about? You
mean he ... (*Gesture.*)?

PYTHIAS.
I think so.

THAIS.
Good god, woman! Is this how you look after the   830
house when I'm not here? Didn't I warn you this
might happen?

PYTHIAS.
Lock her in with the eunuch, you said.

THAIS.
Some eunuch! We've been fooled, Pythias. What
sort of man can he be?

     Whistling offstage.

PYTHIAS.
Madam, madam, shhh!

THAIS.
What?

PYTHIAS.
  He's coming.

THAIS.
  Who is?

PYTHIAS.
  He is! Chaerea! The man himself!

THAIS.
  Where?

PYTHIAS (*pointing*).
  There. Just look at him! Coming back as bold as
  brass to the scene of the ... er ... crime. It's
  disgusting!

  CHAEREA *comes in, still dressed as a eunuch.*

CHAEREA.
840   'Come and change at my place,' he says. 'It's as easy
  as that!' Easy! The first thing we see is his mother
  and father sitting beside the fire, as if they'd stayed
  at home on purpose. I rush into the street, and
  immediately I see someone who knows me. Before *he*
  sees *me*, I dodge into the nearest side-street ... then
  the next ... and the next ... lurking in doorways,
  and dodging in and out in case anyone recognises me
  ... (*Suddenly seeing* THAIS.) Oh my god, Thais!
  Now I've had it!

THAIS.
  Dorus, my dear fellow, how nice to see you! D'you
850   know, someone told me you were trying to escape.

CHAEREA (*in a eunuch's voice*).
  Er ... yes ...

THAIS.
  You surely didn't think you'd get away with it?

CHAEREA.
  Er ... no ... that is ...

THAIS.
  You must have realised you'd be punished.

CHAEREA.
Oh madam, please forgive me ... just this once. I
swear I'll never do it again.

THAIS.
Were you afraid I'd be a cruel mistress?

CHAEREA.
Er ... no.

THAIS.
What then?

CHAEREA.
I was afraid that Pythias there might complain about
me ...

THAIS.
But what have you done?

CHAEREA.
Er, nothing ... nothing much.

PYTHIAS (*furiously*).
Nothing much? You call that nothing much? A
freeborn girl, an Athenian citizen, and you ... you ...

CHAEREA.
I thought she was a fellow-slave.

PYTHIAS.
Fellow-slave? Hold me back before I tear his eyes
out! He's come here to make fun of us!   860

THAIS.
All right, all right ...

PYTHIAS.
Huh! I suppose I'd be the criminal if I gave him
what he really deserves ... the beast! Pretending to
be your slave, and ...

THAIS.
Pythias, that's enough! Chaerea ... yes, we know it's
you ... your conduct has been unworthy of you. You
may think that I deserve to be insulted like this, but
still, what you did was quite unforgiveable. I was

planning to give Pamphila back to her family ...
until this happened. As you'll appreciate, it's rather
870   difficult now ... and I've lost an excellent chance of
making some friends in Athens.

CHAEREA (*in his own voice*).
Oh, don't say that, Thais! I'll always be your
friend ...

THAIS.
You?

CHAEREA.
Well, yes ... I know we've got off on the wrong foot,
but that's often the way lasting friendships start.

THAIS.
What are you saying?

CHAEREA.
Please, Thais! I did this for love, not to insult *you*.

THAIS.
And that's about the only thing in your favour. I
880   know what it's like being in love ...

CHAEREA.
So, please, because I love and respect you ...

PYTHIAS.
Watch out, madam, he's trying to ...

CHAEREA.
I wouldn't dare ...

PYTHIAS.
I don't trust *you* an inch.

THAIS.
Pythias! That's enough!

CHAEREA.
All I ask you to do is help me, Thais.

THAIS.
Help you what?

CHAEREA.
I'm in your hands ... you're the only one who can help me. I'll die if I can't marry her.

THAIS.
But your father ...

CHAEREA.
My father won't mind, if she isn't a slave.   890

THAIS.
Then you'd better speak to her brother. He'll be here soon.

CHAEREA.
What brother?

THAIS.
Chremes. He's gone to fetch her old nurse, who'll be able to prove who she is. Then you can be present at the recognition scene.

CHAEREA.
I'll wait ... but ... er ... (*Pointing to his clothes.*)

THAIS (*amused*).
Perhaps you'd prefer to wait for him indoors rather than standing here in the street?

CHAEREA.
Yes, yes please.

PYTHIAS.
Madam! What d'you think you're doing?

THAIS.
What d'you mean?

PYTHIAS.
Surely you're not inviting him back into the house, after all that's happened?

THAIS.
Why shouldn't I?

PYTHIAS.
He'll cause more trouble ...

THAIS.
Do calm down...

PYTHIAS.
900 Can't you see the sort of man he is?

CHAEREA.
I won't do anything, Pythias.

PYTHIAS.
I wouldn't trust you to ...

CHAEREA.
It's all right, Pythias. You can keep an eye on me.

PYTHIAS.
There's been enough trouble already, from people
keeping eyes on people.

THAIS (*looking offstage*).
Ah, here comes her brother now.

CHAEREA (*agitated*).
Quick, let's go inside. I don't want him to see me in
these clothes ...

THAIS.
You're not shy, are you?

CHAEREA.
Yes, I really am.

PYTHIAS.
Really? Spare his maiden blushes!

THAIS.
Come on, then. Pythias, you wait here for Chremes.

PYTHIAS.
Yes, madam. (CHAEREA *and* THAIS *go inside.*)
910 Oh I wish I could think of something ... some way
of getting my own back on that scoundrel who
palmed him off on us!

> CHREMES *comes in, followed slowly by the aged
> nurse* SOPHRONA.

CHREMES.
Come on, nurse.

SOPHRONA.
Eh?

CHREMES (*loudly*).
Move a bit faster, can't you?

SOPHRONA (*with dignity*).
I'm moving as fast as I can, young man.

CHREMES.
So I see, but not forwards.

PYTHIAS.
Ah, Chremes. Have you shown her the tokens yet?

CHREMES.
Yes, all of them.

PYTHIAS.
And what did she say? Did she recognise them?

CHREMES.
Perfectly.

PYTHIAS
That's good news; I'm really fond of the girl. Go in; the mistress is waiting for you.

> CHREMES *and* SOPHRONA *go into the house.*

Well, well, if it isn't Parmeno. Strolling along as though he owns the street. I do believe I've thought of a way to pay him back for the trick he played on 920 us. I'll just step inside to make sure of the recognition scene and then I'll be back to terrify the life out of him! (*She goes in.*)

PARMENO (*coming along the street*).
I'm dying to know how Chaerea's got on. If he's done well, I'm the one who'll deserve all the credit. (*To the audience, very pleased with himself.*) It was a brilliant plan of mine ... giving him the chance to enjoy, without trouble or expense of any kind, a love affair which could have been very difficult and costly ... you know what's it like when the girl's under the control of a greedy professional ... But my *real* achievement, my masterpiece, was the *educational* 930

aspect ... giving that impressionable young man an inside view of the true nature of such ... loose women ... so he'll be turned off them for life. Yes, that was my real purpose. Women like this ... we all know what they're like in public, dining with their lovers, picking daintily at their food, giving a convincing impression of elegance and good taste. But see them by themselves at home ... (*Getting carried away.*) the filth, the squalor ... dirt on the floor ... stuffing their mouths with stale bread dipped in yesterday's gravy ... Ugh! ... Thank god I've been able to open the eyes of just one young man to all this! ...

940

PYTHIAS (*who has come out of the door and is listening; aside*).
You'll suffer for this, you scoundrel! You'll be sorry you ever played tricks on us! (*Aloud, but pretending not to see* PARMENO.) Oh, what a terrible thing! That poor young man! How could that vile Parmeno have ever let this happen to him?

PARMENO (*aside*).
Eh? What does she mean?

PYTHIAS (*as before*).
I had to come outside: I couldn't bear to watch what they're doing to him.

PARMENO (*alarmed*).
What? (*Aside.*) I've done it this time! (*Aloud, to* PYTHIAS.) For heaven's sake, woman, what are they doing? What's happening?

PYTHIAS (*enjoying herself*).
Oh, the poor young man! You brought him here dressed as a eunuch! Now he must wish he'd never been born ... oh ... oh ...!

PARMENO (*angrily*).
What's ... going ... on ...?

950

PYTHIAS.
What's going on? You know the girl Thais was given today?

PARMENO.
The slave-girl, yes ...

PYTHIAS.
Slave-girl? She's a freeborn Athenian citizen!

PARMENO.
What?

PYTHIAS.
And her brother's a nobleman.

PARMENO (*getting alarmed*).
Well, how am I expected to know ...

PYTHIAS.
It's true! And your young friend ... um ... *you*
know ...

PARMENO.
No!

PYTHIAS.
Yes! This afternoon. When her brother found out ...
he's got the vilest temper I've ever seen ...

PARMENO.
What did he do?

PYTHIAS.
First of all, he tied him up. Oh, it was horrible to
watch!

PARMENO.
Tied him up?

PYTHIAS.
Thais was crying, begging him to stop ...

PARMENO.
I don't believe you.

PYTHIAS.
And now he says he's going to deal with him as they
do adulterers ... something I've never seen, and
never want to ...

PARMENO.
But that's outrageous!

PYTHIAS.
Why outrageous?

PARMENO.
I mean ... whoever saw a man arrested for doing
960   *that* ... in a place like *that*?

PYTHIAS (*mocking* PARMENO's *previous tone*).
Well, how am I expected to know ...

PARMENO.
P-P-P-Pythias, listen, that young man I brought
round today wasn't a eunuch. He was *my master's
son*!

PYTHIAS.
Good heavens! You don't say so!

PARMENO.
Yes! Thais mustn't let anything happen to him. I'll
have to go in and save him.

PYTHIAS (*restraining him*).
Be careful, Parmeno ... you may do him no good,
and yourself a lot of harm. They think this all
happened because of you.

PARMENO.
Oh my god, what now? What on earth can I ...
(*Looking along the street.*) Ahhh! Here's my old
master coming back from the country! What am I
going to tell *him*? (*Resigned.*) Oh well, everything, I
suppose. I got Chaerea into all this and I'll have to
get him out.

PYTHIAS.
970   Quite right. I'll go inside and leave you to tell him
the whole story.

    She goes into the house, leaving PARMENO
    shaking with fright. LACHES *comes in.*

LACHES (*to the audience*).
Ah, what a marvellous holiday I've had! It was a
brilliant idea of mine, buying that farm in the
country ... if you get tired of one house, you simply

go and stay at the other for a week or two ...
splendid idea! But, wait a bit ... isn't that our man
Parmeno? Yes, it is. Parmeno! Why are you standing
out here? Who are you waiting for?

PARMENO.
Oh, sir, I'm s-s-so glad to see you safely back.

LACHES.
What's the matter?

PARMENO (*aside*).
Damn it, I don't know what to say.

LACHES.
What are you shivering for? Aren't you well, or
something?

PARMENO.
S-s-s-s-sir, I'd like you to know, first of all, that
whatever's happened here isn't my fault.   980

LACHES.
Eh?

PARMENO.
A good question, sir, a good question. You see,
Phaedria bought a eunuch yesterday.

LACHES.
A eunuch? What for?

PARMENO.
To give to Thais.

LACHES.
The fool! What did he pay for him?

PARMENO.
Ten gold pieces.

LACHES.
He was robbed. Well, is that all?

PARMENO.
No, sir. Chaerea's girl-friend lives in Thais's house.

LACHES.
Chaerea's *what*?

PARMENO.
G-g-girl-friend, sir.

LACHES (*grimly*).
Girl-friend, eh? I shall have to have a little talk with
Chaerea. Children grow up so fast these days . . . One
calamity after another!

PARMENO.
Sir, don't look at me like that. It was nothing to do
with me!

LACHES.
You can stop the pleading . . . I'll deal with *you*, you
990   scoundrel, when . . . Well, is there anything else?

PARMENO.
Y-y-yes, sir. Chaerea was taken to Thais's house
instead of the eunuch.

LACHES.
Instead of the *eunuch*?

PARMENO.
Yes. And then, when they found out what he'd done,
they arrested him as an adulterer, and tied him up,
and . . .

LACHES.
Oh my god!

PARMENO.
These women will stop at nothing, sir . . .

LACHES (*after a shocked pause*).
Any other disaster you haven't mentioned yet?

PARMENO.
No, sir, that's the lot.

LACHES.
Out of my way!

He rushes into THAIS's *house*.

PARMENO.
Oh dear . . . there's no way out . . . I'm done for this
time. Ah well . . . at least those women aren't going to

get away with it either. My old master won't let *this* one go ... that's for sure. He's been hunting about   1000 for an excuse to do something drastic to them ... and now he's found it ...

PYTHIAS *comes out, roaring with laughter.*

PYTHIAS.
What a magnificent scene! When the old man burst in ... I don't think I've ever seen anything so funny. The trouble was, no one could see the joke but me!

PARMENO *(aside).*
Now what's happened?

PYTHIAS.
Ah, Parmeno! There you are ... *(Goes on laughing.)*

PARMENO *(coldly).*
Would you mind telling me what the joke is?

PYTHIAS.
I haven't laughed at anything so much in years.

PARMENO.
AT WHAT?

PYTHIAS.
At you, you idiot! I've never seen a bigger fool. Oh, I can't tell you what fun you've given us indoors! And I used to think you were pretty smart, too. You   1010 believed every word I said: and then, having got Chaerea into all this, you rushed and told his father. What d'you suppose he felt when his father saw him in those clothes? Well, you've really done for yourself now!

PARMENO.
What?!!! You mean ... you made it all up? Stop laughing, damn you ... it's not funny!

PYTHIAS *(laughing even more).*
Yes it is!

PARMENO.
You wait! I'll pay you back!

PYTHIAS.

> Maybe ... after you've been strung up and whipped!
1020
> After all, you made a young boy commit a serious
> crime and then you informed against him. Both
> father and son will want to see you punished.

PARMENO.

> I'm done for!

PYTHIAS.

> You've served them well, and now you'll get what
> you've deserved.

> *She goes in, still laughing.*

PARMENO.

> I've really had it this time. I should've kept my
> mouth shut ...

> THRASO *and* GNATHO *come in.*

GNATHO.

> But where are we going? What are you planning
> now?

THRASO.

> You'll see. I shall surrender to Thais ... obey her
> orders ... slightest whim ...

GNATHO.

> What?

THRASO.

> Yes, just like Hercules becoming a slave to Queen
> Omphale.

GNATHO.

> Ah, an excellent precedent! (*Aside.*) She'll beat his
> brains out! (*Aloud.*) Look out ... the door's opening.

THRASO.

> Help! More trouble! Who the hell's this ... I've
1030
> never seen him before in my life! Why's he in such a
> hurry?

> CHAEREA *bursts out, dressed in his own clothes.*
> *He does not see them.*

CHAEREA.
  What fantastic luck! There's no one as happy as I
  am! What a wonderful day it's been!

PARMENO.
  Oh, superb.

CHAEREA.
  Parmeno, my dear chap ...! Have you heard the
  news? My darling Pamphila's not a slave-girl!

PARMENO.
  I had heard.

CHAEREA.
  And do you know we're engaged?

PARMENO.
  Engaged? Oh. Congratulations.

GNATHO (*aside, to* THRASO).
  Did you hear that?

CHAEREA.
  And it's all turned out right for Phaedria too. We're
  going to be one big happy family. My father's really
  taken to Thais ... sworn to be her friend and
  protector for ever.

PARMENO.
  You mean Phaedria can marry her?   1040

CHAEREA.
  That's right.

PARMENO.
  So, something else to be pleased about: Thraso will
  be kicked out!

CHAEREA.
  Quick, go and find Phaedria. Tell him the good
  news.

PARMENO.
  I'll see if he's at home. (*He goes.*)

THRASO.
  Er ... Gnatho ...

GNATHO.
Sir?

THRASO.
I'm done for here, wouldn't you say?

GNATHO.
Looks like it.

CHAEREA (*still ecstatic*).
Oh, thank you, Heaven, for everything ... for
Parmeno, who gave me the idea, for me having the
courage to carry it out, for the good luck which
brought it all together on this happiest of days ... oh,
and for my father for being so understanding and
kind ... May it last for ever ...

PHAEDRIA (*rushing out of the house*).
1050   Is it true, this fantastic story of Parmeno's? Chaerea?

CHAEREA.
Here!

PHAEDRIA.
It's wonderful!

CHAEREA.
Yes. And no one deserves to be loved more than your
Thais: she's done so much for all of us.

PHAEDRIA (*laughing*).
I don't need you to praise Thais!

> *They go on talking excitedly. No one has seen*
> THRASO *or* GNATHO *yet.*

THRASO.
It's no use ... the less hope there is, the more I love
her. Can't you do something, Gnatho?

GNATHO.
Pardon, sir?

THRASO.
Go and beg them to let me go on seeing her ...

GNATHO.
What?

THRASO.
Whatever it costs, I'll pay ... just *ask* them!

GNATHO.
H'mm. It won't be easy.

THRASO.
Try. If anyone can do it, you can. Not my right-
hand man for nothing. If you get me this, ask for
whatever you like ... no reward's too great, and all
that...

GNATHO.
You mean ... your house my house, your servants
my servants, your purse my purse ...

THRASO (*dancing with impatience*).
Yes, yes! Hurry up!   1060

GNATHO.
Right. (*Going over to the others.*) Ahem ...

PHAEDRIA.
Who's that? Oh, Thraso.

THRASO.
Good afternoon, gentlemen.

PHAEDRIA.
Er ... perhaps you haven't heard the latest news ...

THRASO.
I've heard.

PHAEDRIA.
Then what d'you think you're doing *here*?

THRASO.
We rely on you ...

PHAEDRIA.
Rely on me? Listen, corporal: if you don't get your
boots out of this street and keep them out, even if
you say 'I was only passing through on my way
somewhere else', you can rely on me all right ... I'll
beat your brains out!

GNATHO.
  That's not very nice ...

PHAEDRIA.
  I mean it!

THRASO.
  I don't like your attitude.

PHAEDRIA.
  Hard luck: that's the way I am.

  They glare at each other.

GNATHO.
  Er ... might I have a little word?

CHAEREA.
  Go ahead.

GNATHO (*to* THRASO).
  Excuse me, sir, would you mind just moving over
  here ...

  He moves THRASO *out of earshot and then returns
  to* PHAEDRIA *and* CHAEREA.

  Now, gentlemen ...

PHAEDRIA.
  Yes?

GNATHO.
  I want to make it clear right from the start that the
1070 only person I'm really thinking about in all this is ...
  me! But it'll do you some good too.

PHAEDRIA.
  What will?

GNATHO.
  I advise you to let the colonel go on thinking he's
  Phaedria's rival.

PHAEDRIA.
  What?

GNATHO.
  No no, listen. You want to go on enjoying life with
  Thais, don't you? But things are going to be a bit

tight financially, aren't they? After all, she's used to
living in style. Now there's the means (*Indicating*
THRASO.) to supply you with everything you need,
without it costing you a penny. In the first place, he's
rich – richer than anyone in Athens. Secondly, he's a
fool: the last of the really great fools. So, don't tell
him about the marriage; let him go on giving her
money. You can always throw him out when you   1080
want.

CHAEREA (*to* PHAEDRIA).
What do you think?

GNATHO.
The main thing is this: he's in a class of his own
when it comes to throwing his money around!

CHAEREA.
It looks as though we do need him.

PHAEDRIA (*reluctantly*).
I suppose so.

GNATHO.
I thought you'd see it my way. Oh, there is one other
thing...

PHAEDRIA.
What?

GNATHO.
Please don't forget all the hard work I've put in for
you with that ... that *millstone* of a man.

PHAEDRIA.
No.

GNATHO.
Very well: in return for letting me become one of
your friends ...

PHAEDRIA *and* CHAEREA (*aside*).
Iuccch!

GNATHO.
... I give you Thraso, the Universal Provider.

CHAEREA.
    We'll take him.

PHAEDRIA.
    He deserves it.

GNATHO (*returning to* THRASO).
    Er, Thraso, sir ...

THRASO.
    Eh? Well, any progress?

GNATHO.
    Oh, it was easy. As soon as I told them what sort of
    man you were ... as soon as I said a few words about
1090   what you really deserved, they gave way at once!

THRASO (*overjoyed*).
    What? My dear chap! (*Preening himself.*) Of course,
    I've always been the same: irresistible.

GNATHO (*to* PHAEDRIA *and* CHAEREA).
    And *so* modest!

PHAEDRIA (*laughing*).
    We couldn't ask for anything more! Let's all go in
    and celebrate. (*To the audience.*) Farewell, and don't
    forget to applaud!

    They all go into THAIS's *house.*

TERENCE

Brothers
(*Adelphoe*)

translated by J. Michael Walton

Characters

DEMEA, an Athenian
MICIO, his brother
AESCHINUS, Demea's son, adopted by Micio
CTESIPHO, his other son
SYRUS, a slave of Micio
DROMO, another slave
STEPHANIO, another slave
PARMENO, a slave of Demea
SOSTRATA, a widow
PAMPHILA, her daughter
CANTHARA, Pamphila's nurse
GETA, Sostrata's slave
HEGIO, a neighbour
SANNIO, a pimp
BACCHIS, slave girl

PROLOGUE.

Your playwright knows well enough that his material
is the subject of critical hostility. As his competitors
have been running down the play we are about to
present, he has decided to serve as his own prosecutor
and let you register your approval or disapproval.

Diphilus wrote a comedy called *Linked by Death*.
Plautus translated it into Latin. In the Greek there is
a young man who takes a girl away from a pimp.
Plautus left this out, so your present author has put
the scene as it stands into his *Brothers*. It's word for   10
word the same. This is the piece which we are about
to perform for the first time. You must decide
whether you regard this as plagiarism or the recovery
of a scene which has been unjustly ignored.

There is a further charge, and a malicious one, that
he received assistance in his writing from certain
men of distinction. He takes this to be less an
accusation than the finest of compliments, if he has
succeeded in earning the respect of those whom you
all and, indeed, the whole population admire, men
whose successful enterprises in wartime and peace-   20
time, as well as in business, have been conducted
with proper modesty.

Don't now expect the argument of the play. The old
men who enter first will explain some of the plot.
The rest will become clear from the action. Give our
comedy a fair hearing and reinforce thereby your
playwright's enthusiasm for writing.

Athens. Two adjacent houses. Enter MICIO.

MICIO.

Are you there, Storax? Aeschinus hasn't come back
from last night's dinner-party and none of the
servants who went with him either. It's true what
they say. If you stay out late or don't come home all
night, the reception you get from a wife, however
angry and whatever she says or suspects, is   30

preferable to the reactions of loving parents. Your
wife will assume, when you don't turn up, that
you've found another woman or that you're off
drinking and having fun while she's at home by
herself and bored. But when it's your son, the things
you imagine! He's had a fall or caught pneumonia.
All manner of disaster. Why do we allow ourselves to
become so vulnerable just by accepting
responsibility for what is dearer than life itself?
Aeschinus is not even my real son. He's my
40   brother's.

We've always had a different outlook on life, my
brother and I, ever since we were little. I've led a
comfortable existence in town and enjoyed myself.
And I'm in the enviable situation, as some might
think, of never having married. With my brother,
quite the opposite, a life of drudgery in the country,
ever thrifty, ever hard-working. He did get married
and had two sons. I adopted one of them when he
was little and have brought him up as my own. And I
love him, always have. He's the greatest joy in my
50   life, the only thing I care about. I try to make him
feel as I do. I pay his way. Overlook things. Don't
make a fuss about a father's rights all the time. As a
result my son doesn't conceal from me all those
peccadilloes which other young men keep quiet
about. The boy who feels he has to deceive a father
or lies to him even once, soon starts treating other
people the same way. Respect and generosity are
what the youth of today need, in my book, not
intimidation.

60   Such views hardly meet with the approval of my
brother. He keeps getting upset and complaining to
me: 'What on earth are you up to, Micio? You'll ruin
the boy. Women? Drink? Extravagance? Why do you
put up with it? And those clothes he wears. Really!
You must be off your head. Truly you must be.'
Well what I think is, *he's* too strait-laced, 'truly he
must be', beyond rhyme or reason. In my opinion

Not fear
love

authority imposed by force will never be as effective
as that based on affection.

That's my belief and I'm sticking to it. If fear of
punishment is all that guarantees good behaviour in
a man, oh he'll behave, as long as someone is
watching. But he'll bide his time until he can get
away with it and revert. Win him over with kindness   70
and he'll repay that kindness whether you're present
or not. It's the same with being a father. Get a son in
the habit of doing the right thing and not just
because he's frightened of you. That's the difference
between a father and an autocrat. If anyone doesn't
agree, he should confess that he hasn't the first idea
about bringing up children.

Why, isn't that my brother now? Yes it is. The very
man. He looks rather down in the mouth. Something
I've done, as usual, I expect.   80

Enter DEMEA.

Morning Demea. Glad to see you.

DEMEA.
Ah, there you are. Good. I want a word with you.

MICIO.
What's the problem?

M'sson

DEMEA.
How can you ask? With Aeschinus treating us like
this, you ask me what my problem is? I told you this
would happen.

MICIO.
What's he done?

DEMEA.
What has he done? Has he no respect for anything,
no concern for anyone, no concept of the law as
something affecting him? Ignore his past exploits,
perhaps. But this . . .

MICIO.
Yes, but what?

DEMEA.

Smashing down a door. <u>Forced entry into a</u>
<u>stranger's house.</u> Beating the master of the said
90   house and his family within an inch of their lives.
And kidnap of some girl he's been messing about
with. The place is in an uproar. I was accosted on my
way here by I can't tell you how many people, Micio.
It's a public scandal. If he needs a decent example,
why on earth doesn't he take note of his brother's
<u>frugal and sober life in the</u> country? It may be
Aeschinus I'm talking about, but the finger's
pointing at you, Micio. You've let him go to the
dogs.

MICIO.

There's no one <u>as unfair as a puritan.</u> Nothing's
right <u>unless he's done it himself.</u>

DEMEA.

Meaning what?

MICIO.

Meaning, Demea, that you've got it all wrong. I tell
100   you it's not <u>such a crime for a young man</u> to do a
little <u>whoring and drinking.</u> It's not. Breaking and
entering too. If you and I never did, it's only because
we couldn't afford to. I hope you're not going to pat
yourself on the back for poverty-driven morality. Oh
really. We'd have behaved like that if we'd had the
wherewithal. Yes, you too. Any sympathetic man
would let his son have a fling at the appropriate age.
Better than storing it up for later when he's got rid of
110   you but should have grown out of such things.

DEMEA.

God in heaven, you'll <u>drive me mad.</u> Are you trying
to tell me that <u>no crime's been committed</u> because
he's young?

MICIO.

Just listen, will you? I'm fed up with this barrage of
criticism. You let me adopt your son. That makes
him my son. If he does wrong, he does me wrong.

But I'm prepared to put up with a great deal.
Expensive meals. Drinking. Perfume. All on me. A
mistress? I'll foot the bill for as long as I please. And
when I don't please, she'll probably kick him out.
Broken doors? I'll have them repaired. A torn coat?
I'll see that it's mended. I can afford it, thank God. 120
And so far, I do not find this a problem. So. Either
lay off, or pick an arbitrator between us. I'll show
you who is the more at fault in all this.

DEMEA.
All I'm asking, for goodness' sake, is that you'll let
those who know advise you on how to be a father.

MICIO.
His blood may be yours. His perspective comes from
me.

DEMEA.
Perspective? From you?

MICIO.
Have it your own way. I'm leaving.

DEMEA.
Is that the way you want it?

MICIO.
Why should I go on listening to you? It's the same
story over and over again.

DEMEA.
I'm concerned.

MICIO.
And I'm concerned. No, I mean it, Demea. Let's
both of us be concerned. You be concerned about
your boy and I'll be concerned about mine. If you 130
start being concerned about both of them, then it's
like asking for your son back. You gave him to me.

DEMEA.
Oh, Micio. Are you angry?

MICIO.
You don't believe me, do you?

DEMEA.

About asking for him back?

MICIO.

That's how it looks to me, yes.

DEMEA.

Really? Very well. You win. He can squander,
seduce and sink without trace. It's no business of
mine.

MICIO.

One more word, Demea, and...

DEMEA.

It's not easy for me, you know. It's not as if I were a
total stranger. If ever I try to prevent ... no, forget
it. Not another word. You want me to make one of
them my concern. He is my concern and, thank God,
turning out the way I would want. The other one
140   will find out when it's too late. But I won't hold him
entirely responsible.

  Exit DEMEA.

MICIO.

I'm not prepared to go all the way with him, but he
does have a point. Aeschinus is a bit of a worry,
though I wasn't going to let on to Demea. He's that
sort of man. The only way to appease him is face him
out and frighten him off. Even then it's touch and
go. Give him any encouragement or fuel that fury of
his and I'd end up as crazy as he is.

On the other hand ... Aeschinus is not exactly doing
any of us a favour carrying on like this. There can't
be a tart left in the place he hasn't had to pay off.
The latest thing was that he wanted to get married. I
150   thought he must have become bored with this sort of
life and grown up at last. Some hope. Back to square
one. Anyway, I'd better try and find out what is
going on, if he's anywhere to be found.

  Exit MICIO.

Enter AESCHINUS *and* BACCHIS, *with*
PARMENO, *followed by* SANNIO.

SANNIO.

Help. Fellow-citizens. Help for a poor man, an
innocent man. Help me.

AESCHINUS (*to* BACCHIS).

Don't worry. Stay where you are. And don't turn
round. There's no danger. As long as I'm here he'll
not touch you.

SANNIO.

I'll get her back, whatever you say.

AESCHINUS.

Rogue he may be, but he'll not risk two beatings in
one day.

SANNIO.

Listen, Aeschinus. You know my trade. I'm a pimp.   160

AESCHINUS.

I know that.

SANNIO.

But I'm straight. None straighter. And when you
turn up full of apologies and tell me how sorry you
are, do you know what I'll say? 'Up yours,' I'll say.
I'm giving you fair warning, I'll have the law on you.
You won't talk your way out of this one. 'I'm deeply
sorry' won't wash. No regrets later. I shouldn't have
to suffer this. But suffer I have, and you're going to
pay for it.

AESCHINUS (*to* PARMENO).

Get a move on. Open the door.

SANNIO.

You won't listen, eh?

AESCHINUS (*to* BACCHIS).

In you go.

SANNIO.

Oh no you don't.

AESCHINUS.
Here, Parmeno. Quick. No, there. Stop hanging
back. Up beside him. That's it. Now, watch me
170 closely. If I give as much as a twitch, punch his head
in.

SANNIO.
If that's the way you want it. You're on.

AESCHINUS.
Leave her alone.

Slave

PARMENO *hits* SANNIO.

SANNIO.
Ow! You shouldn't have done that.

AESCHINUS.
There's another where that came from, so watch it.

PARMENO *hits him again.*

SANNIO.
Hey! That really hurt.

AESCHINUS.
I never even winked that time but he does make that
sort of mistake. In you go, girl.

Exeunt BACCHIS *and* PARMENO.

SANNIO.
What is all this, Aeschinus? Do you think you own
this town?

AESCHINUS.
If I did, I'd see you get the decoration you deserve.

SANNIO.
Why me? What did I do?

AESCHINUS.
Nothing.

SANNIO.
So? Do you know who I am?

AESCHINUS.
I'm not interested.

SANNIO.

Did I take something of yours?

AESCHINUS.

You'd know about it if you had.

SANNIO.

So what gives you the right to take one of my girls? I paid good money for her. Well?

AESCHINUS.

I wouldn't recommend a row at my front door. Any   180
more trouble, we'll haul you inside and beat the
living daylights out of you.

SANNIO.

Beat a free man?

AESCHINUS.

If necessary.

SANNIO.

You bastard. Call this a free country?

AESCHINUS.

If you've finished raving, pimp, hear this.

SANNIO.

Me raving? It's you that's raving.

AESCHINUS.

Come on. Let's get back to business.

SANNIO.

What business? What's there to get back to?

AESCHINUS.

This'll interest you. You want to listen?

SANNIO.

Be fair. I'll listen.

AESCHINUS.

A pimp wants to be fair!

SANNIO.

Look. I'm a pimp, right? Pervert, perjurer,
poxmonger. But I've never done any harm.

AESCHINUS.

190   Not yet.

SANNIO.

Do you mind getting back to the point, Aeschinus?

AESCHINUS.

You paid twenty minae for the girl, worse luck.
You'll get that back.

SANNIO.

Maybe I'm not selling. You going to make me?

AESCHINUS.

Wouldn't dream of it.

SANNIO.

That's a relief.

AESCHINUS.

I wouldn't dream of buying a free woman. Which I
shall claim she is. There's your choice. Take your
money or prepare your defence. I'll be back, pimp.
Think about it.

Exit AESCHINUS.

SANNIO.

God almighty. No wonder assault victims go crazy.
Hauled out of my house. Abused. One of my girls
abducted. Downed under a hail of blows. After all
200   this, what's his offer? Cost price! In the
circumstances, I suppose I'd better cooperate.
Especially if he does have the law on his side. Might
as well. As long as I get my money back. I know
what'll happen. The moment I agree, he'll produce
witnesses that I sold her. And the money? Wishful
thinking. 'Any time. Come back tomorrow.' Which I
could put up with, however infuriating, as long as he
does pay. But that's the way it goes. In this
profession you put up with the young men and you
keep your mouth shut. I'll not see a penny. Profit on
this one, nil, I reckon.

Enter SYRUS, *talking to* AESCHINUS *indoors.*

SYRUS.

Don't go on about it. I'll deal with him. I'll have him
agreeing and thanking you for it. Ah, Sannio, what's   210
all this I hear? A little contretemps with the master?

SANNIO.

The most unfair fight I ever came across. I got
thumped. He did the thumping and we're both worn
out.

SYRUS.

You're entirely to blame.

SANNIO.

What could I do?

SYRUS.

A young man needs humouring.

SANNIO.

I spend the day offering him my face to hit. You
want more?

SYRUS.

You know what I'm talking about. Sometimes
ignoring money is the best way to make it. Here's
you all of a dither over some trifling sum a young
man owes you. You great nitwit. You'll get it back
with interest.

SANNIO.

I don't bank on promises.

SYRUS.

You'll never make it, Sannio. You don't know how
to bait a hook.   220

SANNIO.

I bow to your experience there. I've never been
clever enough not to prefer cash in hand.

SYRUS.

I know what you're thinking. What's twenty minae
against doing Aeschinus a favour? Anyway, they tell
me you're off to Cyprus.

SANNIO.
What?

SYRUS.
Bought a lot of stock. Chartered a boat. There's plenty to occupy your mind. You don't have to tell me. We can sort out all this business when you get back.

SANNIO.
I'm not moving an inch. (*Aside*.) Damn and blast. They knew this all along.

SYRUS (*aside*).
He's worried. That's given him something to think about.

SANNIO (*aside*).
Confound the thing. He's put his finger right on it. I've got this load of girls and other things to take to
230   Cyprus. If I don't get there for the sale, I lose a packet. I can drop this business for now but by the time I get back it'll be a dead duck. 'Oh, you're back, are you? Took your time. Where've you been?' I'll be better off losing her altogether than staying here or trying to chase her up after I return.

SYRUS.
Totted it all up, have you?

SANNIO.
Is this a decent way to behave? Aeschinus stealing her from me by force?

SYRUS (*aside*).
He's teetering. (*To* SANNIO.) Here's an idea. What do you think? Rather than put yourself in the
240   position where you might get the lot or you might equally well lose the lot, compromise. He'll rustle up ten minae from somewhere.

SANNIO.
Terrific. Now my stake's in doubt. Shameless. How dare he? He's loosened my teeth. I've more bump

than head. Now I'm to let myself be cheated? I'm
staying put.

SYRUS.
Up to you. Nothing you want before I go?

SANNIO.
No. Come on, Syrus, confound it. Whatever's
happened, you know perfectly well I don't want to
go to court. Let me have what I paid for her. There's
been no love lost between us, I realise that, up to   250
now, but I'm not one to forget a favour, Syrus.

SYRUS.
I'll see what I can do. Oh, here's Ctesipho. He's
pleased as anything about the girl.

SANNIO.
And that suggestion of mine?

SYRUS.
Hang on.

Enter CTESIPHO. ← other son country o...

CTESIPHO.
Any assistance is a pleasure in one's hour of need: a
pleasure doubled when that assistance is from
someone so suitable. Brother, dear brother, how may
I sing your praises? My tongue lacks words to match
your dazzling qualities. In one respect alone do I
surpass the world. Nowhere is there anyone else with
a brother so superior in every conceivable skill.

SYRUS.
Hey, Ctesipho . . .   260

CTESIPHO.
Ah, Syrus. Is Aeschinus about?

SYRUS.
Indoors. Waiting for you.

CTESIPHO.
Oh . . .

SYRUS.
  What is it?

CTESIPHO.
  What should it be? Oh, Syrus, thanks to him I've
  come to life. It's a wonderful fellow who at every
  turn will accommodate himself to another fellow.
  Harsh words, scandal, my love affair and attendant
  problems: he's taken them all upon himself. The lot.
  He's incomparable.

  A noise within.

  Isn't that the door?

SYRUS.
  Hold on. It's the man himself.

  Enter AESCHINUS.

AESCHINUS.
  Where is the old devil?

SANNIO.
  It's me he's looking for. Has he got the money? Not
  as far as I can see. My bad luck.

AESCHINUS.
  Excellent timing. Ctesipho, the very man. Are you
  all right? Everything's safe and sound. Begone dull
  care, and so on.

CTESIPHO.
  With you as a brother, care can be gone. Aeschinus,
270   oh Aeschinus, my ... brother. Face to face I hardly
  know whether I can tell you just how ... because I
  wouldn't want you to think I was ... or have you any
  doubt how sincerely ...

AESCHINUS.
  You are an idiot, Ctesipho, going on as if we were
  strangers. The only sad thing is that you almost let
  things reach the point of no return. The whole world
  couldn't have helped you then.

CTESIPHO.
  I felt too ashamed.

AESCHINUS.
  That's being dumb, not being ashamed. Almost
  emigrating over a little thing like that? Why, God
  forbid, it's unthinkable.

CTESIPHO.
  I was a silly.

AESCHINUS (*to* SYRUS).
  What's the latest on Sannio?

SYRUS.
  Quite docile.

AESCHINUS.
  I'll go to the forum and pay him off there. And you,
  Ctesipho, get inside to that girl of yours.

SANNIO.
  Now, Syrus.

SYRUS.
  Let's go. Sannio's rushing off to Cyprus.

SANNIO.
  Not such a rush. I can hang on here for a while.

SYRUS.
  You'll get your money, don't fret.   280

SANNIO.
  The lot?

SYRUS.
  The lot. Just shut up and follow us.

SANNIO.
  I'll follow you. I certainly will.

CTESIPHO.
  Syrus. Hey, Syrus.

SYRUS.
  Eh? What is it?

CTESIPHO.
  Do, I beg of you, pay the beastly fellow off at the
  first possible opportunity. If he gets any more upset,

some inkling may filter through to Father and then I'll be crushed. Utterly.

SYRUS.
It isn't going to happen. Chin up. You go and have some fun with the girl. Tell them to set the tables and get ready for dinner. I'll sort out this business and get back here with the shopping.

CTESIPHO.
That's all right, then. Everything's turned out so well, what we need is a party.

Exeunt.

Enter SOSTRATA *and* CANTHARA.

SOSTRATA.
Nurse, please, Nurse, what do we do now?

CANTHARA.
What do we do? We let nature take its course, I trust. Why, her contractions have only just started, pet. There's nothing to worry about. Anyone would think you'd never attended a birth, not even your own children's.

SOSTRATA.
It's so terrible. There's nobody. We're all alone. Geta's not here. There's no one to send for the midwife. Nobody to fetch Aeschinus.

CANTHARA.
Aeschinus will be here. Not a day passes without him coming.

SOSTRATA.
He's my last refuge in adversity.

CANTHARA.
Things being the way they are, it's not worked out at all badly. If someone was going to get her into trouble, it's better it should be a nice lad like that, so clever, so full of spirit. And what a fine family.

SOSTRATA.

I suppose you're right. God save us from losing him.

Enter GETA. ⟵ slave

GETA.

That it should come to this. If all the men from
every town should put their heads together and set
their minds to try to solve our problem, how could
they ever find a way to release this girl, her mother   300
and me from all the trouble we've inherited? We're
under siege, surrounded, under threat from poverty,
injustice, desertion and distress. What times we live
in. Such wickedness, such broken promises. Oh, the
scoundrel!

SOSTRATA.

Lord preserve us. I can see Geta, but why is he so
upset and in such a hurry?

GETA.

His solemn oath, his good faith. Where's his pity?
Will nothing restrain him from carrying on so the
very day of her confinement, poor victim that she is
of his villainous assault?

SOSTRATA.

I don't follow what he's saying.

CANTHARA.

Let's get closer.

GETA.

I'm so furious, I'm scarcely in control. Nothing
would please me more than to line up the whole
family and vomit my anger all over them, now while   310
my blood's at boiling point. For me that would be a
proper vengeance. For them that would be a fitting
nemesis. First the old man. I'd switch off his light
for fathering the brute. Then Syrus, the stimulus,
I'd shred him. Up in the air. Down on his head.
Pavement spread with brains. And the boy. Tear out
his eyes, throw them away and him after them. Rest
of the household, buffeting, bashing, battering,

belabouring, butchering. No point in hanging about.
I'd best go and tell them the worst.

SOSTRATA.

320 We'll call him back. Geta.

GETA.

Leave me alone, whoever you are.

SOSTRATA.

It's me. It's Sostrata.

GETA.

Where are you? Oh, there you are. I was looking for
you. I need to find you. Immediately. Now I have.

SOSTRATA.

Whatever is it? What a state you are in.

GETA.

Oh dear, oh dear.

CANTHARA.

Geta, what's all the panic? Take a deep breath.

GETA.

Altogether.

SOSTRATA.

Altogether what?

GETA.

Altogether done for. Us.

SOSTRATA.

For goodness' sake, tell us what's happened.

GETA.

Well...

SOSTRATA.

Well, what, Geta?

GETA.

It's Aeschinus.

SOSTRATA.

What's Aeschinus?

GETA.
Cut himself off from our family.

SOSTRATA.
That does it. We're finished. But why?

GETA.
He's got another woman.

SOSTRATA.
God help us.

GETA.
Quite blatant about it. He just stole her from a pimp.

SOSTRATA.
Geta, are you sure?

GETA.
Quite sure, Sostrata. I saw him. With my own eyes.

SOSTRATA.
What am I going to do? What can you trust? Who   330
can you trust? Aeschinus, our salvation, the source of
all our hopes and all our expectations. Is this the
man who swore he could not live another day
without my daughter? Who said he'd plant the child
in its grandfather's lap and beg his permission for
the marriage?

GETA.
Dry your tears, mistress. We have to think what
we're going to do. Suffer in silence or tell someone?

CANTHARA.
Are you out of your mind, you silly man? This is not
something we want broadcast all over the place.

GETA.
Of course it isn't. To start with, he's obviously
turned against us. If we go telling people, he'll deny
it, that's for sure. They'll start wondering about
your reputation and your private life. If we do get   340
him to confess, her marriage prospects are hardly
bright when he's already gone and fallen for

somebody else. No two ways about it. We keep this
under our hats.

SOSTRATA.
Not likely. I won't do it.

GETA.
So, what will you do?

SOSTRATA.
Tell the world.

CANTHARA.
Oh, Sostrata. Think of the consequences.

SOSTRATA.
Things could hardly be worse than they are. In the
first place, no dowry. And in the second place, no
second place. She's lost her virginity. No getting
married as a virgin. That leaves this. If he denies it,
here's the ring he lost as proof. No blame attached to
me in any of this, none whatsoever. No money
changed hands, nothing discreditable. I'll take it to
court.

GETA.
350   Whatever you say. I'm easy. I just hope you're right.

SOSTRATA.
Geta. Off with you as quick as you can. Hegio's a
relative. Find him and tell him the whole story. He
was a good friend to my Simulus and he's always
kept an eye on us.

GETA.
Nobody else will, you can guarantee that.

SOSTRATA.
And Canthara. Run and find the midwife. We don't
want her missing at the vital moment.

Exeunt CANTHARA, GETA *and* SOSTRATA.
Enter DEMEA.

DEMEA.
That does it. I've just heard that Ctesipho, my son
Ctesipho, was a party with Aeschinus to abducting

that girl. If Aeschinus can drag a decent lad down to
his level, that will really put the tin lid on it. I
wonder where I can find him. Dragged off to some
dive, I expect. Seduced by that rake, I'm sure of 360
that. Here's Syrus. He can tell me where he's gone.
No. Heavens, he's one of them, come to think of it.
If he thinks I'm trying to find Ctesipho, the
scoundrel will never let on. He mustn't find out what
I'm after.

    Enter SYRUS.

SYRUS.
  We told old Micio the whole story, just as it
  happened. I've never seen anyone so happy.

DEMEA.
  God in heaven. What a fool the man is.

SYRUS.
  He was full of praise for Aeschinus and thanked me
  for my advice.

DEMEA.
  I'm going to explode.

SYRUS.
  There and then he counted out the money and
  tipped us half a mina for expenses. Already wisely
  spent. 370

DEMEA (*approaches* SYRUS).
  The very man, if you want a job well done.

SYRUS.
  Ah, Demea. I didn't see you. Anything the matter?

DEMEA.
  Anything the matter? No, nothing except that I am
  incapable of understanding what you think you're up
  to.

SYRUS.
  You're quite right. It's laughable, I have to admit.
  (*Calling indoors.*) Dromo, clean the fish will you.

You can leave the eel to swim about a bit. It can be
filleted after I get back. Not before, mind.

DEMEA.

Disgusting behaviour.

SYRUS.

I don't approve myself. How often I've said that.
(*Calling indoors.*) The salt fish, Stephanio. Make sure
380   it gets soaked.

DEMEA.

Ye gods! Is he ruining my son on principle or does
he expect someone to congratulate him? It makes me
so miserable. I can see the boy ending up destitute,
joining the army.

SYRUS.

That's good thinking, Demea. Worry less what's
underfoot now than where you'll be treading next.

DEMEA.

Have you got that chorus-girl indoors?

SYRUS.

Yes, she's in there.

DEMEA.

He's going to keep her at home?

SYRUS.

I imagine so. He's a nutcase.

DEMEA.

390   This isn't happening.

SYRUS.

Slackness on his father's part. He's far too easy-
going.

DEMEA.

My own brother, and I'm ashamed of him. He's a
disgrace.

SYRUS.

You haven't a lot in common, the two of you, have
you? I'm not saying this because I'm talking to you.

No, nothing whatever. What's good sense in you, is
nonsense to him, point for point. Would you let your
boy get away with it?

DEMEA.

Would I indeed? I'd have sniffed it out six months
before it started.

SYRUS.

Talk to me about vigilance!

DEMEA.

Let Ctesipho remain for ever as he is at this moment.

SYRUS.

At this very moment. Just as you wish.

DEMEA.

Seen him today, have you?

SYRUS.

Ctesipho, do you mean? (*Aside.*) I'll pack him off to   400
the country. (*Aloud.*) On farm business, I think.

DEMEA.

Do you know he's at the farm?

SYRUS.

I took him myself.

DEMEA.

I'm glad to hear it. I was worried he might be
hanging around here.

SYRUS.

He was in a right old temper too.

DEMEA.

Whatever for?

SYRUS.

He'd had a set-to with his brother in the forum over
that girl.

DEMEA.

Had he indeed?

SYRUS.

Wiped the floor with him. He turned up

unexpectedly while the money was being counted and pitched straight in. 'Oh, Aeschinus,' he cried out, 'what a way to behave. How could you? You put our entire family to shame.'

DEMEA.
You make me want to cry, I'm so happy.

SYRUS.

410 'It's not money you squander but life itself.'

DEMEA.
Thank heavens. I live in hope that he takes after my side.

SYRUS.
Quite.

DEMEA.
You know, Syrus, he has a fund of these sayings.

SYRUS.
Well now. That's domestic example.

DEMEA.
I work at it. A moral for every occasion. 'Hold the mirror up to nature,' I tell him, and 'Find your example in others. Do it like this,' I tell him . . .

SYRUS.
Absolutely.

DEMEA.
'Take care not to do that.'

SYRUS.
Clever.

DEMEA.
'This would be laudable.'

SYRUS.
Quite.

DEMEA.
'This would be unsuitable.'

SYRUS.
Very good.

DEMEA.
And after that ...

SYRUS.
Oh, what a shame. No time to hear the rest.
Beautiful fish I got. Must check they don't ruin
them. All those little things you were talking about, 420
Demea. They're no less important for us slaves, you
know. I try to treat my fellows to a little moral
improvement too, in my own way. 'Too salty';
'overcooked'; 'underseasoned'; 'perfect, don't forget
how you did it'. I encourage everyone, within the
limits of my expertise. 'Hold the pan up, like a
mirror,' I tell them, 'and then see what needs to be
done.' I realise that none of what we get up to   430
matters much, but what are you to do? Treat a man
as you find him, that's what I say. Is there anything
else you require?

DEMEA.
A more moral outlook from the rest of you, that's all
I require.

SYRUS.
Will you be off to the country now?

DEMEA.
Directly.

SYRUS.
You might as well. What can you do round here
when nobody listens to a word you say.

    Exit SYRUS.

DEMEA.
Yes, I'll be off, seeing as the only reason I came to
town has gone back to the country. Ctesipho's my
sole concern, the one person I care for. If my brother
sees things differently, well, Aeschinus is his
business. Hello, who's that? It looks like my old
friend Hegio. Indeed it is, unless my eyes deceive
me. Good lord. We've been friends since we were
boys. There's not many like him around any more, a 440

man of old-fashioned values, a man you can trust.
You won't find him causing trouble in public. It's
good to see him. A man of such traditional virtues is
a reminder that life can still be worth living. I'll stop
and say hello. I'd enjoy a chat.

Enter HEGIO *and* GETA.

HEGIO.
Good God, Geta! What a dreadful story!

GETA.
That's how it happened.

HEGIO.
And from a family like that. Such behaviour! Oh
Aeschinus, not what your father taught you!

DEMEA.
450   He's heard about the girl. He's not part of the family
and he's upset. While the boy's father couldn't care
less. My, how I wish Micio were present to hear this.

HEGIO.
They've got to do the proper thing. I won't let them
get away with it.

GETA.
You're our last hope, Hegio, head of the family and
patron. The old man entrusted us to you on his
deathbed. If you let us down, we're done for.

HEGIO.
No need to tell me. I couldn't let you down. It would
be morally indefensible.

DEMEA.
460   I'll approach him. Hegio, it's good to see you. How
are you?

HEGIO.
Just the same, old man. Well met, Demea.

DEMEA.
Whatever's the matter?

HEGIO.

Aeschinus is the matter, that elder son of yours
whom your brother adopted. He's abused the office
of a gentleman.

DEMEA.

What can you be referring to?

HEGIO.

Our old friend Simulus, you know who I mean?

DEMEA.

What about him?

HEGIO.

His daughter. Aeschinus has violated her virginity.

DEMEA.

He what?

HEGIO.

And that's not all. One could perhaps, put up with
that sort of thing, at a pinch. Led on by the night, by   470
love, wine and youth: human nature, after all. To be
fair, when he realises what he had done, he heads
straight for the girl's mother. Tears and oaths,
protestations of good faith, all that sort of thing, and
he agrees to marry her. All is forgiven; no fuss made;
they believe what he says. Outcome of the assault.
The girl's pregnant. Nine months gone and the
baby's due. What does he do, this admirable fellow?
Runs off with some tart, thank you very much, and
leaves the girl flat.

DEMEA.

Are you sure about all this?

HEGIO.

There's the girl's mother, the girl herself, the fact
that she is pregnant, Geta here, honest and hard-   480
working, as slaves go. He's looking after the whole
family, single-handed, providing for them. Take him
away and tie him up, then see.

GETA.
Torture me if I lie. Aeschinus won't deny it. You ask him.

DEMEA.
This is humiliating. I've no idea what to do. What can I say?

PAMPHILA (*screaming inside*).
Ahhhhh! Juno help me!

HEGIO.
What's that? It isn't her in labour, is it?

GETA.
Indeed it is.

HEGIO.
490   She's appealing to your sense of responsibility, Demea. Why don't you do voluntarily what you'll be forced to do eventually. Show a bit of decency, please God. But if your intentions are not honourable, I give you fair warning, Demea, I'll defend her every step of the way, her and her late father. We were kinsmen. More than that, we were boys together, educated together. On active service and back home we were inseparable. When times were hard, we always saw one another through. I'll move heaven and earth, I'll give my life rather than leave them in the lurch. What do you say to that, then?

DEMEA.
I'll have a word with my brother.

HEGIO.
500   Just get this into your head, Demea. The more comfortable your life, the more blessed with influence, connections, wealth or simple good luck, the greater your obligations in this life. If you want to keep your reputation, that is.

DEMEA.
Don't leave. I'll see that everything is done that ought to be done.

HEGIO.

So you should. Geta, let's go and find Sostrata.

Exeunt HEGIO *and* GETA.

DEMEA.

I *told* them what would happen. That it should come
to this! It was inevitable. Too much freedom ends in
disaster. I'd better find my brother and tell him the
worst.   510

Exit DEMEA. *Re-enter* HEGIO, *talking back
through the open door.*

HEGIO.

Don't worry, Sostrata. Give Pamphila what comfort
you can. If Micio's at the forum, I'll find him and let
him know exactly what's going on. If he intends to
do his duty, well and good. If not, I'll at least get a
straight answer out of him. Then I'll know what we
have to do next.

Exit HEGIO.

Enter CTESIPHO *and* SYRUS.

CTESIPHO.

Are you telling me Father's left for the country?

SYRUS.

Ages ago.

CTESIPHO.

Tell me.

SYRUS.

He went off to the farm. Already hard at work, I
would imagine.

CTESIPHO.

I hope he is. I wish him no harm, of course, but I
hope he's so exhausted, he can't get out of bed for
two days.

SYRUS.

At least. Longer, if possible.   520

CTESIPHO.

Right. I want the whole day to be one long round of
fun, just the way it's started. The trouble with the
country is that it isn't far enough away from the
town. If it were a bit further away, once night had
fallen, he wouldn't be able to get back here. But
when he finds out that I'm not actually there, he'll
come running back here again. I know him ...
'Where have you been?' he'll want to know. 'Haven't
seen you all day.' What am I going to say to that?

SYRUS.

Any ideas?

CTESIPHO.

Not one.

SYRUS.

Well, hard luck. You must have a client, haven't you,
some friend or someone you stay with?

CTESIPHO.

Of course. What difference does that make?

SYRUS.

You were away on business.

CTESIPHO.

530   On business? Oh, I couldn't.

SYRUS.

Yes, you could.

CTESIPHO.

It might work for the day. But what about staying
the night here? What's my excuse?

SYRUS.

Friends never do business at night. A pity that. You
relax. I know how to soft-soap him. The wilder he is,
the tamer I'll make him. Gentle as a lamb.

CTESIPHO.

But how?

SYRUS.

He loves being told how wonderful you are. I tell
him you're an angel and recite your virtues.

CTESIPHO.

My virtues?

SYRUS.

Yes, your virtues. In no time, he'll have tears rolling
down his cheeks as if he were a baby. Hang on.

CTESIPHO.

What's the matter?

SYRUS.

Here comes Mr Wolf.

CTESIPHO.

Not Father?

SYRUS.

The very man.

CTESIPHO.

Syrus, what are we going to do?

SYRUS.

Get inside. I'll handle it.

CTESIPHO.

I wasn't here, if he asks. Have you got that?

SYRUS.

Stop that, will you.

    Exit CTESIPHO. *Enter* DEMEA.

DEMEA.

Just my luck. First, my brother's nowhere to be   540
found. Then while I was looking for him, I met one
of the hired hands from the estate who told me
Ctesipho isn't there after all. Now I can't think what
to do.

CTESIPHO (*from inside*).

Psst, Syrus.

SYRUS.

What is it?

CTESIPHO.
Is he after me?

SYRUS.
Certainly is.

CTESIPHO.
I've had it.

SYRUS.
There's nothing to worry about.

DEMEA.
Damn my luck. Why me? I don't know. I was born
fated. I'm always the first to recognise trouble. The
first to pass on bad news. And the only one to realise
how bad it is.

SYRUS.
He's a laugh, this one. First to realise, he says. He's
the only one who doesn't know.

DEMEA.
Maybe I'll look in and see if my brother's got home.

CTESIPHO (*from inside*).
550   Syrus, for God's sake, don't let him come roaring in
here.

SYRUS.
Will you be quiet? I'm keeping an eye on him.

CTESIPHO.
I'm hardly going to rely on you, not today. I'll lock
us both up in a closet somewhere. We'll be safe
there.

SYRUS.
Well, fine, if that's what you want. I'll shift him
anyway.

DEMEA.
Here's that no-good Syrus.

SYRUS.
How in hell's a man to put up with it? How many
masters do I have? That's what I'd like to know.

DEMEA.
>What's he so upset about? Why the grumbling?
>What's he want? Tell me, my good fellow, is my
>brother at home?

SYRUS.
>You needn't 'good fellow' me. I'm at the end of my
>tether, I am.

DEMEA.
>What is the matter?

SYRUS.
>Well may you ask. Ctesipho all but murdered me
>and that slave-girl, both of us with his bare hands.

DEMEA.
>What do you mean?

SYRUS.
>I've a split lip. Look.

DEMEA.
>Whatever did you do?   560

SYRUS.
>He says I put him up to buying her.

DEMEA.
>I thought you just told me you'd gone off to the farm
>with him.

SYRUS.
>Ah, yes. But then he came back, out of his mind.
>Nothing sacred. Shamelessly batters an old man.
>Why I dandled him when he was so high.

DEMEA.
>Well done. Ctesipho, you're a chip off the old block.
>You're a man, my son.

SYRUS.
>Well done? He'd better keep his hands to himself in
>future, if he knows what's good for him.

DEMEA.
>Congratulations.

SYRUS.

Oh yes. One wretched girl and a slave who didn't
dare hit back. And he won. Very good.

DEMEA.

What could be better? Because he realised, as I do,
that at the bottom of all this, there's you. But is my
brother indoors?

SYRUS.

No, he's not.

DEMEA.

I wonder where I can find him.

SYRUS.

I know where he is, but I can't tell you.

DEMEA.

570   Really? That's all you have to say, is it?

SYRUS.

Yes it is.

DEMEA.

I'll brain you.

SYRUS.

It's who he's with I don't know. Where he is, yes, I
do know that.

DEMEA.

Then tell me where he is.

SYRUS.

You know the food-market? Down the hill by the
arcade.

DEMEA.

Yes, yes.

SYRUS.

Go on past it. Keep straight on and up the hill at the
other side. As soon as you get there, there's a dip.
Straight down to the bottom and you'll see a little
shrine over this side. Near the alley.

DEMEA.
  What alley?

SYRUS.
  By the fig-tree.

DEMEA.
  I know it.

SYRUS.
  Go down the alley.

DEMEA.
  It's a dead end.

SYRUS.
  You're absolutely right. What an idiot. I'm wrong.
  Back to the arcade. This is a much better way. You   580
  can't miss it. You know where Cratinus lives, the
  one with all the money?

DEMEA.
  Yes.

SYRUS.
  Go past his house. There's a road on the left. Down
  there as far as the temple of Diana. Keep to the right
  and before you get to the gate, you'll see a pond
  beside a mill, opposite a small factory. That's where
  he is.

DEMEA.
  What's he doing there?

SYRUS.
  They're making him some garden furniture, with
  little legs, oak legs.

DEMEA.
  For your beer-garden. Wonderful. I'd better go and
  find him.

  Exit DEMEA.

SYRUS.
  On your way. That'll keep you on your feet the rest
  of the day, you corpse's breakfast. Aeschinus is

confoundedly late. Lunch is getting ruined.
590 Ctesipho's head over heels in love. A chance to think
about me for once. I'll nip indoors and have a little
taste of anything that looks good and a sip or two to
wash it down. That'll help pass the time most
agreeably.

Exit SYRUS. *Enter* MICIO *and* HEGIO.

MICIO.
I hardly see that I deserve any credit, Hegio. I have
corrected a wrong and that I consider my duty.
Perhaps you thought me the sort of man who takes it
personally if any criticism is levelled against him and
reacts by making counter-accusations. Are you
thanking me for not behaving so?

HEGIO.
No, not in the least. I have never had cause to change
my opinion of you, Micio. But I would be grateful if
you'd come and see Pamphila's mother. Then you
can tell her what you told me that all this concern
600 about Aeschinus and another woman was no more
than Aeschinus acting on behalf of his brother.

MICIO.
If that's what you think proper, let's go.

HEGIO.
Thank you. She's been under a lot of strain and this
will take a weight off her mind. Then you'll have
more than done your duty. If you're not happy about
it, let me tell her what you said.

MICIO.
No, no. I'll talk to her.

HEGIO.
Thanks again. The worse people's circumstances,
the more sensitive they become, always looking out
for an insult. Poverty's such a restriction.
Explanations would look better coming from you.

MICIO.
I couldn't agree more.

HEGIO.
  You'll come with me?

MICIO.
  By all means.

  Exeunt HEGIO *and* MICIO. *Enter*
  AESCHINUS.

AESCHINUS.
  Mental torture. Beyond belief. I'm overwhelmed. A   610
  catalogue of disasters. I don't know where to turn or
  how to proceed. My limbs won't move. My mind's
  on strike. I haven't a ghost of a plan. How do I get
  out of a muddle like this? I'm the victim of
  suspicion, suspicion justified, with Sostrata
  convinced that the slave-girl is for me. Canthara
  made that clear enough when I met her on the road,
  heading for the midwife's. 'How's Pamphila?' I   620
  asked her. 'Is the baby on its way?' 'Shove off,
  Aeschinus,' she yelled at me. 'Just shove off. We've
  had enough of your fancy talk. We've had enough of
  your protestations.' 'What did I do?' I ask her. 'Keep
  your girlfriend and goodbye,' she says.

  I saw in a flash what they thought. But I couldn't
  reveal my brother's affairs to that old chatterbox. It
  would be all over town. Now what? Admit that the
  girl's my brother's, something we daren't let out?
  Perhaps we could keep it secret, though I doubt if
  they'd even believe me. It's a damning catalogue. I
  was the one who abducted her. I paid off the pimp.
  It was my house to which she was brought. And I
  have to explain to my father? He would have sorted   630
  out the marriage. To date, Aeschinus, there's been
  nothing but prevarication. Right then, first things
  first. Some explanations for the ladies. Here's the
  door. Oh God, I'm petrified. I really don't want to
  knock on this door. Right. Here goes. Hello. It's me,
  Aeschinus. Open up somebody. Help. Somebody is
  coming but I don't know who. I'll back off till I see.

  Enter MICIO.

MICIO.
Follow my instructions, Sostrata. I'll find Aeschinus and tell him what's happening. Now, who was at the door?

AESCHINUS.
Oh lord, Father. I'm done for.

MICIO.
Aeschinus.

AESCHINUS.
What's he doing here?

MICIO.
640   Was that you knocking? No reply. Maybe I'll tease him a bit. Not wholly inappropriate as he declined to let me in on any of this. Not answering?

AESCHINUS.
The door? No, I don't think so, no.

MICIO.
Just as I thought. I was wondering what business you could have here. He's blushing. Good.

AESCHINUS.
Excuse me, Father, but what are you doing there?

MICIO.
It's nothing to do with me really. I met a friend in the forum and he asked me to come and offer my support.

AESCHINUS.
Support for what?

MICIO.
An unmarried girl and her mother.

AESCHINUS.
Go on.

MICIO.
650   The girl's father is dead and my friend is next of kin. Which means he's legally obliged to marry her.

AESCHINUS.
Oh no.

MICIO.
Did you say something?

AESCHINUS.
No, nothing. Yes, of course. As you were saying...

MICIO.
He's come to take her away. He lives in Miletus.

AESCHINUS.
He's going to take her away?

MICIO.
Yes.

AESCHINUS.
To bloody Miletus?

MICIO.
Of course.

AESCHINUS.
It doesn't bear thinking about. What about them?
Don't they have any say in the matter?

MICIO.
You know what women are like. It's nothing. The
mother's cooked up some story about the girl having
had a little boy by another man. But she won't say
who the father is. He got there first, she claims, so
my friend shouldn't have her.

AESCHINUS.
That seems fair enough, doesn't it?   660

MICIO.
Hardly.

AESCHINUS.
For goodness' sake, 'hardly'? He's going to carry her
off.

MICIO.
Why shouldn't he carry her off?

AESCHINUS.

Between you, Father, you've made a decision that is
both harsh and cold-blooded. Forgive me for being
blunt but it's positively barbaric.

MICIO.

Why so?

AESCHINUS.

You need to ask? Did you ever consider the feelings
of the poor fellow she ... er ... got to know first? He
may be madly in love with her for all I know, poor
fellow, and now has to stand by and watch her
snatched away, raped, before his very eyes? It's a
downright crime, Father.

MICIO.

670   I don't see it. Did anyone propose to her? Did
anyone give her away? Has she ever been married?
Where's the man responsible? Why did he make a
grab at something which did not belong to him?

AESCHINUS.

You could hardly expect an eager young thing to sit
around at home waiting for some relation to turn up.
That's the line you should have taken, Father, and
spoken your mind.

MICIO.

Preposterous. Turn against the man I'd come to
support? It's no business of ours, is it Aeschinus?
They're nothing to us, are they? We'll be off. What's
this? Tears?

AESCHINUS.

Father, please, I've got a confession ...

MICIO.

I know. I've heard. Everything. Anything you do is
680   of concern to me, Aeschinus. Because I love you.

AESCHINUS.

And I wouldn't want to forfeit that love, as long as I
live, Father. I shouldn't have done what I did and I
apologise. I'm ashamed and upset.

MICIO.
> I believe you. Indeed I do. You've a good heart. But
> you can be so inconsiderate, I'm afraid. What sort of
> a world do you think you live in? You seduce a girl, a
> virgin you had no right to lay hands on. That was a
> disgraceful way to behave, but it was only human.
> You're not the first, even among decent folk. But
> once it happened, did you never consider the
> consequences? Did you not give a moment's thought
> to what would happen or how it would happen? So   690
> you were too ashamed to tell me. How did you
> expect me to find out? While you've been dithering,
> ten months have passed. You've let yourself down.
> You've let the girl down. And you've let down your
> child. You could scarcely have behaved worse. Did
> you expect the gods to sort it out for you while you
> were asleep? Was that it? And that if you loafed
> about long enough, she'd turn up in your bedroom,
> already married to you? I've had quite enough of
> this. No need to get upset. You're about to become a
> husband.

AESCHINUS.
> Pardon?

MICIO.
> I said 'no need to get upset'.

AESCHINUS.
> Father, are you still having me on?

MICIO.
> Would I? Why should I?

AESCHINUS.
> I don't know, except that I so want it to be true, I'm
> terrified it won't be.

MICIO.
> Off you go inside and ask a blessing on your
> wedding. Go on.

AESCHINUS.
> What? Wedding? To a wife. Right now?   700

MICIO.
Yes, now.

AESCHINUS.
Now, meaning, now?

MICIO.
Now, as ever is.

AESCHINUS.
Oh Father, curse me, heaven, if I don't love you
more than my eyes.

MICIO.
What, more than her?

AESCHINUS.
As much, anyway.

MICIO.
Very generous.

AESCHINUS.
What about the man from Miletus?

MICIO.
Dead, gone. Took the first boat out. What are you
waiting for?

AESCHINUS.
You go, Father. You're the one to ask a blessing.
They're more likely to listen to a saint.

MICIO.
Well, I'll go and make some preparations anyway.
And, if you've any sense, you'll do as I say.

Exit MICIO.

AESCHINUS.
How about that? Is this the model relationship for a
father and a son? Brother and best friend rolled into
one couldn't have been more sympathetic. Isn't he a
710   lovely man? He deserves a big hug. He's been so
obliging I'm terrified of doing anything to upset
him, especially without meaning to. I must be
careful. I'd best get a move on. I don't want to hold
up the wedding.

Exit AESCHINUS. *Enter* DEMEA.

DEMEA

I've walked till I'm exhausted. God damn you,
Syrus, you and your directions. I've scoured the
town. I went to the gate, to the lake. Where wasn't I?
No factory. No sign of my brother or anyone who
admitted seeing him. What I'll do now is camp out
on his doorstep and wait till he does get back.

Enter MICIO.

MICIO.

I'll just go and let them know we're ready.

DEMEA.

It's him. I've been all over the place looking for you,   720
Micio.

MICIO.

What do you want?

DEMEA.

I bring news of yet greater iniquities perpetrated by
that young man.

MICIO.

Really.

DEMEA.

Worse than before. Criminal.

MICIO.

Oh, come on.

DEMEA.

You don't know what he's like.

MICIO.

Of course I do.

DEMEA.

You poor innocent. You think I'm talking about the
slave-girl. This is a crime against a respectable girl, a
virgin and a citizen.

MICIO.

Yes, I know.

DEMEA.
You know about it? And you don't mind?

MICIO.
What's there to object about?

DEMEA.
Confess. Doesn't it make you want to shout and go mad? Doesn't it...

MICIO.
I would have preferred...

DEMEA.
There's a baby.

MICIO.
Bless it.

DEMEA.
The girl hasn't a bean.

MICIO.
So I gather.

DEMEA.
No dowry.

MICIO.
I suppose not.

DEMEA.
So what happens now?

MICIO.
730   The situation speaks for itself. She comes over here.

DEMEA.
God in heaven, what a way to behave.

MICIO.
What else can I do?

DEMEA.
You ask me that? Even if this means nothing to you, you could at least pretend.

MICIO.
He's betrothed to the girl. Everything's set up. The

marriage is taking place. Anxieties all allayed. *That*
was the least I could do.

DEMEA.
And you're happy about all the rest, are you?

MICIO.
If there was anything I could do about it, no. As
there isn't, I might as well resign myself. Life's a
game of dice. If you get a poor throw, you use skill to   740
make the most of it.

DEMEA.
Make the most of it, do you? Twenty minae on a tart.
Down the drain. That's your skill, is it? We'll have
to get what we can for her, or give her away.

MICIO.
I'm not going to give her away and I don't intend
selling her either.

DEMEA.
So what are you going to do?

MICIO.
Keep her at home.

DEMEA.
For heaven's sake. Whore and wife. Under the same
roof?

MICIO.
Yes. Why not?

DEMEA.
I think you're out of your mind.

MICIO.
I don't.

DEMEA.
Lord love us, I can see what you're up to. She's to be
a partner for *you*.   750

MICIO.
And why not?

DEMEA.
Perhaps she could show the new bride a trick or two.

MICIO.
Maybe so.

DEMEA.
With you dancing a jig with the pair of them.

MICIO.
Nice idea.

DEMEA.
Nice idea?

MICIO.
You could join in yourself, if we need a fourth.

DEMEA.
Is there no shame left?

MICIO.
Come on, Demea. Don't look so cross. It's your
son's wedding. Time for a smile and a laugh. I'm
going to fetch everybody, then I'll come back here.

Exit MICIO.

DEMEA.
Heavens. What a way to live. The morality! Sheer
madness. A wife arriving without a dowry. A fancy-
woman installed simultaneously. Extravagance. A
760   young man wallowing in luxury. An old man clean
off his head. Completely beyond redemption, this
family.

Enter SYRUS *from indoors.*

SYRUS.
Syrus, old son, you've done very nicely, thank you.
Handled your duties with aplomb. Off you trot. I've
sampled everything going indoors. Time for a little
constitutional.

DEMEA.

Do you see that? Look at it. What an example of discipline.

SYRUS.

Whoops! Here's the old fellow back. How goes it? Why the long face?

DEMEA.

Of all the diabolical ...

SYRUS.

Hang on. Is this an intellectual discussion?

DEMEA.

If you belonged to me ...

SYRUS.

You'd be a millionaire with sound economic   770
prospects.

DEMEA.

I'd make a proper example of you.

SYRUS.

Whatever for? What did I do?

DEMEA.

Do? What did you do? Confusion reigns and in the midst of a crisis barely contained, you're drunk, you brute, as though there was something to celebrate.

SYRUS.

I should have stayed indoors.

Enter DROMO.

DROMO.

Hey, Syrus. Ctesipho wants you. In there.

SYRUS.

Push off.

Exit DROMO.

DEMEA.

Did he say Ctesipho?

SYRUS.

No, not at all.

DEMEA.

You vulture, you! Ctesipho's in there, isn't he?

SYRUS.

No, he isn't.

DEMEA.

Then why did that fellow say Ctesipho?

SYRUS.

It's a different Ctesipho, a little bit of a sort of a parasite called Ctesipho. Know him, do you?

DEMEA.

I'll find out if I know him.

SYRUS.

780   What are you doing? Where do you think you're off to?

DEMEA.

Leave go.

SYRUS.

I don't want to.

DEMEA.

Take your hands off me, you scoundrel, if you don't want your brains scrambled.

    Exit DEMEA.

SYRUS.

He's gone. Not the most welcome of guests, especially to Ctesipho. What am I going to do? Find a corner and sleep it off till the rumpus dies down. That's what I'm going to do.

    Exit SYRUS. *Enter* MICIO, *talking to* SOSTRATA.

MICIO.

We're all ready, Sostrata, as I told you. As soon as you like. What's all the racket at my house?

    Enter DEMEA.

DEMEA.

Oh dear, oh dear. What am I going to do? How can I
face it? Shall I rant and rave? 'Heaven above. Earth
beneath. Oh rolling sea...'   790

MICIO.

Ah, it's you. The cat's out of the bag. No wonder
he's yelling. Now they are in trouble. I'd better lend
a hand.

DEMEA.

There he is. The consummate corrupter of my
children.

MICIO.

Calm down will you. Get a grip on yourself.

DEMEA.

I'm perfectly calm, thank you. I have a grip on
myself. No more swearing. Let us consider. We
entered into an agreement – your idea, as I recall –
that you would not interfere with my son. Isn't that
right?

MICIO.

Quite right.

DEMEA.

Then what is he doing in your house at this precise
moment drinking? What are you doing entertaining
my son? Why, Micio, did you purchase a whore for
him? And what possible reason can you adduce for   800
expecting me to respect our arrangement while
ignoring it yourself? I've stopped bothering about
your boy. Leave me mine.

MICIO.

That's hardly fair.

DEMEA.

Oh, isn't it?

MICIO.

You know the old saying: 'Among friends, share and
share alike.'

DEMEA.

Most amusing. It's a little late for that sort of remark.

MICIO.

Demea, listen a moment, will you ... please. In the
first place, if it's the extravagance of the boys you're
concerned about, I would ask you to look at it this
810   way. Originally you undertook to bring up the pair
of them because you thought you could afford both
of them. It also seemed likely that I would one day
get married. So go back to the original plan. Penny-
pinch, overwork, do without. Build up something to
bequeath and the reputation that goes with it. My
money comes from a windfall anyway. Let them
make use of it. Your capital won't be affected.
Anything from me is a bonus. Think it over, Demea,
and you'll see that this is in the best interests of
everyone – you, me and the boys.

DEMEA.

Forget the money. It's their behaviour...

MICIO.

820   Hang on a minute. I realise that, and I'm coming to
it. There are lots of indications of character, Demea,
which allow you to predict that what might be
acceptable in one man would be unacceptable in
someone else, even when the action's the same. It's
not what is done but who does it. When I look at
these boys of ours, what indications of character do I
see, indications that give me confidence that they
will turn out as we would wish? I see that they have
common sense, intelligence, caution when it's called
for and mutual affection. You can tell that they're
830   easy-going in heart and mind. You could rein them
in any day you please. Yes, I know you're concerned
about their extravagance. But, my dear Demea,
discernment is a matter of age and experience. Do
you know the greatest mistake that we make when
we get old? We worry too much about money.
They'll learn.

DEMEA.
An elegant argument, Micio. I just hope that this
fine philosophy isn't our undoing.

MICIO.
Don't talk about the future like that. It may never
happen. Put such things out of your mind and award
today to me. Unfurrow that brow.

DEMEA.
I can see the way the wind blows. So be it. But at   840
dawn tomorrow, I'm off to the farm with Ctesipho.

MICIO.
Before dawn, if you like. But today you're going to
enjoy yourself.

DEMEA.
I'm taking that slave-girl along too.

MICIO.
You win. Ctesipho will be bound to the farm for life.
The girl will need watching.

DEMEA.
I'll keep an eye on her all right. She'll be covered in
ash, smoke and flour from cooking and grinding. I'll
send her gleaning at midday. She'll look like a burnt
offering.

MICIO.
Just the job. Now you're making sense. And let's   850
make your son sleep with her however much he
objects.

DEMEA.
Are you joking? You're lucky you can. I still feel . . .

MICIO.
Not again.

DEMEA.
All right. That's it. I've finished.

MICIO.
Then in you come and spend the day as it ought to
be spent.

Exit MICIO.

DEMEA.

No man can ever be so ordered and organised in his life that some circumstance, some novelty, won't catch him out. There's always a lesson to learn, something to discover you never knew. A priority to relegate in the light of experience. Well, it's happened to me. Here I am, getting on in years. I've had a hard life and now I'm turning my back on it. And why? Because I've discovered that it is preferable to be easy-going and amiable. Look at my brother and me. It's obvious, isn't it? He's had a life of ease. He enjoys company, is mild-mannered, never harms a soul and always wears a smile. He suits himself how he lives and how he spends his money. Result. He's popular. Everyone likes him.

What about me? I lived like a peasant, surly, miserable, stingy and bad-tempered. I got married. That was a mistake. Fathered two sons. More trouble. I put all my efforts into trying to provide for them and in the process contrived to miss out on living. Now in my old age, what's the reward for my labours? They can't stand me. There's my brother picking up all the joys of fatherhood by doing nothing. They adore him as they avoid me. They take his advice, never leave his side, either of them. And here I am, all by myself. I wouldn't be surprised if their prayers are for his long life and my prompt demise. He's taken over the education of my sons and it's cost him nothing. I get the problems, he gets the fun.

Very well then. Time for a new approach. Let's see if I can out-blandish and out-charm him. I'll only be following his advice. I have a right to the love and respect of my own children. If that means giving and agreeing all the time, so be it. And if it means bankruptcy, so what? He's younger than I am.

Enter SYRUS.

SYRUS.

Demea, your brother says he hopes you won't go too far away.

DEMEA.

Who's there? Ah, Syrus, good old Syrus. How are you? Everything all right? How's it going?

SYRUS.

Fine.

DEMEA.

How nice. (*Aside.*) That's three unfamiliar additions to my repertoire, 'Good old Syrus', 'Everything all right?' and 'How goes it?' (*To* SYRUS.) You've proved yourself to be a grand slave and I'd like to see you looked after.

SYRUS.

Thanks very much.

DEMEA.

No, really, Syrus. You'll soon find that I mean it.

Enter GETA.

GETA.

Mistress, I'll just go and find out when to expect the girl. Demea, there you are. Good day to you.   890

DEMEA.

And what's your name?

GETA.

Geta.

DEMEA.

Geta, of course. Well, I tell you Geta, you're a pretty valuable fellow, if today is anything to go by. The slave who gets my vote is the one who follows his master's requirement to the letter. And that's you, eh, Geta? And for that reason, Geta, should the chance arise, I'd like to see you looked after. (*Aside.*) This affability's going well.

GETA.

Thanks very much, sir. A kind thought.

DEMEA (*aside*).
My first steps in currying favour.

Enter AESCHINUS.

AESCHINUS.
900 This formal wedding is murder. It's taking all day to get ready.

DEMEA.
Aeschinus! How's everything?

AESCHINUS.
Ah, Father, is that you?

DEMEA.
Yes, by God it is, your dear old father who loves you body and soul and more than his eyes. Why are you not fetching the bride?

AESCHINUS.
I want to but we've got to wait for a musician and the choir.

DEMEA.
Will you take a bit of advice from your dear old dad?

AESCHINUS.
Yes?

DEMEA.
Don't bother with any of that stuff: wedding hymns, congregation, torch-bearers, musicians. Knock down the garden-wall and carry her over. Turn the two into a single house. Bring her mother, the whole family. They can all live with us.

AESCHINUS.
910 That's terrific. Oh, yes! Father, dear old Father, that's terrific.

DEMEA.
Now I'm an old dear. Fine. My brother will be living in a thoroughfare, with a whole mass of people. It'll cost him the earth. But why should I bother? I'm an old dear, thanks very much. Let the nabob fork out twenty minae. Syrus, go and get on with it.

SYRUS.
With what?

DEMEA.
The demolitions. And you, Geta, off and fetch the women.

GETA.
Bless you, Demea. You're a good man, I can see that, the saviour of the family.

DEMEA.
No more than you deserve.

Exeunt SYRUS *and* GETA.

What do you say to that, then?

AESCHINUS.
I agree.   920

DEMEA.
You don't want the poor girl wandering through streets when she's not well.

AESCHINUS.
You're absolutely right, Father.

DEMEA.
That's my way. Oh look. Here comes Micio.

Enter MICIO, *talking back to* SYRUS.

MICIO.
My brother said that? Where is he? Demea, did you give these orders to Syrus?

DEMEA.
I certainly did. I told him to use every means at his disposal to make a single family, paying their way, giving them help, linking us to them.

MICIO.
It's not quite what I had in mind.

DEMEA.
We have to do the decent thing, damned if we don't. There's his wife's mother.

MICIO.
Yes. What about it?

DEMEA.
930   A good woman. Upright.

MICIO.
So they say.

DEMEA.
Not as young as she was.

MICIO.
That's true.

DEMEA.
Well past child-bearing age. No one to look after her.
All alone in the world.

MICIO.
What's he driving at?

DEMEA.
The obvious thing is for you to marry her.
Aeschinus would like that, wouldn't you, Aeschinus?

MICIO.
Me? Get married?

DEMEA.
You.

MICIO.
You mean me?

DEMEA.
Of course, you.

MICIO.
You're being ridiculous.

DEMEA.
A decent man would.

AESCHINUS.
Father . . .

MICIO.

You've been listening to him, have you, you damned
fool?

DEMEA.

Don't get so upset. You can't get out of it.

MICIO.

This is insane.

AESCHINUS.

Please, Father, I beg of you.

MICIO.

You're off your head. Leave me alone.

DEMEA.

Humour the boy.

MICIO.

Are you quite mad? I'm almost sixty-five. What do I
want to go and get married for? And to a clapped-out
old hag! Is that what you're lining up for me?

AESCHINUS.

You'll have to. I promised.   940

MICIO.

Promised did you? Honour your own promises,
young man.

DEMEA.

Come, now. He could be asking for something
major.

MICIO.

This is major enough for me.

DEMEA.

Be generous.

AESCHINUS.

Don't sulk.

DEMEA.

Come on. You're committed.

MICIO.

Couldn't you uncommit me?

AESCHINUS.

Not until you say yes.

MICIO:

This is coercion.

DEMEA.

Micio, what happened to your generosity?

MICIO.

I find this whole business indecent, inappropriate
and insane. It goes completely against my principles.
Nevertheless, if you're both determined, I give in.

AESCHINUS.

You're doing the right thing and I love you for that.

DEMEA.

There is one point. (*Aside.*) Dare I try this on now
that he's agreed to the marriage?

MICIO.

Now what. There's nothing else, is there?

DEMEA.

It's Hegio. He's their closest relation which links
him to us. He's a poor man. We ought to do
something for him.

MICIO.

Like what?

DEMEA.

You rent out a smallholding just outside the city. He
could work that, perhaps.

MICIO.

950   It's not that small.

DEMEA.

Even if it were an estate, we are under an obligation.
He's been a father to Pamphila. He's a good man,
one of the family now. Let him have the place. You
yourself made me see the light when you expressed
the sentiment so wisely, so sensibly, I thought, what
was it? 'Do you know the greatest mistake we make
when we get old? We worry too much about money.'

We must be very wary of such a failing. Admirable
sentiments become moral obligations.

MICIO.
Happy to. Anything else? He can have anything he
takes a fancy to.

AESCHINUS.
Oh, Father.

DEMEA.
Now we're brothers indeed, body and soul. (*Aside.*)
And he's hoist on his own petard.

Enter SYRUS.

SYRUS.
Orders carried out, Demea.

DEMEA.
What a good lad. Well, in my considered opinion,
Syrus is eminently worthy of being given his
freedom.   960

MICIO.
Freedom? Him? Whatever for?

DEMEA.
Plenty of reasons.

SYRUS.
Bless you, Demea, you're a fine man. I've done my
best for those boys, both of them, ever since they
were so high. I educated them, advised them, taught
them everything I know.

DEMEA.
Anyone can see the result. And don't forget the
extra-curricular activities. Credit-shopping. Whore-
negotiation. Daytime-partying. No ordinary man's
duties.

SYRUS.
Oh, you're a lovely man.

DEMEA.
Well, you were the middleman in negotiating for

today's slave-girl. You managed everything. He deserves some recognition, if only as an example to the others. Last but not least, it's what Aeschinus wants.

MICIO.

Is it what you want?

AESCHINUS.

Oh, I do.

MICIO.

970   In that case, come here, Syrus. Syrus, you have your liberty.

SYRUS.

Thank you. I'm indebted to you all and especially to you, Demea.

DEMEA.

I'm delighted for you.

AESCHINUS.

Me too.

SYRUS.

I know you are. There is one thing that would make my happiness complete. To see my wife, Phrygia, standing by my side, a free woman.

DEMEA.

An excellent lady.

SYRUS.

And did you know? She gave your nephew's son his first feed this very morning.

DEMEA.

Did she indeed? His very first feed? Well, no question about it. She deserves her freedom.

MICIO.

For that?

DEMEA.

Oh yes. I'll pay you the price.

SYRUS.

God grant you your heart's desire, Demea.

MICIO.

He's certainly been on your side today.

DEMEA.

True enough. As long as you offer him a bit of cash
in hand to get started. He'll repay you in no time.   980

MICIO.

So much the worse for me.

DEMEA.

He's a good fellow.

SYRUS.

I'll pay you back, of course I will. Hand it over.

AESCHINUS.

Hand it over, Father.

MICIO.

I'll consider the matter.

DEMEA.

He will.

SYRUS.

You're a wonderful man, sir.

AESCHINUS.

The best, Father.

MICIO.

What's going on, Demea? How come the
transformation? What's got into you? Why the fit of
generosity?

DEMEA.

I'll tell you. So that I can demonstrate something to
you. People may find you good-natured and
cheerful, Micio, but that doesn't mean you live a
decent life. It doesn't mean what you do is fair or
correct. It simply shows what you can buy by being
complacent, permissive, and extravagant. I put it to
you, Aeschinus. If you and your brother reject my   990

way of life because I am not prepared to overturn basic decencies, then I reject you. Waste money. Spend all you like. Do what the devil you want. If, on the other hand, you would prefer someone to offer advice when a young man's appetite overrules his discretion; if you want someone to restrain you and tell you when you make a mistake; if you need someone who will always be there when you need him, here I am. I'll be your man.

AESCHINUS.

Father, we are in your hands. We'll respect your experience. But what'll happen to Ctesipho?

DEMEA.

He can keep the girl. I don't mind. But there I draw the line.

MICIO.

You're right.

ACTOR.

And now, audience, your applause, please.

A Note on the Translators

RICHARD BEACHAM is Professor of Theatre Studies at the University of Warwick. His numerous books and articles on theatre history include *The Roman Theatre and its Audience* (Harvard, 1992) and *Spectacle Entertainments of Early Imperial Rome* (Yale, 1999). He directed the EU-sponsored THEATRON Project, a multimedia research and teaching module based on Virtual Reality depictions of historic theatres. He also directs the Pompey Project, a major investigation of Rome's first permanent theatre. He has worked as a Getty Scholar at the Getty Museum, where he oversaw the production of *Casina*, and is currently working with a team of specialist VR modellers at Warwick, directing VR-based theatre projects, for which they were honoured as a 'Laureates' of the Computerworld Honors programme, an award given to those who have 'achieved outstanding progress for society through visionary use of information technology'.

KENNETH McLEISH's translations, of plays by all the Greek and Roman dramatists, Ibsen, Feydeau, Molière, Strindberg and others, have been performed throughout the world on stage, film, TV and radio. His original plays include *I Will If You Will*, *Just Do It*, *The Arabian Nights*, *Omma* and *Orpheus*. His books include *The Theatre of Aristophanes*, *Guide to Shakespeare's Plays* (with Stephen Unwin), *The Good Reading Guide* and *Guide to Greek Theatre and Drama*. He was editor of the Drama Classics series for Nick Hern Books and a Fellow of the Royal Society of Literature. He died in 1997.

MICHAEL SARGENT's career has been mainly in education. As teacher/lecturer/inspector in Classics, English and Drama, he directed plays by Aristophanes, Shakespeare, Wycherley, Sheridan, Chekhov, Wilde,

Shaw, Coward and Genet, as well as Kenneth McLeish's translations of Molière (*The School for Wives*), Feydeau (*The Girl from Maxim's*) and Labiche (*The Italian Straw Hat*). For Xenia Theatre Company, in addition to *The Haunted House* and *The Eunuch*, he directed a touring production of McLeish's original play *Omma*. He was also the founder and artistic director of Focus Opera Group, for whom he directed over 30 operas and music-theatre works.

J. MICHAEL WALTON worked in the professional theatre as an actor and director before joining the University of Hull, where he holds the Chair of Drama. He has published four books on Greek theatre, *Greek Theatre Practice, The Greek Sense of Theatre: Tragedy Reviewed, Living Greek Theatre: A Handbook of Classical Performance and Modern Production*, and *Menander and the Making of Comedy* (with the late Peter Arnott). He is Series Editor of Methuen Drama Classical Greek Dramatists, edited *Craig on Theatre* and, with Marianne McDonald, *Amid Our Troubles: Irish Versions of Greek Tragedy*. He has translated plays by Sophocles, Euripides, Menander and Terence, and was founder director of the Performance Translation Centre in the Drama Department at the University of Hull.

CPSIA information can be obtained at www.ICGtesting.com
Printed in the USA
LVOW06s1046120814

398740LV00001B/1/P